D0120960

BACKBEAT

Described by the *Western Morning News* as the 'A. J. P. Taylor of the pop world', Alan Clayson is the author of several books on music, including biographies of George Harrison and Ringo Starr. He has also written for journals as disparate as *Record Collector*, *The Times Educational Supplement*, *Mediaeval World*, *Folk Roots*, *Country Music People*, *The Beat Goes On* and, as a teenager, the notorious *Schoolkids Oz*.

As leader of the group Alan Clayson and the Argonauts in the late 1970s, he was thrust to 'a premier position on rock's lunatic Fringe' (*Melody Maker*). His cult following continued to grow as well as demand for his production talents in the studio and the number of cover versions of his compositions by such diverse acts as Dave Berry – in whose Cruisers Clayson played keyboards in the mid-1980s – and (via a collaboration with ex-Yardbird Jim McCarty) New Age behemoths, Stairway, Britain's foremost exponents of New Age music.

Pauline Sutcliffe was, in her own words, 'the original Beatles groupie' and now works as a psychotherapist.

POLYGRAM FILMED ENTERTAINMENT and SCALA PRODUCTIONS In Association With
CHANNEL FOUR FILMS Present A SCALA/WOOLEY/POWELL/DWYER
and FORTHCOMING PRODUCTION SHERYL LEE STEPHEN DORFF BACKBEAT
Introducing IAN HART Casting Directors JOHN & ROS HUBBARD and DIANNE CRITTENDEN
Costume Designer SHEENA NAPIER Production Designer JOSEPH BENNETT Photographed by IAN WILSON Editor MARTIN WALSH
Original Score Composed & Produced by DON WAS Screenplay IAIN SOFTLEY, MICHAEL THOMAS and STEPHEN WARD
Executive Producer NIK POWELL Produced by FINOLA DWYER and STEPHEN WOOLEY Directed by IAIN SOFTLEY
Original Soundtrack Album available on Virgin Movie Music Cassettes and Compact Discs

BACKBEAT

STUART SUTCLIFFE: THE LOST BEATLE

Alan Clayson and Pauline Sutcliffe

PAN BOOKS
in association with
SIDGWICK & JACKSON

First published 1994 by Pan Books Limited
and Sidgwick & Jackson Limited

Divisions of Pan Macmillan Publishers Limited
Cavaye Place London SW10 9PG
and Basingstoke

Associated companies throughout the world

ISBN 0 330 33580 4 (paperback)

579864

A CIP catalogue record for this book is available from
the British Library

Typeset by CentraCet Limited, Cambridge
Printed and bound in Great Britain by
Cox & Wyman Ltd, Reading, Berkshire

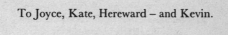

To Joyce, Kate, Hereward – and Kevin.

CONTENTS

PROLOGUE
The Fifth Man
1

CHAPTER ONE
The Father Figure
7

CHAPTER TWO
The Young Sailor
34

CHAPTER THREE
The Passenger
56

CHAPTER FOUR
Pop Goes The Easel
76

CHAPTER FIVE
Mädel Ruck-Ruck-Ruck
98

CHAPTER SIX
Homesick For St Pauli
110

CHAPTER SEVEN
Peace Of Mind
136

CHAPTER EIGHT
Cry For A Shadow
162

Contents

EPILOGUE
Just A Beginning
176

Appendices
195

In my primary school playground in the summer of 1963, it was obvious that the world was changing. The term before it was cowboys and Indians, then all of a sudden we were arguing about who would play John, Paul, George or Ringo. It was no longer Airfix kits but the latest Beatles Parlophone EP that became the object of our pocket money. Then in 1967 my father bought me a copy of *Sgt. Pepper*, and I remember thinking, at eleven, they must be getting too respectable. In fact, it was just that the rest of the world was becoming weirder.

Sixteen years later, when I was making my first films at Granada TV, I saw Astrid Kirchherr's self-portrait photograph – a beautiful young woman with cropped hair looking directly into the mirror above her Roleiflex camera – and I was hooked. In the photographs that Astrid took of Stuart and herself I saw not only two lovers with striking looks and a sense of style ahead of its time, but a hint of something else that marked them as people apart.

Instinctively I felt that here was a story worth telling, a universal love story about the synthesis of two worlds – boy and girl, England and Germany, rock'n'roll and art – set against the backdrop of the biggest rock'n'roll band of all time. I knew too that it was important to experience as much as possible at first hand.

In the houses of Stuart's mother Millie and sister Pauline, I first saw Stuart's paintings, the work of an artist pushing himself, experimenting with new techniques and materials, all of them, canvas or collage, possessing a haunting beauty.

Then, finding a number, I picked up a phone and spoke to Astrid in Hamburg. At first she was reluctant to talk about her past, not wanting to exploit her association with the Beatles. I told her it was *her* story I was interested in, and her relationship with Stu and John. She became less reserved. If I happened to be in Germany sometime, why didn't I give her a call? So the next week I went to Germany.

Foreword

Over the next few years there followed several meetings: in Klaus's Hamburg apartment – the bass guitar that Stuart gave Klaus leaning in the corner, his paintings and Astrid's photographs all around us; in a Baltic coast farmhouse, where for several days I recorded interviews with Astrid and Klaus, the years slipping away as we talked into the night.

When it seemed that I would spend my life trying to make this film, in the spring and summer of 1993, ten years after I first met Astrid, filming began on *Backbeat*. My collaborators were more talented and committed than I had dared hope: the producers from Scala Productions, Finola Dwyer, Steve Woolley and Nik Powell; fellow screenwriters Michael Thomas and Stephen Ward; the inspired cast led by Sheryl Lee, Stephen Dorff and Ian Hart, all of the crew, and Polygram, our major backers.

Just before Christmas 1993, Astrid and Pauline saw the film for the first time. What for me was a ten-year struggle for them had lasted a lifetime. Their involvement in this project has been a bitter-sweet experience. The pain of reliving a personal tragedy has been mixed with the hope, so important to both of them, that at last Stuart's work will be seen and appreciated in its own right.

This book is the first and long overdue biography of Stuart. It continues the re-evaluation begun by the film *Backbeat* so that now, hopefully, Astrid and Stuart will be known for who they were and what they did, and not for who they knew.

IAIN SOFTLEY, director/screenwriter *Backbeat*
London, February 1994

THE FIFTH MAN

D oes anyone recollect the following Andy Capp cartoon in the *Daily Mirror*? Capp – a beer-swilling, womanizing Geordie – is dissecting his best pal Chalky's character over a pint. A chap on the next bar-stool adds a scathing comment of his own about Chalky. Capp's response is not grim agreement but an uppercut that sends the other sprawling: 'That's my mate you're talking about!'

The friendship between the late Stuart Sutcliffe and John Lennon embraced territory just as forbidden and often as inexplicable to outsiders. How else can be explained abrupt reconciliations after hours of verbal and emotional baiting; a tacit implication in a seemingly innocuous remark sparking off a slammed front door, and jokes side-splitting to nobody else.

During the turbulent adolescence that prefaced a turbulent man-hood, hardly anyone knew Lennon as intimately as Stuart. For just over a year, he too was a member of John's then-struggling beat group. Even though he resigned in June 1961, just the wrong side of the 'Love Me Do' watershed, Sutcliffe is less peripheral to the old, old story of the Beatles than certain more celebrated characters. The concept of a firm artistic link between rock 'n' roll and Lennon's abandoned art college course work was exemplified by the group's conscious musical progression – and was received wisdom from Sutcliffe.[1] With his fiancée, Hamburg photographer Astrid Kirchherr, he also anticipated the 'look' (including the gimmick haircuts) adopted by the Moptopped Mersey Marvels on their emergence as the showbusiness sensation of the century.

It is intriguing to note how many other important acts from every phase of the mid-1960s beat boom had roots in British art schools. Off-the-cuff examples are the Rolling Stones, the Yardbirds, the Kinks, the Animals, the Pretty Things, the Bonzo Dog Doo-Dah Band, the Move and the Pink Floyd, while Roxy Music, the Portsmouth Sinfonia, Deaf School, the Sex Pistols and Ian Dury and the

Blockheads were among those that informed pop undercurrents in the next decade.

It is often too easy to forget that this tight-trousered lead singer or that clenched-teeth guitarist may have once aspired to fine art with music merely an extra-mural pursuit in which personal popularity and financial gain were irrelevant. After the coming of Beatlemania, many such dabblers let themselves be sucked into a vortex of events, places and circumstances that hadn't been dreamed of before record industry talent scouts searched the kingdom for if not *the* New Beatles then *a* New Beatles.

The Fab Four's long shadow also provided Stuart Sutcliffe's posthumous career with the best and worst start. In 1964, his first major retrospective, in Liverpool's Walker Gallery, was attended by coachloads of Beatles fans with only the vaguest notion of what they had come to see. They may have shared the *Liverpool Daily Post* reviewer's 'impressive and moving experience'[2] – but, to them, Stuart was less an artist than the 'Fifth Beatle', the One Who Died, the auburn-haired one when the others were dark, the one whose name was less likely to trip off the tongue than those of John, Paul, George and even Ringo's predecessor, Pete Best.

Touchingly, Stuart's image was included among more fabled celebrities on 1967's *Sgt. Pepper's Lonely Hearts Club Band* album sleeve montage. Before the year was out, the Beatles also made veiled reference to their departed colleague in the *Magical Mystery Tour* soundtrack package. Nearly a quarter of a century on, 'Stuart Sutcliffe of The Beatles' was also pictured among 'absent friends' (as were Lennon and Brian Epstein) in the souvenir programme for a Liverpool charity concert where re-formed Merseybeat outfits performed before a spooky photo enlargement of Rory Storm, another local lad in the legion of the lost. During the early 1990s, small fortunes changed hands for a letter to Stuart from George and a Sutcliffe oil painting – not in the murmur of a museum or art gallery committee room but in the unrefined bustle of a pop memorabilia auction.

In a 1975 letter to Stuart's mother, John Willett, who had been prominent in the organization of the Walker retrospective, deplored a London gallery's reluctance to grant her son an exhibition as

they assume that the work must be artistically suspect because of the Beatle connection. I think they are wrong, but it will take a showing of the work itself to convince them so, and, of course, that is just the question at issue. It does seem rather an *impasse*. I wish I could do something to break it, but [I] am not at all active in the Art business, and find it difficult to go back to the people I think might listen to me – whether in the commercial or the 'official' Art world – and repeat things which I already told them several years ago. All I can say is that those are pictures which I don't forget, and that my opinion of them hasn't altered; your son was an artist, and the greater part of the work which I've seen was a good deal more than merely 'promising'.

According to Astrid, 'Stuart was a genius and would have been a very, very great writer and painter'.[3] More objective critics tend to bracket Sutcliffe with esteemed post-war Merseyside artists like George Jardine, Millicent Ayrton, John Edkins, Arthur Ballard and Nicholas Horsfield, of whom an uncanny number chose not to seek renown beyond Merseyside but to return to their old colleges as staff.

Would Stuart have done the same – or would he have become a second Picasso? We could speculate for ever. Perhaps he would have wound up back on the Beatles' payroll. While his ghost will hover over them always, their fairy-tale has given his surviving paintings a similar poignancy – if unwanted and less undeserved – to that of the daubs and sketches of such as Bob Dylan, the Prince of Wales, Syd Barrett, Captain Beefheart[4] and – yes – John Lennon: goods bought principally as investments for their historical and curiosity value, even out of morbid inquisitiveness.

Consequently, there will remain division over whether Sutcliffe was gifted – even brilliant – in absolute terms or just a minor talent in the Beatles' saga. If technically astounding, his earliest output as a student in Liverpool developed the ideas of others, but the final months in his Hamburg studio produced abstracts that had little obvious precedent, and were, indeed, 'a good deal more than merely "promising"'.

Regardless of how regrettable a loss he was to the world of fine art, as a figure in time's fabric, Sutcliffe's period as a Beatle was still central to most considerations of him in Dick Clark's made-for-TV *Birth of the Beatles*[5] in 1980. Neither did 1990's 'challenging' (i.e. incomprehensible) Granada TV documentary about him add any further information or in-depth assessment of motive. However, a silver screen bio-pic, *Backbeat* – *the* British movie of 1994 – might allow him to move at last into an orbit separate from that of the Beatles.

While Stuart Sutcliffe's deeds and personality have become more ambiguous and vague in retrospect, care has been taken to define as widely as possible the myriad social, cultural, economic, environmental and other factors that polarize and prejudice what is generally known about him already, and the new and rediscovered evidence and information that recent research has brought to light. Often pop biography – and that is all this account is – has tended to shy away from these areas, even though they form a more tangible basis for investigation than treating, say, John Lennon's most flippant remarks as gospel or squeezing a few paragraphs from an idle afternoon when George Harrison and Klaus Voorman spray-painted a friend's 1966 Citroën 2CV.

Those whose lives are devoted to collating facts about the Beatles may pounce on mistakes and omissions while scrutinizing *Backbeat*. All we can say to them is that it is as accurate as it can be after the synthesis of personal memories and interviews with most of the key *dramatis personae* – not to mention a filing cabinet of Sutcliffia, and exercise books full of doctor's prescription-like scribble drawn from press archives – some of them quite obscure.

For much of the secondary research, the authors would like to thank Ian Drummond who was always on hand at a moment's notice in his capacity as a scholar and observer of the Beatles and Stuart Sutcliffe. Thanks are also rendered to Bryan Biggs, Peter Doggett, Pete Frame, Spencer Leigh, Sam Leach, Steve Maggs, Andy Pegg and John Tobler for their faith and very real assistance, especially as consultants over apparent trivia.

We are also grateful to Susan Malvern, Jilly Easterby, Sophie Brewer, Hazel Orme and the rest of the team at Cavaye Place, particularly our commissioning editor Helen Gummer who, as expected, went far beyond the call of duty from this biography's sluggish genesis to its final publication.

Special tribute must also be paid to Arthur Ballard, the late Lord Clark of Saltwood, Finola Dwyer, Mike Evans, Adrian Henri, Nicholas Horsfield, Ken Horton, Michael Kenny RA, Rod Murray, Nik Powell, Muriel Radforth MBE, Iain Softley and John Willett. Let's hear it too for June Furlong, Bill Harry, John Hart, Philip Hartas,

The Fifth Man

Rod Jones, Astrid Kirchherr, Mark Lewisohn, Eduardo Paolozzi, Alan Peters, Jürgen Vollmer and Sir Harold Wilson.

We have also drawn from conversations with the following musicians: Ian Amey, Don Andrew, Roger Barnes, Alan Barwise, Cliff Bennett, Dave Berry, Don Craine, Tony Crane, Dave Dee, Keith Grant, Mike Hart, Tony Jackson, Garry Jones, Billy Kinsley, Jim McCarty, Mike Pender, Ray Phillips, Lord David Sutch, Mike Sweeney, Geoff Taggart, John Townsend, Paul Tucker and Twinkle.

Invaluable, too, was the clear insight and intelligent argument of Stuart Sutcliffe's elder sister, Joyce Whitelock Wainwright, and the patience of Kate Kilroy who, with the expertise of a short-order cook, was always ready to provide refreshments for up to a dozen people at once.

It may be obvious to the reader that we have received much information from sources that prefer not to be mentioned. Nevertheless, we wish to thank them.

We are also grateful to B and T Typewriters, Stuart and Kathryn Booth, Carol Boyer, Eva Marie Brunner, Ron Cooper, Brian Cresswell, Kevin Delaney, Mary Emmott, Tim and Sarah Fagan, Ross Fergusson, Beth Foster, Katy Foster-Moore, Ann Freer, Gary Gold, Dave and Caroline Humphreys, Allan Jones, Graham Larkbey, Brian Leafe, Dave and Helen Maggs, Russell Newmark, Mike Ober, Mike Robinson, George Rowden, Charles and Deborah Salt, Michael and Ann Towers, Andrea Tursso, Ted Woodings – and Inese, Jack and Harry Clayson for letting us get on with it.

Alan Clayson and Pauline Sutcliffe
London, 1993

NOTES

1   John Willett, a respected art critic and longtime champion of Stuart Sutcliffe's work, became aware of this at an early stage. He noted in 'The Arts in Liverpool', a *Liverpool Daily Post* article (19 March 1964), 'the embryonic and still unconscious relationship between the visual arts, jazz and the rock groups. We shall become more aware of this when the late Stuart Sutcliffe's pictures are shown here in May.'

2   *Liverpool Daily Post*, 19 March 1964.

3   *John Winston Lennon* by R. Coleman (Sidgwick and Jackson, 1984).

4   In fairness, Beefheart – as Don Van Vliet – has had around twenty-five exhibitions of his art shown around the world since retiring from the music business in 1982 to devote himself to painting. Most buyers are unfamiliar with his pop past.

5   According to one bizarre report, Pete Best was to play the teenage George Harrison. Actually, the sacked drummer had been engaged as the project's unheeded factual adviser.

chapter one

THE FATHER FIGURE

'I didn't think Liverpool had anyone like him'[1]
Brian Epstein

**'We'd hoped he'd become a doctor. "My son a
painter!" said Daddy, "I'll never live it down"'**[1]
Millie Sutcliffe

In 1940, Stuart Fergusson Victor Sutcliffe was born at the Simpson
Memorial Maternity Pavilion, Edinburgh, on the twenty-third
day of the warmest, driest June that Scotland had had for over
eighty years. The 'Fergusson' came from his thirty-five-year-old
father, Charles Fergusson Sutcliffe, the youngest of a tall, well-spoken
brood. Charles's immediate forebears were army-officer class, High
Anglican in religion, Tory in politics and prominent members of the
Freemasons. With an ingrained certainty about everything they said
and did, his parents had thrust their own deeply held values on their
children.

For almost the first twenty years of his life, little suggested that
Charles would be different. While at public school, he came up
through the ranks of its Boy Scout troop to become a King's Scout,
the highest honour that the meritocratic, paramilitary organization
could confer. Though the possibility of university might have beckoned, he joined the Civil Service at eighteen, climbing the executive
ladder almost straight away.

There was, however, another Charles Sutcliffe, who painted, did
pen-and-ink drawings, and took photography seriously enough to
develop films himself rather than trust the chemist. He also had a
natural aptitude and love for music. Having studied keyboards from
infancy, Charles had no qualms about performing in public, whether
tinkling incidental music as silent movies flickered in local cinemas;
taking his place on a palais bandstand to begin the night's veletas and
square tangos, or accompanying the hymns, canticles and psalms at
evensong in the local church.

In his early twenties, he cut back on the extra-curricular Te Deums and Charlestons after wedding Martha, a local butcher's daughter, in the teeth of parental disapproval. This union and its issue of four children propelled Charles up the career ladder; focusing more on his job, he landed the post of Head Assessor with the National Assistance Board for Scotland's east coast region. Even so, other members of the family couldn't help thinking that he had ruined his life by marrying beneath him and so young.

He was the fount of even fiercer gossip several years after this first marriage had broken down when his name was linked with Martha – though Charles was calling her 'Millie' to distinguish her from the other one. Two years his junior, 'Millie' Cronin was from an area of rural Lanarkshire. Her people were known to have Socialist sympathies, but were wealthy enough to have contributed quite substantially to the building of the village church – a Roman Catholic one, mind, at a time when Papism was still seen on a par with Fascism in many quarters of Scotland.

Millie spoke in a refined Hibernian trill, and was a distant relation of author A. J. Cronin of *Doctor Finlay of Tannochbrae* fame. However, as might be guessed from her contentious religion, Miss Cronin's background was as much Irish as Scottish. Through lingering Victorian custom, she was also the last of an unbroken line of nine daughters. Her parents' disappointment manifested itself in their hasty adoption of a longed-for son, and the emotional deprivation of sickly, diminutive Millie. One message, therefore, became clear early on: sons were special.

Had she had the benefit of psychoanalysis, Millie would have had to confront the crippling sense of loss and rejection she experienced from the cradle. This was exacerbated when, earmarked for the Church, she entered a Franciscan convent to be prepared for missionary work, but left before her final vows due to ill-health brought on by such a calling's harsh disciplines and self-denials, both physical and psychological.

She had begun training as a school teacher when she met Charles Sutcliffe. Though there were shared interests – for example, Millie, too, was an able pianist and had had the benefit of a private education – theirs was the proverbial 'attraction of opposites'. She was short and slight; he was tall. He was an adored son; she, a disregarded daughter.

The Father Figure

She had run into the arms of one who seemed a sophisticated man-of-the-world by the standards of her rustic upbringing. Unlike the former Boy Scout, well nurtured by his mother, Millie wasn't self-sufficient enough even to cook for herself. Charles was able to provide her with the care and instruction her own parents had never given.

Charles set the wheels in motion for the dissolution of his first marriage that had muddled on because neither partner had the motivation to finish it. Nevertheless, preferring marital fetters at any price to the scandal of divorce, the Sutcliffes cast the erring Charles adrift. To all intents and purposes, the Cronins had likewise disowned Millie.

For nine guilt-ridden years before she found a sympathetic priest, Millie attended Mass as a nominal outsider, barred from taking Holy Communion or having her confession heard. Her husband was punished for his hand in her sin by being required to resign his senior civil service position. On top of his professional ruin, the personal and legally imposed complications that would always yoke Charles to his daughter and three sons by his first wife was to place a frequently intolerable strain on his marriage to Millie.

There were, however, no perceptible signs of danger when the couple fled their horrified relations. For a while, they accepted any suitable work to be had over the border in Manchester and then London, but the outbreak of the Second World War and Charles's new vocation as a marine engineer found them back in Scotland.

This new post paid enough for the mortgage on an elegant terraced house in Edinburgh's Chalmers Street. For once, the couple seemed settled. Charles commuted to a Glasgow shipyard while Millie looked after Stuart and his sister Joyce, on the understanding that she would apply for teaching jobs as soon as the two babies were old enough to be assigned to a minder.

Nevertheless, she was determined to ensure that the children had everything she had missed during her emotionally impoverished upbringing in Lanarkshire. Stuart especially was treated as a wondrous gift, a notion applauded by her husband because he had been raised like that himself. It seemed natural to both parents that boys should hold sway over girls in the family structure.

More than Charles, Millie was glad to be back in the old country. She had never been quite comfortable among the English. A year after Joyce's arrival in 1942, however, the fever of mobilization took the family away from Scotland again. The War Office was anxious about the stalemate the Allied forces had reached against the Axis powers and Japan. They sent for Charles Sutcliffe. Millie, too, was called upon to teach.

As a tiny cog in the machine provisioning the distant bloodshed, he was dispatched to the Cammell Laird munitions depot in Birkenhead where barrage balloons hung over cranes and giant chimneys levelled at the sky like anti-aircraft guns. Ordered to remain there until further notice, Charles arranged for Millie and the toddlers to follow after he had been allocated 17 Sedbergh Grove, a council house in Huyton-with-Roby. This twin borough was then more Lancashire than Merseyside; within twenty years, however, it would be lost in the encroaching urban renewal programme that had been both helped and hindered by the malevolent shadows of Goering's Luftwaffe.

Though the house in Edinburgh was sold, Millie still assumed that their stay in Huyton was only for the duration of the war. Afterwards, they would go home to Scotland. She ran the household accordingly; porridge rather than less troublesome cornflakes was served for breakfast, and everyone donned national costume – sporrans, gorgets, clan tartans *et al.* – on Burns Night, Hogmanay and similar occasions. These customs continued even after months turned into years, and a second daughter, Pauline, was born in Huyton in 1944 when Millie was thirty-seven.

As all three children caught and held a Scouse intonation, Millie became increasingly maudlin about a Scotland she saw through a rosy haze, exiled as she was to this forlorn side-road where every strangely accented neighbour was potentially as much of an enemy as a German. Interrelated with this despair were the maladies that poleaxed her before the war was even half over. The most tangible were an operation to remove her gall bladder, and a miscarriage of twins. Then came a chest infection with its lifelong legacy of chronic bronchial asthma, though she gave this condition no help whatsoever with her inability to stop smoking.

She held her painful homesickness at arm's length to a degree by occupying herself with the patriotic chore she was most precisely qualified to do. After delivering the children to a nursery, she took a clattering rush-hour tram through tangles of Liverpool suburbs caked in grime and soot. In West Derby, she taught youngsters whose parents had been lost in the hostilities. Orphaned and bewildered, they had been housed – temporarily, they had been told – in the outbuildings of the Hospital for the Aged Poor on Belmont Road. Stirred by the wild boys and girls in an infinitely worse predicament than she was, Millie proved an efficient, caring schoolmistress with a valuable knack for scrounging materials to supplement the meagre supply of textbooks, pencils and other necessities that was all a harassed education authority could spare.

After the war, she transferred to the first of several Roman Catholic schools that would benefit from her skills. She also became an active and evangelical supporter of the Labour party, canvassing during the build-up to elections, posting manifestos (assisted by one or more of her children) and hosting campaign meetings in their living room.[2] On the periphery of debate at these gatherings, Stuart, Joyce and Pauline drank in an early if biased understanding of political doctrine and national and world affairs. While their play-mates may have heard vaguely of a man named Winston Churchill, the Sutcliffes could explain the different shades of Socialism, the Suez crisis and prison reform. They understood why their mother was nearly requested to leave the party over her vehement opposition – because she thought standards could not be maintained – to the 'education for all' comprehensive system, then so new that schools of this ilk were unknown in the north-east before the late 1950s.

The younger Sutcliffes' well-developed social consciences embraced both needy individuals in their immediate playground environment and a more sweeping concern about, say, the need for voters to badger the Government to do something about the slums. From their comparatively sheltered perspective, they had noticed but hardly spoken to rough children hopscotching and footballing in the greyer streets of the blackened city, and catcalling in the coarsest glottal intonation of a region where even the most refined speakers sounded ambiguously alien and 'common' to anyone south of Birmingham.

If Tory by instinct, Charles viewed his wife's political activities with benevolent neutrality. While you wouldn't catch him pushing her pamphlets through letter-boxes, he was only too pleased to help with research, writing pages of notes while delving into books either borrowed from the library or hauled off one of the shelves at home.

Backbeat

More steeped in literature than most, Millie and Charles had bred in Stuart a compulsive reader who was digesting Huxley, Kafka and Dostoevsky when others his age hadn't yet got past *Biggles Flies East*.

Such maturity might be expected of the son of older parents, one of whom was a teacher, but that alone didn't account for the questioning candour that carried Stuart and the girls into adulthood. Probably, it was rooted in Charles and Millie's own rebellion against the beliefs of *their* parents, and, according to Pauline, 'You've got to look at the polarity – Catholic mum, ex-nun, Church of England father, King's Scout, his father's background in the Regular Army, but the mother on the renegade side of it'.

No child of such parents could have avoided exposure to the arts. Van Gogh prints on the walls, and Charles's dark-room in the cupboard under the stairs were symptomatic of the perpetuation of his adolescent pastimes, as were the upright piano in the living room and the wheezy old harmonium that Charles had saved from destruction and repaired. Sensibly, neither father nor mother goaded the children to over-formalize what they might have assumed were innate artistic strengths.

Stuart's investigative pounding with plump fists on the piano was not, as it turned out, an indication of prodigious musical talent, but all the children were fascinated listeners when Mum or Dad was seated at the keyboards for those 'musical evenings' that were a frequent occurrence before television became an indispensable fixture in most homes. The sounds that tinkled from the Sutcliffes' front room ranged from Mozart, Chopin and Schumann to selections from the latest film musicals like *South Pacific* and *Oklahoma*. Before being packed off to bed, Pauline might be cajoled into piping out her party piece, 'Polly Put The Kettle On'. Stuart and Joyce considered themselves above nursery rhymes.

All three endured weekly piano lessons on the same evening from a lady who was always ostensibly delighted with their progress, especially that of Stuart whom she saw first. The others followed in order of age. This policy was, conjectured Pauline, 'the wrong way round because I was usually the sleepiest and the least inclined to do it when it got round to my turn'. None of them practised much, partly because they had come to believe the marvellous reports given to Millie by the tutor as she pocketed her fee.

Soon, they felt sufficiently confident to venture into the avant-garde – albeit when both tutor and parents were out of the house. One such piece, the wittily titled 'Music For Per*cushion*', began, remembers Pauline, by 'putting a cushion on the piano, then we would sit on the cushion and bounce up and down'. In later recitals, they grew bold enough to remove the front board from the instrument so that Stuart could pluck the wires, breaking off occasionally for ballet leaps across the room. Precocious though they were, they were not aware that 'Music For Percushion' was comparable in its way to the buzzings and rattlings of US composer John Cage's works for pianos 'treated' with objects from household and office.

The cover was blown on the piano teacher after she had kept her sessions going for a full year. Her impressive written assessments had little substance, as Charles realized on testing Stuart who couldn't manage the most elementary exercises. Without bothering to hear the girls, he cancelled all further lessons.

Stuart compounded his father's disappointment by proving himself as inept on the bugle during a spell with the Air Training Corps.[3] Neither did he master an acoustic guitar bought for him by Charles. Yet despite the depressing discoveries that he was no natural instrumentalist with little capacity to try, try again, Stuart was self-contained enough to disassociate the music itself from the carping tutorials and the prescribed drudgery of daily practice.

Like his father's, Stuart's musical genesis was ecclesiastic as well as domestic. His singing voice was put to use in the choir at St Gabriel's in Hall Lane, Huyton Quarry. In cassock, ruff and surplice, he warbled at three services every Sunday and, when required, at weddings and St Cecilia's Day oratorios. Before his voice deepened to baritone, he was appointed head chorister. As befitted this office, he was privileged to bear the processional cross as priest and choir filed to and from the vestry. He also snuffed out the altar candles after the General Confession during Matins. However, the holy sounds he sang every Sunday were novel and intelligible at seven, over-familiar and rote-learnt by thirteen: like every intelligent teenager, he questioned the motive of adult communicants. Was praising the Lord once a week a stockpiling of spiritual ammunition for the defence when their cases came up in the afterlife?

He and his sisters were inclined to be conscientiously 'good' for similar reasons after Charles joined the Merchant Navy in 1947. For over a decade he was a more remote figure in their lives, prompting opaque memories of life during the war. However, in some respects, he governed his children's behaviour from the high seas via Millie's 'just wait till your father gets home' litanies whenever they were naughty, although unless they had done something beyond redemption, Dad's homecomings were usually akin to the arrival of Santa Claus with his sack of presents and other intriguing objects from foreign parts.

Life without Charles wasn't easy for Millie at first. For a northern male, he had been unusually attentive to household tasks, particularly cooking. This was fortunate as his spouse was no great chef. Nevertheless, without it impinging on either her teaching career or her work on behalf of the Labour party, she ensured that her – thankfully, healthy – children were as comfortable and contented as her new station as a virtual single parent would allow.

Stuart, Joyce and Pauline helped according to their varying capabilities with the initial enthusiasm children often have for the onerous jobs on the rota their mother had drawn up. Yet though the situation nurtured self-reliance, Stuart's childhood was shorter than it needed to have been. At times, Millie – vulnerable both socially and physically – was unable to separate her needs of Stuart from his needs of her. He became the confidant and comforter her husband had been, a rock for her to lean on. It wasn't surprising, therefore, that the girls, plainly aware of their secondary place in their mother's hierarchy, came to look on him in the same way.

Aged seven when his father's impact on the family lessened, Stuart was living evidence of the precept, supported by developmental theories, 'Give me the child till he's seven and I will show you the man.' Having absorbed his father's attitudes towards the women of the household, he slipped easily into the paternal role thrust upon him during Charles' absences. As a result, he emerged as an astoundingly self-confident, purposeful young man, able to differentiate between his own passions and those of others.

He was an unlikely looking father figure. Short, bespectacled and bookish, he had had all the makings of a swot when, gaberdine-raincoated and short-trousered, he began his formal education at nearby Park View Primary School. Perhaps to allay guilt about her growing dependence on him as the man of the house, Millie, with her insider's awareness, enquired into problems Stuart encountered at school with a zeal that other parents might have thought excessive.

The Father Figure

With a possessive intensity that both they and Stuart might not have welcomed, she spoke to his teachers whenever he got into trouble.

He was to indulge in petty shop-lifting, stealing fruit from local orchards and similar pranks of normal boyhood. At school, though he was placatory in the uglier playground confrontations, he was not the sissy bigger boys might have imagined. His father's son, he would put up his fists, look fierce and hope for the best rather than swallow insults. The most public playtime disputes were usually concluded in the Head's office, as often as not with the swish of a bamboo cane on buttocks or outstretched palm. The rap of a cane on an inkwelled desk might also regulate the mechanical chanting of multiplication tables.

Under the unimaginative and often frightening regime prevalent in Park View and most other state schools in the late 1940s, Stuart made steady progress. His retentive memory and methodical tenacity (that he wouldn't apply to piano lessons) helped an already advanced and sometimes encyclopaedic perception of people and places, interactions and outcomes. Arithmetic was a trying subject but, even in the infant department, he betrayed a flair for art and creative writing.

It was supposed by Millie that he would pass the eleven-plus examination and gain a place at a grammar school rather than a secondary modern – where all the 'failures' went. This was then a desirable social coup for ambitious parents. When the soap opera *Coronation Street* was young, 'Ken Barlow', then fourth-year teacher at a junior school, was once depicted refusing a bribe to rig the eleven-plus results so that a town councillor's son could attend Market Wetherby Grammar. Such illicit strategies were, of course, anathema to Millie – and so was the traditional bribery of a new bicycle. Stuart would have to pay for most of one with his earnings from a paper round.

Just in case Stuart was below par on that day of days, Millie left as little as possible to chance by giving him extra coaching in mathematics. 'She used to drum formulae into him,' said Pauline, 'teach him tricks for learning.' His weakness in the subject had mystified Charles who played chess like a master and regarded numerical posers as an amusing game.

Millie's efforts were not wasted, and Stuart, ill at ease in the regulation uniform of black 'bombhead' shoes, grey flannels, blazer, white shirt, tie and cap, boarded the Liverpool bus for his first day at

Prescot Grammar in September 1951. As far as he was concerned, he had suffered enough maths to last a lifetime merely to get there. Therefore, he was going to exert himself in that area, and others he disliked, just enough to avert punishment.

If indifferent to logarithms and Euclid's knottier theorems, Stuart shone in those subjects that the ordinary working man, whether navvy or ledger clerk, saw as having doubtful practical value. Never mind, it could provide inadvertent fun – like the time when an abstract by Arthur Ballard, a Liverpool painter, was exhibited upside down.

A keen interest in music and art was treated with humorous scepticism – and Prescot's respective teachers in these disciplines only helped to reinforce such prejudice. Flamboyant in a flapping cloak, Joseph Kirk tried to increase attentiveness to music by means other than the tedium of diminished fifths and Brahms' German Requiem. He was the sort who would start a lunchtime guitar club in the hope that it might lead participants to study flamenco. Among his star pupils were Neil Foster, a classmate of Stuart, who played woodwinds, and Ken Horton, who slid trombone. Ken was, perhaps, Stuart's closest friend at school.[4]

William Walters, the art master, was of a similar type to Mr Kirk. Burly in build, his artificial leg, suede shoes, creased corduroy jacket and halo of powder paint set him apart from smarter-looking colleagues in their academic gowns. To Ken Horton, 'Art teaching was more or less copying and learning off the blackboard', but Walters did not always stick to a curriculum that made only cursory reference to modern movements like Dada and surrealism.

Under Mr Walters, Stuart's technical expertise was more noticeable at first than any creative inclinations. By the time his O level (General Certificate of Education) exams loomed, he could duplicate any known artistic style, and his appreciation of what was worth looking at and what wasn't became more acute. He was drawn in particular to the Impressionists and the then unfashionable Pre-Raphaelites. From these new aesthetic and intellectual experiences were forged the naïve beginnings of both a personal style and an as yet unspoken fancy that he would like to make his way in the world as some sort of visual artist.

He didn't mention it immediately as he wasn't sure how Mum – and Dad when he was around – would react. Though both had sought to stimulate his interest in art from the cradle, they wouldn't allow it to gain unrealistic proportions. Put crudely, art was all right as a hobby but you couldn't make a living at it. Mr and Mrs Sutcliffe's vocation-minded attitude was not uncommon: a Liverpool contemporary, Michael Kenny, had to appease his parents by taking a soul-destroying job in a blood transfusion laboratory before he found the courage to chuck it in and enter the city's Regional College of Art.

Kenny became a well-known sculptor, but he had to move to London to be recognized as such. Merseysiders treated their local artists less deferentially than Londoners. As late as 1960, no artist based in Liverpool had been able to rely solely on his work for a reasonable income. This had much to do with the dearth of effective commercial and promotional outlets within the region. A typical case was that of Roderick Bisson. Painting was his life but the closest he came to doing it full-time was as an architect's draughtsman and then as the *Liverpool Post*'s shrewd and well-informed art critic.

Musicians were in the same boat. If on a business trip to Manchester, which with its radio and television stations was 'Entertainment Capital of the North', moguls from the kingdom's four major record companies rarely found time to negotiate the thirty-odd miles west to sound out talent. In the realm of popular music, it had been necessary for 1950s palais vocalists Lita Roza, Frankie Vaughan and Michael Holliday to tramp a well-beaten path south to Make It. 'In the noise and heat of a tailor's shop,' cooed *Everybody's Weekly* in 1956, 'a nineteen-year old negress from Liverpool thinks of crooning in a West End night club.'[5]

Millie Sutcliffe's thoughts had lain in the opposite direction. Though the family's upmarket move in 1951, to 43 St Anne's Road, was an unquestionable material improvement – 'From a council house to something more Huyton villagey,' recalled Pauline – it represented a deeper entrenchment in the bleak conurbation she had never liked. During Stuart's second year at Prescot Grammar, her yearning for 'home' became so overwhelming that she abruptly upped and left for a probationary term in a Scottish school. It was triggered by some frank exchanges with Charles after she found out that he was still very much in personal touch with the avowedly half-forgotten children of his first marriage, about whom Stuart, Joyce and Pauline had only a generalized suspicion. On his last voyage, he had even holidayed with his eldest son, now a naturalized Australian.

Charles was compelled to throw down the anchor in Huyton for months while Millie decided what to do. He didn't use the word 'separation' in front of the children, preferring them to think of it as a journey from which their mother would return – just as he did from abroad. As it happened, he was right. The ghost of Scotland as some kind of Promised Land was exorcized, and Millie did not sign on for a permanent post.

In vain, she had defied a seemingly preordained fate. Prosperity had been just as thin on the ground in urban Scotland as it was on Merseyside. All such regions were riven with queues as the country paid for its war. Well into the 1950s, food and clothing continued to be rationed. As bad in its way was life's overall drabness. With geometrically patterned lino the only hint of frivolity in middle-class homes, you would get stuck on a post-dinner crossword and wander over to the front window to stare glumly through the lace curtains and wonder if this was all there was. There was nothing on the horizon to indicate openings other than in secure but dead-end jobs with a gold watch on retirement to tick away the seconds before you went underground.

You were lucky to have a job at all around Liverpool. Time was, when a third of Britain's exports from the tropics and North America passed through its docks, clerking offices and processing mills. Thanks to the investment of old money in the shipping boom, it was recognized as the second largest city in the kingdom when it was created a bishopric in 1897. A year before, the University of Liverpool had opened on the site of the old lunatic asylum.

Heat from this high summer was still felt half a century later, although, as an economic base, Liverpool had been outflanked by the gouging of the ship canal to Manchester. Even in boom years, the unemployed were a civic nuisance. With demand for labour rock-bottom by the late 1930s, the only visible reminders of former glory were promenade edifices such as the statue of Edward VII staring towards the clouded hills of North Wales.[6] By the end of the war, commuter ferries on the Mersey were chugging past a shoreline sliding into seediness; a desolation of used-car lots, silos, advertising hoardings, derelict warehouses and moorings for corroded barges. Gradually, this mean hinterland gave way to the worn grandeur of marble, granite and sandstone round the Pier Head. Raw red bricks, however, were the principal building blocks of the overspill estates that were swallowing the city's surviving parks and tree-lined avenues, which had once been admired by Daniel Defoe.

Liverpool was already bleeding into Huyton village in 1953 when the Sutcliffes changed residence from St Anne's Road to 22 Sandiway, nearer Joyce and Pauline's primary school. The first tower block had appeared. The view from the top floor was perversely spellbinding: the creeping smog, the sulphurous light, miles and miles of Coronation Streets and arteries of traffic that droned constantly.

To the affluent south, it was a place with a football team stuck in the middle of the Second Division; a corner of the map where penury and unemployment clotted, and nothing happened except dock strikes. It was assumed that the further north you voyaged, the more primitive the natives. Past Birmingham, people still wore clogs and shawls, didn't they? Disregarded by the rest of the country, 'the pool of life', as Jung tagged it, bubbled in its isolation and built-in resilience.

More comedians than other types of artist emerged from the city. Nevertheless, before high rents priced out all but the most affluent, the streets within earshot of the unfinished Anglican cathedral's bells were a Scouse bohemia that intermingled with a Scouse Harlem. As well as West Indian immigrant families, it teemed with would-be poets, painters, musicians and the like, ekeing out a living in studio flats within crumbling town houses built originally for slave merchants. Once the acme of elegance, these buildings now held each other up like drunks rolling home after closing-time. Their state of disrepair was expressed to passers-by in peeling pillars, window-ledges off-white with pigeon droppings, and rubbish sogging behind railings. Thunderous door-knockers would shake lumps of brittle plaster from walls in hallways where naked light bulbs were coated in dust.

The main thoroughfare was Hope Street which, aptly enough, linked the Roman Catholic and Anglican cathedrals. Along one of its tributaries, Mount Street, stood most of the city centre's seats of learning outside the university campus. The Mechanics Institution with its imposing Greek façade had occupied an entire side of the street until 1905 when it split into the Institute High School for Boys, a sister school, a dance-and-drama academy and the Regional College of Art.

Backbeat

The best known of Merseyside's art schools, the college's catchment area embraced North Wales, Preston and Blackpool. Its intake dwarfed that of art faculties within the university and Liverpool Polytechnic and, indeed, every other art establishment in the northwest whether the vibrant Laird School of Art over the water at Birkenhead or Wallasey School of Art, which, in 1938, contained only six students and one master.

Even when it had been a pivot of Victorian commerce, the city offered numerous opportunities for cultural development matching those of any other British city bar the capital. While Augustus John taught at the art college, and Dickens gave readings at the Institute, Liverpool also benefited from the bequest of private artistic purchases by John Rankin, James Smith and other enlightened industrialists in its close-knit business community. Such gifts were exhibited in all manner of public galleries, some of them purpose-built by the givers. Works could be hung and mounted in the Walker, the Bluecoat, the Academy, the Allerton, the Williamson, the New Shakespeare Theatre and in the university. Otherwise, they could be seen in the less rarefied atmosphere of arty coffee-bars-cum-clubs like the Blue Angel, Streate's, the Zodiac and the Jacaranda.

The latter was a watch-repair shop prior to its transformation in 1957 with newly painted walls, benchseats and a dropped trellis-work ceiling with dangling fishing-nets and coloured glass balls. A convenient stone's throw from the art college, it became a rendezvous for the students and staff as well as those with business at the nearby Labour Exchange. You could sit there for hours on end for the price of a transparent cup of frothy coffee. Entertainment was usually coin-operated but, as a change from the juke-box, musicians were hired to play evening sessions on the small dance floor in the basement.

After its opening in 1959, tutors and students alike could also hold court in the cellar bar of Hope Hall (later, the Everyman). As well as exhibitions of local art, 'the Hope' hosted poetry recitals and the kind of films that, having faded from general circulation, are watched as either an intellectual duty or as a wallow in nostalgia. Millie Sutcliffe was a keen patron of the Hope and other specialist film clubs as far away as Hoylake and Birkenhead. Stuart often went too. However, though he professed a liking for early Chaplins and other silent movies, Pauline 'didn't know if he used to go to keep her company, or whether it was an active choice'.

The Father Figure

Cinema proprietor Leslie Blond had financed the building of Hope Hall, but the city's most famous commercial patriarch was the late John Moores, founder of the Littlewoods Organization in 1934. After a shaky start, he amassed his first million with the football pools, a competition with cash prizes. Ramsay MacDonald pronounced it 'a disease' as it spread across the nation, countless households filling in the weekly coupon that might win them a fortune. By the 1950s, Moores, an adventurous if old-fashioned businessman, controlled a retailing empire that employed ten thousand on Merseyside alone.

The paternalistic firm's art society, seventy-strong choir and similar recreational facilities were inspired by the boss himself. Nevertheless, Moores the man was a self-effacing fellow with a harelip and spectacles who shunned publicity. If parsimonious in small matters, he lent generous hands-on support to children's charities. A painter himself on the quiet, he was a collector and connoisseur of modern British art. Indeed, much of his wealth had been spent on the fostering of art in Liverpool via scholarships and, in conjunction with the Walker Gallery, his inauguration in 1957 of the biennial John Moores Exhibition of Contemporary Art, one of the few British arts institutions known simply by its benefactor's name. Its declared aim was 'to encourage living artists, particularly the young and progressive'. Motivational sub-texts were rooted in Moores' municipal pride, justified when the winning of a John Moores prize became one of the proudest boasts a British artist could make.

Quite a few of these winners came from Merseyside itself. While it was not steeped in the same cohesive traditions as Paris or Venice, the region had produced a respectable crop of parochially renowned artists. Yet the world at large remained ignorant of the likes of Neville Bertram, Millicent Ayrton, Thomas Rathwell, Josh Kirby, Clifford Fishwick, Nicholas Horsfield, Roger Leigh, Mavis Blackburn and even George Jardine, who carried off a 1957 Moores prize with a surreal landscape, reminiscent of Dali.

The man-in-the-street may have read about them occasionally in the *Liverpool Post*, but he poured contempt upon a lot of these so-called artists' efforts. They could talk all they liked about 'isms', 'periods' and 'movements', but he would still scratch his head over the squiggles and explosive blots or even the clean geometry of Mondrian or Malevich before asking, 'What's it meant to be?' Like some twentieth-century music had left key, scale and the common chord behind, so the modern artist didn't have to produce a nice picture of a specific subject any more; photography took care of that. Whether Fauvist, Cubist, Dadaist or Surrealist, a painting or sculpture no longer needed to be of anything recognizable. Like music, its sole object was to touch you in some way, perhaps for reasons you couldn't put into words.

Abstract expressionism was all the rage in the 1950s, not so much the Americans as the more lyrical Tachism of the École de Paris. Outlines dissolve between Tachism and action painting. 'Unconscious calligraphy' was the blanket term coined by one critic. It involved the unplanned application of colour to 'represent' nothing but itself. Sounds pretty easy, eh? While it was true enough that anyone could do it, like a stand-up comic with old jokes, it's the way you tell 'em. A Tachist painting was supposed to express the emotional condition of the artist at the time he did it. If he was in an interesting emotional condition, the result was interesting. There was a difference between the intelligent implementation of technique, and just squirting and splashing it on any old how.

Philosophically, Tachism is sometimes linked with existentialism and its 'nothing matters' preoccupations with fed-upness and death. Among Tachism's leading exponents are Willem de Kooning, Jackson Pollock – and Nicolas de Staël, a former French Foreign Legionnaire. His subsequent career in Paris epitomized the popular romantic ideal of the bohemian, right up to his self-administered exit in 1955 at the age of forty. 'He died with his work as it were,' theorized Nicholas Horsfield. 'His work was developed and I think the reason why he committed suicide was, like Van Gogh, he'd said it all and didn't know where to go.'

During his final years, de Staël reverted to figurative painting, though not in a realistic style. Some of his portrayals of footballers found their way to showrooms in central Liverpool, such as the Times Furnishing Co. and Lewis's Show House.

In extreme terms, de Staël – and, in method, England's David Bomberg – may be seen as a shadowy link between abstract expressionism and another major trend of the 1950s, the austere 'kitchen-sink' realism that articulated the post-war mood of the 'Angry Young Men'. Titles from the movement's books, plays and films – *Billy Liar*, *Look Back In Anger*, *Room At The Top* – are more familiar than the output of Jack Smith, Edward Middleditch, Derrick Greaves and – another 1957 Moores winner – John Bratby. Vigour not subtlety was the name of the game. Brushwork was always conspicuous, and bright, harsh *impasto* slapped on so aggressively that it stood out in lumps. Its usual subject matter was domestic squalor and sordid scenarios from the inner city – just the thing to nail over your mantelpiece.

It wasn't done to be both an abstract expressionist and a social realist. Unless you were of a truly independent spirit, you were either one or the other. In Liverpool, lines were drawn in noisy argument in Ye Cracke, the pub in Rice Street frequented by those denizens of the art college who patronized the Jacaranda outside licensing hours. Certain ex-students had returned to teach at the college after the war: Bertram, for example, had been appointed initially to the sculpture department while Horsfield and Jardine, respectively, took art history and graphics. A younger old boy, John Edkins, painter of neat, emblematic canvases, joined the staff in 1961 only to die under the scalpel five years later, just before his thirty-sixth birthday. Unlike de Staël, he can be eliminated from any league of legend by a relatively uneventful if industrious life.

Owing to poor health, Edkins was an irregular participant in lunchtime symposia. The most celebrated local artists to prop up the bar at Ye Cracke and the Everyman were the two Arthurs, Ballard and Dooley. An ex-shipyard welder, the self-taught Dooley exhibited his first metal sculptures at the Jacaranda. These were as brutish as his anti-everything personality. Never one to forgo opportunities for self-promotion, he was particularly outspoken about the question of working-class children getting into art college. Dooley reckoned that the system favoured 'doctors' daughters'.

Bill Harry, an art college student who was the product of as tough a childhood as Dooley's, agreed. During his maiden term in 1954, he was struck that 'a lot of the young girls there were from middle-class families, whose parents had put them in art school until they were about eighteen or so, so they can get married and everything without having to do a job in the meantime. They were more or less dilettantes, dabbling in everything, and there didn't seem to be all that much of a creative spark.'

Dooley instigated a sensational punch-up in the Everyman with Arthur Ballard after belabouring him over the issue. He was either a brave or a foolhardy man. Ballard was, like William Walters, a middleweight boxer in his youth, resembling more closely a PT instructor than an art lecturer. However, as television wrestler Mick McManus was an expert on fine porcelain, and comedy film actor Will Hay a noted astronomer, so pugnacious Ballard was the most omnipotent of post-war Merseyside-born painters.

On leaving school in 1930, he enrolled at the art college. Specialized in painting, he was accepted for teacher training, and was working in a Wavertree school up to his conscription into the army. While he was stationed in Egypt, he exhibited some watercolours, mostly landscapes, in Cairo's British Institute. Upon his demobilization, these and other items created in the theatre of war appeared in the Bluecoat.

He was then headhunted by the college principal, Henry Huggell, for the painting department. Before a lengthy sabbatical in Paris in 1958, he could be categorized as a social realist, albeit one with overtly abstract tendencies. France, however, caused him to cut back on representationals in favour of an uncompromising form of abstract expressionism. The prosaic titles of his new works (such as *Abstract Painting*) betrayed no clues. The pervading influence (and not only on Ballard at the college) was de Staël, although Ballard claimed never to have heard of him until a comparison was made in a *Times* review.

Further critical feedback from Ballard's periodic exhibitions down south intimated that had he moved to London, the art world might have been his oyster. Yet he preferred to be a big fish in a smaller pond with a regular income supplemented by prizes in the 1959 and 1961 Moores events, and sales of about one painting a year. He would always defend these modest windfalls, saying, 'Van Gogh never sold a picture in his life.'

By the early 1960s, however, the quality of Arthur's work showed signs of inconsistency and self-doubt, failings connected with bouts of depression and the worry over his wife's cancer. Nevertheless, he was strong-minded enough to remain, outwardly at least, the lively, popular college tutor, respected as both a figurehead and *éminence grise* of the local art scene.

Arthur was a family friend of the Sutcliffes; while he found Millie 'difficult', he drank socially with Charles, 'very much a man's man'. Of the eldest child, Ballard would 'always remember one rather amusing incident I had when I first knew him. He went to London for the first time with a school party, and when he came back, the thing that impressed him more than anything else was that middle-aged men were wearing drain-pipe trousers. He couldn't believe it of middle-aged men.'

The latest films and plays were quicker to reach Liverpool than Cecil Gee menswear. At Prescot and other secondary schools, boys were still supposed to dress like little men, men like most of their masters, smooth in the 1950s 'quiet' style of cardigan and dark business suit with baggy trousers. Those who still lived with parents risked disinheritance if they dared to come downstairs in an American tie.

During the decade after the war, GIs on leave from bases in Lancashire would descend on Liverpool City centre in snazzy check jackets, hip-hugging slacks, bowling shoes and those provocative hand-painted ties with baseball players or Red Indians on them. Sartorial visions, they would acknowledge bemused stares with waves of fat wands of cigars.

Other stares were in envy. The United States seemed the well-spring of everything glamorous from Coca-Cola to the Ink Spots, whose humming polyphony had enraptured the Liverpool Empire in 1947. 'Are we turning our children into little Americans?' bleated *Everybody's Weekly*.[7] Still a principal port of embarkation for the Americas, Liverpool was more prone to such a metamorphosis than other cities. Like Stuart Sutcliffe, many Merseyside teenagers had fathers or brothers at sea who would import Davy Crockett mock-coonskin caps, classic literature in comic form, otherwise unobtainable records and further treasures long before they filtered even to London.

There was also much to please British children in US movies. Throughout the late 1940s and early 1950s, Stuart and his sisters would queue with a million others for Saturday morning cinema. It was always fun there; the convulsions of laughter at the same joke; the lump in the throat during the sad bits, giving way to giggles; the Pearl and Dean commercials; choc-ice and Kia-Ora, and the muted buzz as the half-lights dimmed before the main feature. While dipping involuntarily into a rustling packet of Murraymints, you'd feast visually on a diet of Walt Disney, cowboys-and-Injuns and swash-buckling 'historical' epics. Closer to home were the offerings of UK companies like Ealing and Gainsborough with their hello-'ello-'ello policemen, monocled cads and happy endings.

Backbeat

Their antitheses, as Stuart discovered when old enough to watch them, were the A- and X-rated flicks pertaining to Hollywood's cynical *film noir* apotheosis. Whether an espionage thriller like *Pickup On South Street* or the backstage plot – debonair radio star with a sinister secret – of 1947's *The Unexpected*, the overall thrust was similar: platinum blondes in sleazy dives; rain-sodden nights lit by neon advertisements; and lonesome anti-heroes, narcissistic and defeatist. Stuart was inclined towards the more thought-provoking movies of the genre, particularly the crafted high tension of Hitchcock and the psychological analyses of underlying violence when Tennesse Williams's dramas were adapted for film.

In 1951, Williams's *A Streetcar Named Desire* starred Marlon Brando. Three years later, Brando was the leather-clad leader of a motorcycle gang, mumbling his way through *The Wild One*. Much banned, because he and his hoodlums' raid on a small sir-and-ma'am town went unpunished. *The Wild One* did not appal the generation later blamed for the 'generation gap'. Instead, the moral crusade – if it was one – backfired, the gap widened, and the delinquent Brando character became a role model: a 'fast boy' oozing sullen introspection, despised by your parents for coming from the wrong side of town. On uncovering your sister's illicit trysts with him, a responsible father would order her to never see him again. Flighty girls like Brigitte Bardot revelled in their disobedience. Acned youths everywhere slobbered over Brigitte, but the Thinking Man's French actress was Juliette Greco. A singer, too, she was a high priestess of popular existentialism, and a pioneer of white lipstick that, coupled with black mascara, tent-like sweater and trousers, made her the heroine of intellectual adolescent females in dim-lit middle-class bedrooms.

If they had heard of them, their sixth-form brothers could identify with the German actor Horst Buchholz and his Polish opposite number, Zbigniew Cybulski, but the secondary-modern yobs who weren't shackled to homework in the evenings went for James Dean, the rock 'n' roll rebel prototype, who left this vale of misery in his silver Porsche Spyder at 86 mph on 30 September 1955. Of Dean's three movies, the posthumously released *Giant* was one of the highest grossing of all time – simply because he was in it for forty minutes.

Nineteen fifty-five's *Rebel Without A Cause*, however, surfaced as all-time favourite, partly because it demonstrated that you didn't have to be from the wrong side of town to qualify as a charismatic ne'er-do-well. On Merseyside, even middle-class boys from Huyton mooched down to corner shops with hunched shoulders, hands rammed in pockets, and chewing gum in a James Dean half-sneer.

If the attitude was derived from Dean, the appearance of the most menacing teenage cult of the 1950s was almost entirely British. Teddy Boys went around in packs to barge *en bloc* and without paying into dancehalls, especially those where Teds were barred. If there was no other action going, they might wreck a Church youth club, snarling with laughter as a with-it vicar in a cardigan pleaded with them ineffectually. Pedestrians would cross the road to avoid lamp-post clusters of hybrid Edwardian rakes and Mississippi riverboat card-sharps with brass rings decorating their fists like knuckledusters.

A meek reproof by the victim had sparked off the first Teddy Boy murder in 1954. After that, there had been questions in Parliament, hellfire sermons, plays like Bruce Walker's *Cosh Boy* – that suggested flogging was the only answer – and films such as *Violent Playground* and 1957's *These Dangerous Years*, both set in Liverpool.

These Dangerous Years – teenage troublemaker reformed by a spell in the army – had a title song performed by Frankie Vaughan who, in 1958, rivalled Dickie Valentine as the country's most popular male vocalist. Their music, like most of that aired on British radio and television before the mid-1950s, was directed at the over-thirties. For the adolescent listener – and a mighty 'square' one at that – there was *Quite Contrary*, a show built round the light-opera style and heavily masculine image of Ronnie Hilton who, for want of anyone better, had preceded Dickie Valentine as the UK's singing demi-god.

For pre-teen listeners, there was the BBC Light Programme's *Children's Favourites*, a weekly hour of mostly lightweight novelties like 'Where Will The Baby's Dimple Be', 'The Runaway Train' and 'The Ballad Of Davy Crockett'. Stuart Sutcliffe was particularly fond, apparently, of 'How Much Is That Doggie In The Window', not Lita Roza's cover but the US original by the more personable Patti Page, 'The Singing Rage', who headlined a weekly spectacular on Independent Television which broke the BBC's stranglehold over the nation's electric media in 1956.

Some teenagers might have supposed that the 'quality' adult schmaltz they picked up on TV or wireless was because they had cheap sets, but it was the same on all of them: programmes monopolized by such as Billy Cotton, *Housewives' Choice* idol Lee Lawrence and Donald Peers ('The Cavalier of Song') with his maddening 'By A Babbling Brook' signature tune, plus musical interludes in shows spotlighting such as ventriloquist's dummy Archie Andrews, Richard 'Mr Pastry' Hearne and Lancastrian 'schoolboy' Jimmy Clitheroe. While *Round About Ten* was a bit racy in its embrace of Humphrey Lyttelton's Jazz Band, the inclusion of the Teenagers, a winsome boy-girl troupe in 'Forces Sweetheart' Vera Lynn's *Melody Cruise*, was something of a false dawn.

December 1955 brought a vague glimmer of hope when Dickie Valentine's 'Christmas Alphabet' lost a hard-fought battle for supremacy in the recently established *NME* record sales chart ('hit parade') against a disc by Bill Haley and the Comets, a paunchy North American dance combo. Incited by the newspapers, Teddy Boys snapped cinema seats off their spindles to make room for themselves and their girlfriends to jive when the metronomic clamour of Haley's 'Rock Around The Clock' and other 'rock 'n' roll' ditties punctuated the flimsy plot of 1956's low-budget B-feature of the same name.

It was never as bad as the tabloids made out. Enterprising cinema managers even began offering 'Teenage Shows' during intermissions on Saturday mornings when possessed local youths knee-dropped, swivelled their hips and rolled about as if they had wasps in their pants. These gyrations, together with the lop-sided smirk and the hot-potato-in-the-mouth singing were not an aping of Haley, but of a more suitable teenage champion in a twenty-year-old Tennesseean named Elvis Presley. As the first photograph of him[8] published in Britain testified, he was of the Brando-Dean persuasion and, like the Teddy Boys, had a brilliantined but effeminate cockade offset with scimitar-like sideburns. Attired in outrageous 'cat' clothes of pink and black, he was a seedy-flash cross between a pool-hall hoodlum and a homosexual GI gone berserk on a weekend pass.

Presley's first single had been a hillbilly treatment of a negro blues. From then on, his go-man-go 'rockabilly' and sulky balladeering came to be both adored and detested throughout North America. The staid *NME* dismissed 'Heartbreak Hotel', the first of his singles to be issued in Britain, with 'If you appreciate good singing, I don't suppose you'll manage to hear this all through.'[9] Later, a *Melody Maker* correspondent would call it 'emotionally embarrassing and intellectually ridiculous'.[10] What more did Elvis need to be the toast of teenage Britain?

Stuart Sutcliffe was approaching his sixteenth birthday when he first heard 'Heartbreak Hotel'. He was instantly 'gone'. Elvis Presley was surely the greatest man ever to have walked the planet and listening to him either sent Stuart into a reverie or brought on an onset of high spirits. Sometimes his discovery cried out to be shared with others, and so it was that he drew in Joyce, Pauline – who had the same birthday (8 January) as Elvis – and even Millie. On other occasions, it was something no one else could be allowed to touch. The spotty Prescot Grammar pupil would place, say, 'All Shook Up', the King of Western Bop's first UK Number One, on the Dansette turntable, and get into position in front of the mirror. From the opening bars to the final chord, he would curl his lip, hip-shake and pretend to slash chords and pick solos with negligent ease on the guitar his father had given him. He would mouth the lyrics, yeah-ing and uh-huh-ing to imaginary thousands of ecstatic girls. Some only-too-real girls – a group of Joyce's schoolfriends – once burst in on one of Stuart's rituals of frustrated eroticism. He froze, gaped at the stunned faces in the doorway, and felt no end of a fool.

Who said rock 'n' roll wouldn't last? Every week seemed to bring another US maniac into the hit parade. Even wilder than either the proper or make-believe Presley was shrieking Little Richard in billowing drapes, beating hell out of a concert grand in Bill Haley's second movie, *Don't Knock The Rock*, which arrived in Liverpool in 1957. Then came Chuck Berry with his duck-walk, crippled Gene Vincent, 'the Screaming End', and another piano-pumping fireball, Jerry Lee Lewis, who, just as the Sutcliffe children had in 'Music For Percussion', hit the ivories with parts of the body other than fingers. Next up were a pair of duck-tailed brothers called Everly, two Elvi for the price of one, a mute Elvis in guitarist Duane Eddy, and a gangling, bespectacled one, Buddy Holly. He made up for a deficit of teen appeal with his ability to compose simple but atmospheric songs tailored to his elastic adenoids.

Britain clung on to the new fad's coat-tails, at first with jazz musicians forming contingent groups in the Haley image, and an ultimately innocuous 'answer' to Presley in Tommy Steele, a former sailor, who was superseded by the less uncomfortable Cliff Richard.

Steele's first hit, 'Rock With The Cavemen', had been overtaken in 1956's autumn Top Twenty by both 'Dead Or Alive' by Lonnie Donegan – 'The King of Skiffle' – and 'Bloodnok's Rock 'N' Roll' by the Goons. This was the high summer of the Light Programme's *Goon Show* which developed the off-beat humour and topical parodies of an earlier series, *Crazy People*, which also featured Spike Milligan, Peter Sellers, Harry Secombe and Michael Bentine. Incongruous parallels, casual cruelty and stream-of-consciousness connections not only made it different from mainstream shows like *Educating Archie* and *The Clitheroe Kid*, but also ushered in that stratum of fringe-derived comedy that culminated in the late 1960s with *Monty Python's Flying Circus*.

Stuart rarely missed *The Goons*, although he wasn't one of those irritating people who re-enacted 'I Was Monty's Treble' or 'Bridge Over The River Wye' the next day on the school playground. 'I would guess he was much more reflective and thoughtful about it,' said Pauline, 'and more interested in the construction of it and what the links were.'

Skiffle wasn't quite as peculiar to mid-1950s British culture as the Goons. It had evolved from the speakeasies, rent parties and dust-bowl jug bands of the US Depression and its musical melting-pot of bluegrass breakdowns, Cajun, blues, Western swing ('hillbilly jazz') and most other shades of American folk music. However, unlike rockabilly – likewise based on primeval rowdiness and sparse instru-mentation – it never gripped the imagination of young North America as it did that of their British cousins in the late 1950s. The form was bossed throughout its prime by singing guitarist Donegan, a Glasgow-born Londoner who was to add pub singalong, music-hall ditties and like British ingredients to skiffle's cauldron. In his lordly opinion, 'Rock 'n' roll has no musical value, no variety in sound, nondescript lyrics and a rhythmical beat about as subtle as that of a piledriver. A section of the public likes it – but it's only the youngsters who have to be "in the swim". You know, when marbles are the craze, they all play marbles – and rock 'n' roll just about comes into the marbles category. I'm a folk singer, and I intend to stay that way. No rock 'n' roll gimmicks for me!'[11]

Despite himself, Lonnie was a precursor of the 1960s beat boom, bearing in mind those future stars who began to master their assorted crafts in amateur outfits based on his precedent. As well as Cliff Richard, Adam Faith and others who received more immediate acclaim, among hitmakers from later pop eras who started as skifflers were the Beatles, the Spencer Davis Group and Gary Glitter.

Like punk after it, anyone could have a go. The more home-made your sound, the better. Though most units were formed for the benefit of performers rather than audience, there were thousands of skiffle groups nationwide thrumming tea-chest-and-broom-handle basses, tapping washboards, rasping comb and paper, clanking dustbin-lid cymbals, hollering in an energetic Donegan whine, and thrashing that E-chord on finger-lacerating six-strings for all they were worth.

Rhythm guitar was at the core of skiffle's contagious backbeat. Once it had been associated with Latinate heel-clattering but now the guitar was what Elvis and Lonnie played. In April 1957, the *Daily Mirror* cracked 'Springtime Is Stringtime!' as 'Cumberland Gap' became Donegan's first chart-topper, and a London musical instrument company with two thousand unfulfilled orders for guitars indented a West German manufacturer for a further six thousand, although 'some of the lads,' believed leading guitar tutor Ivor Mairants, 'are buying them just to hang on their shoulders.'[12]

Though Stuart Sutcliffe might have resumed his miming ritual after the shaming incident with Joyce's chums, skiffle did not re-awaken his interest in extending his grasp of the guitar beyond a handful of chords. Nor did he respond to either the jocund encouragement of his father, who took the trouble to transpose piano music for him, or the easy availability of *Play In A Day*, a manual by Bert Weedon, a middle-aged session player who was equally at ease with Dickie Valentine as Tommy Steele. If Stuart couldn't or wouldn't play guitar, and his choirboy voice was too plummy for such as 'Cumberland Gap', what else was there? Washboard players had trouble joining the Musicians' Union and were thus prohibited from defiling the stage at many venues.

Stuart had absorbed Elvis deeply, but perhaps it was time to cast aside adolescent follies. Rock 'n' roll was the most exciting music ever but maybe he'd grow out of it. There was no reason why it should last much longer than previous short-lived crazes. It just chanced to be going a bit stronger than hula-hoops and the cha-cha-cha. He had read in *Melody Maker* that many skiffle musicians were switching their allegiance to less-than-pure traditional jazz, the next big thing, so they said. Unlike skiffle, anyone *couldn't* have a go.

Yet it wasn't how good you were, it was being in the right place at the right time. More than that, it was who you knew. He didn't know anyone apart from lads in a couple of school bands that trod warily amidst official disapproval – all pop musicians took drugs and had sex, didn't they? In truth, the only stimulants available to skiffle ensembles were in local pubs, where they played as a change from providing interval music at school dances. None of them had been born into showbusiness, and it was unwise for anyone to see it as a viable career – especially as, in the wider world, a Merseyside singer or instrumentalist was regarded as a contradiction in terms, unless they were a music-hall clown like 'Big-Hearted Little' Arthur Askey or ukelele-plinking George Formby.

Feeling the chill of reality, Stuart took his O levels during 1956's rainy June. Two months later, the results landed on the Sandiway doormat. He had passed English language, English literature, geography, woodwork – and art. In the interim, he had finally come out with it: he was going to be a painter. If he couldn't make a living at it, he would teach it. Entry standards for art college weren't very tight: you could get in without any official qualifications at all. They didn't care if you were hopeless at maths.

After token attempts at appealing to his common sense, Millie gave up, even finding vague enchantment in the idea. Stuart was trying to escape too, to save himself from a more mundane life. Nevertheless, she knew how Charles was going to take it. For all Arthur Ballard's capacity to hold down the ale, painting somehow wasn't a man's trade. As Millie predicted, 'Daddy was shocked. We'd hoped he'd become a doctor. "My son a painter!" said Daddy. "I'll never live it down." '[1]

NOTES

1 *Music Echo*, 6 November 1970.
2 Huyton's Member of Parliament at the time was Harold Wilson who was prime minister from 1964 to 1971. During his administration, he advised the Queen to invest the Beatles as MBEs, supposedly for their contribution to the export drive. No such decoration before or since has been as controversial.
3 A more palpable legacy of this episode were the model aeroplanes of balsawood that dangled from his bedroom ceiling.

The Father Figure

4   An initial point of contact between Stuart and Ken had been that they shared the same birthdate.

5   *Everybody's Weekly*, 23 June 1956.

6   Now obscured by the upper windows of a Berni Inn.

7   *Everybody's Weekly*, 3 July 1957.

8   *Record Mirror*, 21 January 1956.

9   *New Musical Express*, 24 February 1956.

10   *Melody Maker*, 29 March 1958.

11   *Picturegoer*, 1 September 1956.

12   *Daily Mirror*, 8 April 1957.

chapter two

THE YOUNG SAILOR

'We young artists are like young sailors: unless
we encounter rough seas and are buffeted by
the winds, we'll not become real sailors. There
is no mercy for us, everyone has to go through
a period of worry and struggle if he wants to go
into deep water'

Stuart Sutcliffe

'His wit was so prostituted to the lust of
applause that he would sacrifice his best friend
for a scurvy jest'

Charles Johnson on John Wilkes

Stuart held out against his father, and enrolled for the National
Diploma in Design (NDD) at the Regional Art College in
autumn 1956. At sixteen, he was below the normal admittance
age. For the first two years, he was to be an Intermediate student,
concentrating on the basics of all disciplines while deciding on a
specialist subject. A compromise might have been A level art in the
sixth form at Prescot, but the claustrophobia of suburbia was not
conducive to *la vie bohème* that was the background to his self-picture.

Bohemia was a distant land as he suffered banal chit-chat, fuggy
warmth and body pressure on the bus that took him – and often
cumbersome art apparatus – to and from Mount Street. The six-mile
journey dogged from the outset Stuart's involvement in any social and
recreational activities that the college offered, unless they were held
in the lunch hour. To attend, say, an interesting evening lecture
meant hanging about for hours after dismissal. When it was over, he
would arrive back in Huyton after dark, ravenous, tired and with
course work to do. It didn't seem fair. Everyone who was anyone
lived in their own studio within the environs of college. He felt totally
square sometimes – particularly as the rest of the class were quite a
lively shower. 'The thing about Stuart's lot was that a couple of his

year had actually done National Service,' a youth named Rod Jones would notice after he began his course in 1958. 'They'd been places and done things, so there was a bit of spice in that year to start with.'

Within weeks, Stuart had fallen in with Rod Murray, a willowy older boy who had to travel in from West Derby – but, unlike Stuart, he did it by car. He was one of those people for whom the hand and foot co-ordination needed to drive one had become second nature long before he was officially entitled to take a car on the public highway. Furthermore, he could speak with authority about how cars worked, the differences between them and the sorcery of the whizzing springs and pistons under the bonnet. From earliest youth, he had been able to take a motor engine to bits and put it back together again. At college, his eventual transference from sculpture to kinetics – a 'building' discipline – could be foreseen by Stuart in his perpetual tinkering with cars, and, particularly, in his construction of a flashy fibre-glass-bodied red vehicle to enliven the lugubrious streets of West Derby and Liverpool 8.

If manipulative and too self-protecting at times, 'there was a paternal quality about Rod,' observed Pauline Sutcliffe, 'where he showed him the ropes a bit, as a man of the world.' Nevertheless, it was Stuart who first heard of a vacant flat at 83 Canning Street, next door to a now-demolished post office and literally round the corner from the college. It had a sitting room, a small kitchen with gas-ring and sink, an outside toilet and another room – perpetually cold – with space for a couple of beds. It was what an estate agent might describe as 'compact'.

Rod and Stuart were permitted to kick over only some of the traces: 83 Canning Street was for daytime use, pronounced their respective parents. They were to come home each night until they found somewhere more congenial. Eventually, a decision was made for the boys when the soft-hearted landlady moved a destitute Irish family into the freezing bedroom. Unable to work with the new intruders around, Stuart flitted between the comforts of Sandiways and roughing it where he could in Liverpool for what remained of the academic year.

After the summer vacation, he left home with Millie's blessing, although Huyton remained his official address. As it was technically beyond the city limits, he didn't qualify for a maintenance grant for living expenses. Therefore, while collecting his laundry once a week, his mother would leave cash for groceries, but soon began to buy them herself after she realized that Stuart was spending most of the money on art equipment.

His first home from home was on the opposite side of Canning Street. A few weeks later, he was a few hundred yards away, on the middle floor of 9 Percy Street. Bill Harry remembered 'a very bleak room with hardly anything in it'. As Stuart was the official resident, and Rod merely a 'hiding' tenant, he slept on the bed while Rod took the sofa until another room became available. Neither could complain of any shortage of romantic squalor – well, squalor anyway – as it quickly acquired the sock-smelling frowziness common to adolescent male student accommodation. What marked them as artists was the film of coloured dust on chairs and tables that had been painted either black or white to denote ownership, although they were the property of the freeholder, a Mrs Plant.

It was understood, wrongly, as it turned out, that as long as you didn't fall behind with the rent, you could get carried in drunk at seven in the morning, stay in bed till the street lights came on, leave crockery unwashed in the sink for as long as you liked – and entertain girls. Murray and Sutcliffe also took further liberties with the furniture. 'They'd cut the wardrobe in half,' gasped Rod Jones, 'not longways, but sideways, so they each had a wardrobe about three foot high.' If the toilet was blocked – as it frequently was – you could either urinate in the sink or (if no one was about) out of the front window, trying for a direct hit on the seat of a moped belonging to one of the disliked architecture students from the floor below.

'There were easels there as they were both painting at the time,' explained Ron Jones. 'It was the thing to do – you got an easel from College and did your work at home quite a lot.'

Stuart's preference for painting alone rather than in the chattier ambience of class was expressed in telling sentences in his essay, 'The Function of a Door'. 'I find in the silence of isolation the element in which all great things fashion themselves. One plunges one's eyes into one's heart and into one's self; one feels the charm of ethereal being which is not like the mundane beauty of physical experiences.' Master Sutcliffe had a mature awareness that 'college-bred' did not mean a three-year loaf. The point of being there wasn't just to piss on mopeds. His higher self cared enough to jot down artistic experiences that were not necessarily relevant to his diploma course, homing in on details that others in the class might be too lackadaisical to consider or even notice. However, they were rarely irritated when he aired his knowledge or steered group discussions into tangents that extended into break time.

He was more *au fait* than most with the historical traditions and classical conventions of painting, and his cultivation of a truly personal style was, therefore, more advanced. Moreover, he was not one to be swayed by fashion although he incorporated into his efforts whatever aspects of the latest fad suited his purposes. Jackson Pollock's huge action paintings were shrugged off in his notes as the work of one who had 'failed to become anything more than a decoration . . . nothing more than an erroneous burp', but Stuart became notorious for working with Pollock-sized canvases that required him to jump or stand on a chair so that his brush could touch the top.

Very much knowing his own mind, Sutcliffe then preferred discernible structure and tangible substance. Just as he had been when he was still at Prescot Grammar, 'He was keen on the pre-Raphaelites,' recalled Rod Murray, 'about five years before they came back into fashion.' It was not, therefore, surprising that Monet's more feathery paintings 'seem terribly weak and have no excitement for me'. He was only fractionally kinder to Cézanne, another father of modern art, who was 'too sophisticated but not in an alluring way'. Yet, with regard to the same late Victorian era, Stuart was moved by the similarly figurative Vlaminck ('terribly exciting, the reddish trees are strong and solid') and Rouault who had rejected Fauvism to devote his life – as Graham Sutherland and Arthur Dooley would – to religious art.

In the same spiritual vein, the earlier and more obscure Filippo Lippi was admired and, simply as an exercise, copied by Stuart. He half liked the elaborate if then outmoded local landscapes of George Mayer-Marton, a lecturer in art history throughout Stuart's time at college, but was more receptive to the London views ('the most beautiful harmonies') of Vienna's Oskar Kokoschka, seen during a visit to the Tate in 1958.

Stuart also absorbed an unofficial curriculum through taking on various holiday jobs. A stint as a corporation dustman brought him closer to the everyday during a social-realist phase ('we are shocked back into reality') that included paintings of dustbins and watercolours from a quarry round Garston, a grim suburb on the city's outskirts that had once been fields. With Rod Murray, he was as gainfully employed to decorate a bar wall in Ye Cracke with an abstract dock scene. This was executed in as pedantic a fashion as possible because part of his payment was free drinks for as long as it took. Another commission was for a bacchanalian mural in the rifle range of a Territorial Army centre.

Back in class, too, 'He would tend to work for effect, rather than really to search,' perceived Nicholas Horsfield, one of his more distinguished tutors, 'but his answer to that might well have been Picasso's answer at an equivalent age: he said something to the effect that "I don't seek, I find", and I think that could well have been Stuart's answer if ever I made that point.' As de Nerval and other symbolist poets recognized dreams as a bridge between reality and the supernatural, so the young man saw art as linking the objective outer world with the inner world of feeling: 'We owe it to ourselves to endeavour to cross the threshold of self-knowledge.' We should, he continued, 'give our soul to our work' and avoid 'confusing our real conscience with a would-be conscience'. These and other philosophical confidences in Stuart's writings coincided in many respects with the enlightening nectar that was falling from the lips of the robed and ascetic Mahesh Prasad Varma who, espousing a doctrine of cosmic consciousness, founded the London branch of the International Meditation Society in 1959. In less than ten years, the world would come to know him as 'The Maharishi Mahesh Yogi'.

Sutcliffe's cerebral musings were forged as much from pragmatism as theory. The actual process of putting oil paint on canvas was but the culmination of much painstaking preparation. In exchange for a denim jacket, Bill Harry's curly head was immortalized in a portrait by Stuart, and had the opportunity to observe his methodology: 'First he had hordes of pink foolscap paper, and he had me sit down and rapidly he did all these sketches at different angles. He must have done about forty sketches, and then he started the painting proper on a piece of board, and he completed the entire oil painting in the afternoon, and I was surprised at how easily it seemed to come from him. It just sort of flowed.'

Though painting was to be the main content of his work, he proved no slouch at collage, life studies, charcoal drawing and other areas of study in the Intermediate years. Three-dimensional work held no terror for him either. Neville Bertram, his sculpture tutor, recalled a Sutcliffe wood-carving of 'a mother and child that could have been a Henry Moore'. In charge of foundation sculpture, Philip Hartas maintained that 'He could have been a sculptor as easily as he could have been a painter.'

Until he gave himself more fully to abstracts, the most recurrent painting style of Stuart's early days at college was reminiscent of kitchen-sinker John Bratby both in content and tonal clarity, though David Bomberg, another British painter, was evoked in brushwork made more nakedly expressive by mixing sand and even coal particles with oils. In differing ways, both Bratby and Bomberg were derivative of Van Gogh. A Sutcliffe depiction of fellow students in *The Cracke* achieves much the same mood – if a little more joyous – as Van Gogh's *Night Café* in its greenish tinge and deliberate distortion of shape. Both the picture of Bill Harry and a 1959 self-portrait, in spectacles, owe something to Van Gogh – Bratby too.

After a painting of a church *à la* Van Gogh was displayed in the entrance hall, and eight more canvases in a main corridor on the first floor, Stuart, though he rarely signed his work, began to be noticed. Horsfield had already gauged that 'he was, of course, far more stimulating than most of the rest. My criticism was – and I was hoping too much, really – of his restlessness, his passing on rapidly from one thing to another. I wanted him to try and dig deeper, to spend longer on a work, try to achieve a more substantial, lasting thing, which was, of course, echoing myself, and not realizing his quite different and much younger attitude.'

Likeable and unassuming though he was, Stuart had become a being apart from his immediate academic contemporaries as the mainstream of his scholarship loomed. This change was not received willingly in some quarters. 'Rod Murray was no longer able to keep being paternal in his relationship with Stuart,' said Pauline, 'but had to acknowledge that they were peers.' The attention Sutcliffe was attracting as a college *wunderkind* filtered through to freshmen like Rod Jones: 'All I knew about Stuart was that he was rated as a painter. Rod wasn't.'

The word reached the staffroom too. 'It wasn't until I heard from other tutors how clever he was that I became interested in his work,' conceded Arthur Ballard. 'I had not needed to see it earlier. I wasn't his tutor. So then I made it my business to have a look at what he was doing.' Before the class of '56 came under his aegis, Ballard had already developed a soft spot for Charles Sutcliffe's lad: 'One couldn't ignore Stuart, and there was something very beguiling about him, very wistful, and he was very inventive and very inquisitive, which is a very important instinct in an artist. He got fed up with most of the instructors who thought he was running before he could walk. They thought he'd taken the leap too quickly and that he should learn how to draw. He *could* draw! You don't have to draw any better than he could draw. I have met other gifted students who were more competent in the disciplines, and probably much better technicians than Stuart, but few if any had that particular kind of spark that was genius.'

If too young to lose his hair, Arthur had clocked up a lot of miles in Sutcliffe's eyes. Armed with a sustaining half-bottle of whisky, he would bowl round to Percy Street to oversee work-in-progress. As he refilled glasses at regular intervals, and the star pupil continued painting, they would speak of textural surface, the chemistry of paint, Fauvism *et al.*, and, very occasionally, of their respective families. These days, Stuart was looking hard at de Staël – and Ballard – and it showed in the essence and stark titles of such as *Blue Non-Figurative Painting* and *Totem II 1960*.

Ballard was then engaged in uncertain experiments with Pop Art, predicted by some to be the coming trend, but scorned by the art establishment as a novelty. Its British pioneers included Peter Blake, Richard Hamilton and Edinburgh-born Eduardo Paolozzi. Pre-empting Warhol's soup cans, the aim was to bring humour and topicality back into painting via the paradox of earnest fascination with the brashest of junk culture, a mannered revelling in hard-sell advertising hoardings; magazines such as *True Confessions*, *Tit-Bits* and *Everybody's Weekly*, escapist horror flicks about outer-space 'Things', and artefacts of this Coca-Cola century, usually disparaged as silly, vulgar and fake in their custard-yellows and tomato-reds. In the interests of research, nascent Pop artists listened avidly to turn-of-the-decade Top Forty radio, clogged, as it was, with one-shot gimmicks, dance crazes and – just arrived this minute – the all-American piffle of insipidly handsome boys-next-door like Bobby Vee, Bobby Rydell and Bobby Vinton, all hair-spray and bashful half smiles.

The other side of the same coin, and one more acutely felt in art circles on Merseyside, were the beatniks. They tended to consume specific paperback books rather than records. Caught in the general drift, Stuart Sutcliffe actually read some of the literature bought mostly for display by other students. To Rod Murray's occasional displeasure, he would journey into the graveyard hours with Joyce, Somerset Maugham, Dostoevsky, Chekhov and Rimbaud. After limbering up with, perhaps, a chapter or two of Hemingway, Henry Miller or Colin Wilson's *The Outsider*, his brow would furrow over Soren Kierkegaard, the Danish mystic, and his existentialist descendants, chiefly Jean-Paul Sartre. He was less enraptured with Kerouac and Burroughs, foremost prose writers of the 'Beat Generation', and associated bards such as Corso, Ginsberg and Ferlinghetti. Now a television scriptwriter, Johnny Byrne, one of Liverpool's archbeatniks, was more enthusiastic: 'I fell in with a group of people who, like me, were absolutely crazy about books by the beats. We were turning out our own little magazines. In a very short time we were into jazz, poetry – straight out of the beatniks – and all around us were the incredible beginnings of the Liverpool scene.'[1]

While it was to become homogeneously Liverpudlian in outlook, beatnik culture was as North American as the pop charts. Moreover, in most cases, it was intrinsically as shallow in the sense that it wasn't so much being anarchistic, free-loving and pacifist as being seen to sound and look as if you were. With practice, you would call everybody 'man', and drop buzz-words like warmonger, Zen, Monk, Stockhausen, Greco, Bird, Leadbelly and Brubeck into conversations without too much obvious affectation.

The uniform for both sexes was an army-surplus duffel coat draped with a long scarf, sunglasses even in a midnight power cut, polo- or turtleneck pullover down to the knees, CND badge, sandals or desert boots, and corduroy trousers that looked like they'd hung round the legs of a particularly disgusting building labourer for the past three years. Had the wearers got round to reading Molière, they might have quoted, 'Guenille, si l'on veut: ma guenille m'est chère' – Rags they may be: my rags are dear to me.

Girls wore either no make-up at all or emulated Juliette Greco's black-eyed, skull-white face. Hair was either long and straight – like Greco again – or elfin like Audrey Hepburn in *Roman Holiday*. They hid their figures inside baggy sweaters annexed from boyfriends, who either contrived to keep a day away from a shave or went half the whole hog with bumfluff beards like half-plucked Fidel Castros.

Backbeat

Risking your father's accusations of transvestism, you let uncombed locks curl up an inch or two down the ears. Otherwise, you bristled with a crew-cut.

As sartorial a magpie as he was an artistic one, Stuart married elements of the beatnik – like a beard that hadn't really taken – to pink shirt with tab collar, hip-hugging jeans, *Rebel Without A Cause* zip-up jacket and Cuban-heeled 'winkle-picker' shoes: gear that, pre-rock 'n' roll, only the boldest homosexuals would be seen dead in. 'James Dean was his hero,' said Arthur Ballard, 'and he looked like him too.' Indeed, he did – bar the facial hair and one other detail. The advice that drummer Jerry Allison had given to Buddy Holly – 'If you're going to wear glasses, then really make it obvious you're wearing glasses'[2] – was also put into practice by Sutcliffe who offset his pale complexion with an impressive pair of black horn-rims. In canteen conversations, he would gesture with a cigarette from a lung-corroding intake of over twenty a day. The embodiment of adolescent narcissism, 'he had this wiry, sticking-out hair which he used to plaster down with a piece of soap,' remembered Ken Horton, who, likewise, had graduated from Prescot to the art college, 'so it just used to go straight out like that. You'd see him in the cloakroom with a bar of soap, combing his hair.' Without the least embarrassment, he'd go back to Huyton to subject the spiky quiff that anticipated punk to the lacquer, setting lotion, highlights and rollers wielded by his sister Pauline who had blossomed as an amateur hairdresser, and was the self-appointed stylist of Millie's and Joyce's coiffures too.

He distanced himself further from beatnik friends at college by his taste in music, that most abstract of all the arts. Ostensibly snooty about Teddy Boy rock 'n' roll, intellectual types Living in the Shadow of the Bomb were more likely to be 'sent' by Lewis, Meade Lux, than Lewis, Jerry Lee. A 'sign of maturity' was an apparent 'appreciation' of either traditional or modern jazz, but, sighed Ken Horton, 'it didn't do anything for Stuart at all. I used to play my records, like Chris Barber, but he seemed to take no interest.' The nearest he got to jazz was black, blind and heroin-mainlining Ray Charles who, as the Twisted Voice of the Underdog, caused the likes of Kerouac and Ginsberg to get 'gone' on even the 'heys' and 'yeahs' he traded with his vocal trio, The Raelettes, during 1959's 'What'd I Say', with all the preacher–congregation interplay of an evangelist tent meeting.

The Young Sailor

Jerry Lee Lewis and Little Richard were products of the same equation, but they didn't punctuate their catalogues of vocal smashes with instrumental albums and collaborations with such as Count Basie and Milt Jackson of the Modern Jazz Quartet.

When Stuart painted, you were likely to hear, hovering in the background, an Everly Brothers B-side on instant replay. Strewn around his monophonic Dansette record-player, too, were discs by Buddy Holly, Gene Vincent, Chuck Berry – then without major UK hits – and, of course, Presley. 'He was a big Elvis man,' agreed Rod Murray. 'He was the first to bring rock records into college, even when most people still thought pop was rubbish.'

If his musical perversity and idiosyncratic dress sense bemused other students, it courted downright antagonism from more conservative members of staff as an epitome of both the post-war breed of irreverent, anti-everything youth, as opposed to 'young people', and the questionable sea changes in the international art scene. Nicholas Horsfield – himself resembling an absent-minded French onion seller without the onions – conjectured that 'college at that time was going through a curiously rather respectful phase. There was then a certain separation of staff and students. There wasn't the easy mixing that exists now, for example. At the same time – and this is interesting – teaching staff, whose initial artistic experience was more or less pre-war, had not given up their own values and denied their own experience. Now I wasn't aware of that, and looked upon myself as being avant-garde or fairly advanced at the time, but I now recognize that all sorts of things were happening that I was unable to accept – the arrival of American painting and all the rest – which would, of course, have been very stimulating for someone like Stuart. I saw a brittleness in his tonality, and tried to get him to reach for better harmony, but I was teaching something valid in the 1930s and 1940s . . . I didn't impede him, but was not able to guide him in the way Paolozzi eventually was. His painting never toed the line but was limited by the system.'

Such phlegmatic detachment and retrospective honesty was not Arthur Ballard's way. He was a left-wing bastion between promising if wayward students and intransigent college authorities, waging a constant war against the compounding of mediocrity. Sometimes, as he explained, he put his own career in jeopardy in the process: 'The man in charge of the painting department then was the most bourgeois, reactionary customer I'd met in my life. We had fight after fight, until finally he tried to get me sacked.'

By 1959, the unconventional Ballard's unconventional protégé had risen to a position of authority: Stuart Sutcliffe was now on the Students Union committee, which also included Bill Harry, now transferred to the college's new commercial design faculty. He and Stuart might have been destined to be nothing more than acquaintances had it not been for Bill who, intrigued by 'the buzz about how good his stuff was, made up my mind to get to know him. I sought him out and we used to chat and we found that we connected. I found him a very introvert person in many ways, very quiet and, though he had this burning talent, he was a bit . . . not only shy but, in some ways, timid.'

In contradiction, Nicholas Horsfield 'wouldn't call him a quiet person. He generated so much energy, it was felt. He would be painting away and not talking or anything, so in that sense he might be quiet, but certainly he was very noticeable. He was in no sense a hidden personality.' Rod Murray concurred that 'basically, he was a most determined character. He had great belief in himself and he'd defend himself fiercely if any of the teachers put his work down.'

Evidence supports Horsfield and Murray rather than Harry. No shrinking violet would tear ill-prepared or stick-in-the-mud lecturers to pieces as Stuart did. He exempted nobody. His earliest known remark in a Ballard master class was after the tutor expressed surprise at the speed of modern aeroplanes, 'and Stuart was sitting in the front row and said, "You might be surprised, Mr Ballard, but we're not." He put me right in my place as the old fogey.'

Stuart also had the self-confidence to have a belated if half-hearted crack at skiffle with Rod Murray: 'There was a guy called Roger Taylor, a few years on from us, who was trying to form a sort of skiffle thing – tea-chest bass and washboard, comb-and-paper and a kazoo and all those sorts of things. I think we all had a go at it, but it didn't last very long.' Further musical activity was confined to the retractable privacy of Murray's tape-recorder back at the flat: 'We made all sorts of really screamingly funny tapes.'

Was there no end to this man's talent? There he was again as 'Fairy Snow' (after the detergent) in a college pantomime and, while a second-year student, on a regional television chat-show as one of a hand-picked audience submitting pre-ordained questions to members of the Goons. Stuart quizzed Spike Milligan about the connection 'if any' between surreal art and surreal humour.

No one under Ballard would have lasted long as a hermit anyway as it was incumbent upon all to participate in the seminars he conducted in Ye Cracke. Even thirty years later, this was regarded as extremely unorthodox. In the late 1950s, it verged on lunacy.

Stuart was also a regular attender of Ballard's Saturday morning life classes. The centre of attraction at these meetings were the models Sue Lee and hard-wearing – or wearing nothing at all – June Furlong, a talkative, gregarious college fixture since the 1940s. These ladies were required sometimes for private sessions in student flats. 'He [Sutcliffe] liked me in one particular pose – with my hands behind my head – and he did several,' reminisced June Furlong.

She and Sue were battle-hardened by frequent bouts of fending off amorous advances when unclothed and alone before the canvas of some young brute with raging hormones. By the standards of most other seats of learning, a pimpled fumbler of a bra-strap stood more chance of completing his sexual pilgrimage at Liverpool Art College than anywhere else. A beatnik girl was less inclined to 'save herself' for her future husband than a truer daughter of the 1950s who would have none of it.

His lofty ideals and the allure of his studies did not prevent Stuart from meditating on the fast flashes of knicker that caught his glance as girls jived in gingham whenever the Students Union held a ball-cum-cattle market in the canteen. As agile at cutting a rug as the next man, Stuart enjoyed many romantic encounters at college dances. Another forum for initiating carnal adventures were coffee bars – particularly in the light of Sunday newspaper condemnations of such houses of ill-repute where boys smoked and girls were deflowered.

These allegations were not always unfounded. In the Jacaranda, for instance, 'there used to be office girls who'd go up there to get laid because all the art students used to hang around there.' Amused by a memory, Rod Jones elaborated: 'We got these two birds, Ann and Janet. I got one of them, and Rod [Murray] and Stuart got the other one. The outcome was that we all got a bit itchy. We either drew straws or cards to decide who was going to the doctor's – and I lost. He gave me this ointment and said, "You go home and shave, and put the ointment on. Three weeks." I said, "Excuse me, doctor, could

I have enough for three?" So I took this stuff back and that seemed to sort things out, but that was my real introduction to bohemia, getting a severe attack of the crabs.'

Grubby one-night stands apart, Sutcliffe was walking proof of the adage that it's always the so-called quiet blokes who pull the most gorgeous birds. Pop artist Adrian Henri has a wistful recollection that one of Stuart's paramours was 'the local high school's answer to Brigitte Bardot'. He appeared to like girls in the plural as, affirmed Rod Murray, 'There were a hell of a collection of ladies that were in and out of that flat in Percy Street. When he did fall for a girl, he used to paint her like buggery. I think he was into Modigliani at the time, and there was this particular girl who had a sort of longish neck anyway, quite a pretty girl, nothing to do with the art school, just one he'd found somewhere. I think he went out with this girl for about six or eight months, and did hundreds of drawing and paintings and pastels of her – and then somebody else came along, and he painted over them all.'

Other girlfriends included a Brenda, mentioned because she and Stuart used to babysit for novelist Beryl Bainbridge, then a Juliette Greco lookalike married to long-bearded art-college lecturer Austin Davis. More permanent an attachment than Brenda was Veronica Johnson, a de Staël disciple who would visit Paris in 1960 to see his work at the Musée Nationale d'Art Moderne. Another student, Ann Mason, had a brief fling with Stuart before running into the arms of the late Jeff Mohammed, a Mancunian of the same lecture-disrupting bent as Rod Jones and an amazing young man called John Winston Lennon.

Mohammed was asked to leave college, and so, eventually, was Jones: 'I blew my Intermediate because of too much skiving and larking about, and left for London in 1960.' Lennon's expulsion seemed as inevitable but was never carried out. He had Arthur Ballard to thank for that, but it was open season on John once more after Ballard transferred to a new department. Lennon, too, tried to change from lettering to graphics with his friend Bill Harry, but the teacher, George Jardine, a pruny-looking gentleman in sports jacket and patterned tie, wouldn't have it. He knew all about John Lennon.

John was a product of the draconian affectations and futile rigmarole of Quarry Bank Grammar – nicknamed 'The Police State' – over in Calderstones. After a valedictory sermon in the headmaster's study, he had left the school in July 1957 as an academic failure, with a reputation as a round peg in a square hole – and with a kinder testimonial than he deserved. This would assist his passage a few weeks later into the art college.

An incorrigible rock 'n' roller, he dressed the part for his first day on the Intermediate course. In preparation for The Entrance to class, he had risen early to spend an inordinate amount of time squeezing out blackheads and whorling his hair into a precarious pompadour, gleaming with brilliantine. For quick adjustments, he stuck a comb in the top pocket of his three-quarter length drape jacket. This Teddy Boy garment made him seem top-heavy on thin legs that from a distance gave the illusion that they had been dipped in ink. He promenaded up Mount Street in a somewhat pigeon-toed gait, his feet adorned with blue suede loafers and fluorescent socks with a rock 'n' roll motif. At the college portals, he narrowed his eyes and jutted his chin forward.

He was like someone who had stepped out of a novel. Yet the new student's self-image was at odds with the only subject he kept silent about: a comfortable if rather strait-laced middle-class upbringing by his devoted aunt in Woolton, a suburb as village-like as Huyton. His adored – and recently departed – natural mother had lived nearby with her second family, and had been a bolt-hole whenever her sister's regime became oppressive. The innate confusion of 'Who am I to regard as mother?' affected his ability to trust adult authority figures whom he mocked and abused as a defence against being rejected by them.

An inverted snob, he had embraced the machismo values of both Teddy Boys and proletarian Merseyside males, and generally came on as the Poor Honest Wacker – a working-class hero, in fact. By the end of his first term, he was speaking in a raw Scouse that, laced with incessant swearing, was still transparent to Arthur Ballard: 'I think Lennon put it on. He had quite a posh accent at the time by Liverpool standards.'

Not peculiar to Lennon alone was the notion that northern women were mere adjuncts to their men. John's overwhelmed girlfriend, Cynthia Powell, seemed to tolerate this role. With it came a dual code of morality whereby John could mess around with other girls but wouldn't stomach any infidelities from her. Trying to blinker his roving eye, she let her blonde perm go to Hilton-highlighted seed so she would look more like a slightly buck-toothed Bardot. She also made a radical transition from tweed twin-set and brown stockings to tight sweater and skirt, fishnet and high-heeled stilettos.

In the beginning, she had forced her Cheshire reserve to drop whenever his butterfly concentration alighted on her. John had chased her until she caught him, and, though it was beyond him to admit it publicly, 'He clearly loved her,' said Pauline Sutcliffe. 'She was clearly the most important person to him for some time.' Nevertheless, he became evasive when the topic of wedding bells and babies reared up. With a reputation as a hard case yet to be secured, he didn't want it to seem that he'd gone soppy over Cynthia Powell.

As one of an entourage united in terrified admiration, Cynthia's diffident personality was lost in his shadow as he, Jeff Mohammed and another of the same mind, Tony Carricker, lunaticked round college and the middle of Liverpool. 'He was like a fellow who'd been born without brakes,' exclaimed Philip Hartas. 'His objective was somewhere over there, that nobody else could see, but he was going, but in that process, a lot of people got run over. He never did it to me, but he had this very sarcastic way of talking to people – and at other times, he could be very charming and he would be charismatic.'

Few were capable of having a sensible conversation with him. 'He worked so hard at keeping people amused, he was exhausting,' said Rod Murray, an impressively witty fellow himself. 'He could be very cruel at times, but he was hilarious and everyone was dominated by him. One day, I saw him running down the street, holding a steering-wheel – no car, just the wheel. He said he was driving down to town.' Lennon's buffoonery and extreme behavioural strategy would sometimes deteriorate into a nonsensical frenzy, and soon would come the antics that would get him barred from Ye Cracke by Doris, its long-suffering landlady. 'John would get pissed out of his mind,' groaned Arthur Ballard, the pot calling the kettle black, 'he was a bloody nuisance in pubs.'

As a student, he was impatient of prolonged discussion on art. His tutors could not help but imagine that he did very little reading on art or anything else: 'I'm sure that John Lennon had never read anything except a comic in his life. He was totally uninformed in every kind of way' (Ballard); 'You had the feeling that he was living off the top of his head' (Philip Hartas).

The Young Sailor

It was his veneer of self-confidence rather than any heavily veiled air of learning that swiftly made John the centre of attention in canteen and classroom. 'They wanted everyone there to be an art teacher or go to this section or that,' he'd rail later, 'rather than what I could do.'[3] In his defence of Lennon against those at college who wanted him out, Ballard insisted that he had some messy aptitude as an illustrator and writer of surreal stories and comic verse. As John was even more of a Goon fan than Stuart Sutcliffe, facets of the comedy team's *oeuvre* were apparent in his literary style. A compliment paid by Bill Harry when he read it was that it wasn't like Kerouac, Corso and a mythical America: 'You could see in his work the heritage of Lewis Carroll and all the rest of it, the Englishness of it, and he reminded me a bit of Stanley Unwin, his malapropisms et cetera, but there was an Englishness about it, and everyone was copying the San Francisco people and reading Ginsberg.'

With deceptive casualness, it was through Bill Harry that John came into the life of Stuart Sutcliffe. By early 1959, Bill had been editor and main (some would say sole) contributor to some short-lived and narrowly circulated magazines, one of which was for Frank Hessy's Music Store ('and he [Hessy] crippled it with the terrible name of *Frank Comments*'). Undaunted, Harry's next plan was more ambitious: he was going to write a book about Liverpool. Stuart could illustrate it, and John could throw in a few of his funny poems. The project had been motivated through Bill being 'very annoyed and frustrated that whenever I had to go to the cinema, it was all American films – the best comics were supposedly American comics, but I personally liked the *Eagle* and things. I was staunchly liking British things and in particular a Liverpool thing. I said, "Why can't we do something about Liverpool?"'

An informal working party assembled in Ye Cracke to mull over Bill's latest idea. It was a cordial discussion that ultimately led nowhere, but Stuart's and John's eyes met through the cigarette smoke.

Though they were the same age, John was in the academic year below Stuart. Because of this and their greatly contrasting standpoints over course work, many college lecturers were surprised later that they even knew each other, let alone became the best of pals. 'Stuart was a totally different character in the sense that he was a very reflective chap,' maintained Philip Hartas. 'He would fall into quiet moods, and he'd be thinking a lot or he'd go off and he'd come back in, that sort of thing. There were things going on in his head, and he wasn't living at the tempo that Lennon was living at.'

The bedrock of the rapport between them was the potential of each to outfit the other with vestments of personality he had wanted but never dared to wear before. Why should Stuart have wanted to be like Lennon? Why should a youth with two cherishing parents during his formative years need to rebel? Mostly, it was the emotional pressure to 'be good', to 'be worthy' of all they had given him that had led to a more constructive if covert form of revolt than that of John.

While the differences between Stuart and John consolidated their friendship, so equally did all that they had in common. For a start, they were both short-sighted but were generally too vain to wear spectacles in public. Both were 'special sons'. Neither had an omnipresent father as a guiding (or restricting) influence. Indeed, John's was a seaman too though he had vanished altogether when his son was five.[4]

For all their loutish affectations, they both knew how they were supposed to behave when among other middle-class folk. Although John was to be remembered years later as a 'working-class hero' his was a genteel background with access to the likes of the complete works of Winston Churchill and BBC symphonies on the radio, in complete contrast to the truly working class roots of other Beatles such as Paul McCartney and Ringo Starr.

Because they had read books and were art students, Stuart and John modelled themselves on idols other than Dean, Presley, Vincent *et al.* Emulation of pop heroes became a vital part of growing up from the mid-1950s onwards, with a bearing on the clothes you couldn't afford, the hairstyle you were forbidden to have, and the way in which you mouthed into a hairbrush-as-microphone in front of the bedroom mirror. While Lennon and Sutcliffe might not have copied their modes of dress and hair sculpture, the impact of older figures from other cultural genres was as insidious if less demonstrated. Though Elvis was a hero of Lennon and Sutcliffe, both were just as deeply absorbed by any number of famous romantic bohemians who inhabited a decadent Europe during the previous two centuries.

Stuart's yardstick of 'cool' was now as much Amedeo Modigliani as Elvis Presley. The Italian painter's post-Impressionist portraits of fragile females with long necks were recognized as masterpieces. Nevertheless, the Modigliani personality cult hinged more on the hand-to-mouth existence of this gifted but neurotic and improvident chap whose noble visage effused melancholy and poor health. These traits were aggravated in part by a propensity to alcoholic black-outs. In 1920, he endured one of such depth that he never came round. This was followed immediately by the suicide of the young wife who had loved him to distraction.

The idea of aping self-destructive Modigliani – starving in a garret, burning his furniture against the cold of a Parisian winter, and going to an early grave for his art – might have held vague enchantment for Sutcliffe and Lennon, but a less uncomfortable option might have been the happy(ish) ending in *The Horse's Mouth*, a light film comedy that they saw at the Jacey cinema in 1958. Starring Alec Guinness, and with 'kitchen sink' sets designed by John Bratby, it was about an obsessive artist, a social liability who might have been Modigliani's frightfully refined English cousin. He's frightful to live with too, but his friends stick by him – antedating what one college contemporary was to say of Lennon: 'He was a terrible fellow really – but I liked him.'

John had learned as much about self-destruction from his drunken exploits with Jeff, Rod, Tony and the lads as from discussing Modigliani with Stuart. Unlike Modigliani, the *Horse's Mouth* character and, indeed, Stuart, John was basically lazy. His student notebooks were as empty as his friend's were conscientiously full of information gleaned from lecture theatre and library. When course assessment work was pending, he cadged assistance as he would a cigarette. 'John was at the Intermediate stage, and I don't think he was going to get through,' said Rod Jones. 'I was doing some of John's work because he was no good at it, and Stuart was doing some of mine because I was no good at it.'

Yet, through Stuart, Lennon shook off enough ingrained indolence to transfer from lettering to painting and actually do some work. With Stuart showing him how, he grew less cautious about the marks he made on the canvas. He also became more interested in the theory side to the extent that, now and then, a lecture was not approached as an avenue for either dozing off or exercising his wit at the tutor's expense. 'It was Stuart who nurtured an interest in John to want to know more about things than he knew,' said Arthur Ballard. 'In other words, he was educating him. Lennon wouldn't have known a Dada from a donkey. He was just so ignorant.'

In turn, John fascinated Stuart because he wasn't like the rest of the college crowd. Often, Stuart was content to be a passive listener as John, angry or cynically amused by everything, held forth during their wanderings along street and corridor, giving his lightning-bright imagination its ranting, arm-waving head. Occasionally, Stuart would let slip a seemingly uncontroversial comment that might spark off a sudden and inexplicable spasm of nastiness in John. He would take a long time to calm down. Then, again, Lennon would tease his comrade more jovially on occasions. 'Hanging's too good for it,' was his view of one of Stuart's early abstracts. As a figure of growing renown at college, Stuart had all the makings of a 'sitting duck' for John's 'rejecting' behaviour. Moreover, Stuart had not been abandoned by his mother whereas John, despite the extenuating circumstances of a stable upbringing by his aunt, felt himself to have been so. John had had enough experience of his natural mother to know what he was missing – hence the bitterness inherent in his outbursts.

'I can imagine John taking the mickey out of Stuart mercilessly in private,' reflected Bill Harry. 'He'd try it on, and if you stood up to it – fine. If you put up with it, he'd keep on.' Though Stuart struck back occasionally with barbed rejoinders that even shut John up, he was able to shrug off his friend's hurtful and, at times, humiliating attacks without needing to retaliate or sulk. Yet nothing John said or did could belittle him in Stuart's eyes and vice versa. Outlines dissolved and contents merged. They started to dress similarly and copy each other's mannerisms. John, for example, flicking his cigarette away just as Stuart always did. Both came to know almost precisely how the other felt about anything. 'Lennon's no hero of mine,' glowered Johnny Byrne. 'His one saving grace was that someone like Stuart Sutcliffe, who I respected enormously and liked very much, liked him – and Stuart knew Lennon in a way that perhaps no one else did at the time.'[5]

If they weren't exactly David and Jonathan, June Furlong had 'never seen two teenagers as close as those two'. Without purposely snubbing anybody, they evolved a restricted code that few outsiders could crack, not even Rod Murray or Ken Horton – who had been persuaded by Stuart to pack in his job as a laboratory technician to enrol at the art college to specialize in ceramics, and had been introduced to Stuart's network of acquaintances there. Utterances unamusing to Ken, Rod or anyone else would set the new best friends howling with laughter. Ballard would cite Stuart as source of 'a lot of that goofy kind of humour – which was really a Dadaist sort of humour. It's entirely Stuart's influence on John Lennon that introduced that Dada element.'[6]

Whether they understood the jokes or not, both Millie Sutcliffe and John's guardian, Mary 'Mimi' Smith, approved of the boys' friendship. Both women seemed of a kind: strong, passionate and protective. Hence, none of John's delinquent exploits at Quarry Bank and the art college filtered through to the Sutcliffes nor any of Stuart's to Aunt Mimi. To an extent, a self-deceiving Millie maintained the illusion that Stuart had, indeed, sidestepped the developmental stage known as 'rebellious adolescence'. To Aunt Mimi, Stuart was the proverbial 'good influence', a nice little friend: 'He was the only other boy he really enjoyed being with for long periods of time.'[7] This was praise indeed, as tight-lipped Mimi usually blamed doubtful company for John's mischief.

It was their fault, for example, that 'the stupid fool' got involved in a skiffle group, the Quarry Men, although it was John's own innate bossiness that ensured his walkover in the power struggle for leadership of this grammar school outfit that, via wary amplification, had mutated to Johnny and the Moondogs a year before he was introduced to Stuart. By then, groups who still used instruments made from household implements had become *passé* and, worse, insufferably square after professors with clipped beards had conducted 'experiments with skiffle' at London University, and Dr Vivien Fuchs had been welcomed back to Scott Base after his epoch-making trans-Antarctic trek in 1958 by a hastily assembled combo going to town on 'My Bonnie Lies Over The Ocean'. With this *Boys' Own Paper* episode as the spur, youth club big shots saw skiffle as a medium for keeping teenagers out of the coffee bars. Another nail in the coffin was a Camberwell vicar's self-penned 'Skiffle Mass' making a joyful sound unto the God of Jacob.

Some skiffle groups that didn't fall by the wayside made a transition to traditional jazz and a booking network where watching enthusiasts were likely to know more about the music's history than did the players. It was not unknown for certain purists to boo if a trad band deviated from Louisiana precedent by including saxophonists or committing the more cardinal sin of amplification.

Liverpool's principal bastions of jazz were contained mostly within the lofty ravines of warehouses around Whitechapel. These included the Cavern, the Temple and – 'No Weirdies, Beatniks or Teddy Boys admitted' – the Storyville (later, the Iron Door). Students Union dances at the art college were generally headlined by a trad band, but with friends in high places, such as Rod Jones as union president, and Bill and Stuart still on the committee, Johnny and the Moondogs were often engaged as support, despite every other item in their repertoire being an act of homage to Presley, Vincent, Lewis, Berry, Richard and other giants of classic rock. The only concession to trad was Louis Armstrong's 'When You're Smiling', albeit with John singing in a Goon voice and inserting cheeky references to college staff into its lyrics.

Though engagements were few and far between, and undertaken for as little as a round of fizzy drinks, Lennon's preoccupation with Johnny and the Moondogs took its toll on his college course. What did stereoplastic colour, tactile values and Vorticism matter when the group were opening that night for the Merseysippi Jazz Band at Stanley Abattoir Social Club? They were able to make twice as much row now that Bill, Rod and Stuart had inveigled the Students Union into buying Johnny and the Moondogs – regarded as 'the college band' – an amplifier which could also be used as a public address system. It mustn't leave the Mount Street premises. That was what the committee had emphasized, more fool them.

Notes

1   *The Times*, 24 September 1988.
2   *Buddy Holly*, J. Goldrosen (Granada, 1979).
3   *Student*, September 1969.
4   John Lennon's mother had been killed in a road accident in 1958. However, to all intents and purposes, he had lived with his aunt from babyhood. John was not to understand the profundity of the less absolute loss of his father, Alfred Lennon, until much later.
5   *Days In The Life*, ed. Jonathon Green (Heinemann, 1988).

The Young Sailor

6   This is probably putting it too bluntly, but the essential tenet of Dada is that all art is mindless rubbish, just as all modern civilization is. The movement began in Zurich in 1918 as a reaction against the mass slaughter of the First World War.

7   *Music Echo*, 31 October 1970.

chapter three

THE PASSENGER

'George and Paul used to come round and practise when we were at Gambier, and make a hell of a lot of noise'

Rod Jones

Mrs Plant had had her fill of the present crop of lodgers. It wasn't that each room looked as if someone had hurled a hand-grenade into it, nor was it the greasy fish-and-chip papers in the fireplace or them using the backyard as a receptacle for old newspapers, paint cans, abandoned canvases, maggoty mattresses and more odious objects. It wasn't even the pissing out of the window. What she didn't like was the dismantling of the white marble fireplace – 'which in those days we considered awful,' elucidated Rod Murray – and painting the furniture in funny colours. Black or white, she could take, but that Stuart boy had daubed it with these ridiculous stripes and polka-dots. Whatever would a prospective tenant being shown round think? The last straw was hearing that the students were burning tables and chairs to keep warm. Some of them were antiques – or, at least, they looked it. 'Once we'd done it, we realized that it wasn't a sensible thing to do,' confessed Murray. 'We were determined that there was no way Mrs Plant could ever get into that room to collect the rent. We'd always take it round because [otherwise] she'd find out.'

The formidable landlady of Percy Street had a purge the morning after an autumn party. Every hung-over occupant was given two hours' notice. Although she was persuaded to extend it to two days, she sent the furniture on to Rod and Stuart's next address with a written demand: '*I want this cleaned up and back as soon as possible, or else you're going to be in trouble.*' 'Masses of all this furniture, painted black and white, enormous great mahogany sideboards and tables and beds,' Rod moaned. 'We did make a half-hearted attempt at cleaning it, but it's an absolute swine to get off. We found we were taking the varnish off. Anyway, the novelty wore off and nothing happened about it.'

Rod Murray was next seen in a first-floor apartment at 3 Hillary Mansions, Gambier Terrace, two parallel roads from Percy Street. As it had been understood from the Canning Street days – how long ago that seemed now – Stuart was expected to move in too. For a while, John was there as well before returning to Woolton where the sugar was in its bowl, the milk in its jug, the cups unchipped on their saucers on an embroidered tablecloth, and Aunt Mimi served up three meals a day. It went without saying, however, that he could still use Gambier Terrace for dalliances with Cynthia and, to the exasperation of the two middle-aged ladies in the flat below, for Johnny and the Moondogs rehearsals.

Through thin walls, Stuart's train of thought would also be disturbed by the stirrings of Rod and what would now be called his 'live-in lover'. Nevertheless, he had a lot more space than at Percy Street, and he endeavoured to keep it that way. His room was dominated by his easel, the Dansette and, over in a corner, his divan bed from Huyton beneath the large curtainless window, dim with grime, that opened on to a small balcony and a view of not social-realist gasworks but the vast Anglican cathedral.

As bare as the sixty-watt bulb above, the floorboards were pocked with oil paint from the half-used tubes on the mantelpiece. Spots had also congealed upon the kitchen knives he used for de Staël-like linear structure. Just as farms always smelt of manure, so Sutcliffe's bedroom-cum-studio smelt of the turpentine necessary for cleaning the knives and brushes. Canvases leaned against walls on which charcoal sketches and the odd picture scissored from a magazine were pinned.

The Hillary Mansions flats were not salubrious, even by the standards of Liverpool 8. There was only one communal toilet which became so inconvenient that a solution was found in items from the Aladdin's Cave of 'No Waiting' signs, roadworks bollards and other street furniture stolen by tenants for decoration. 'There were a lot of Belisha beacon tops,' said Rod Jones. 'These were used as piss-pots before the police came and picked them up, and we were quite impressed that the police didn't press any charges.'

There was a bathroom, converted on occasion into sleeping quarters for overnight guests, but hot water was far from constant.

Damp, however, was not. In places, the walls were so mildewed that it was as if they were covered with black-green wallpaper. Living in the basement, Johnny Byrne recalled 'a cruel and bitter winter, and the water used to come up through the flagstones when it rained, and we were living on a loaf in which we made a hole and filled it with a packet of chips and which you carved up like a meatloaf.'[1]

For all its faults, a stay at Gambier Terrace seemed to be a prerequisite for renown in Liverpool. Byrne was on the verge of a future that would embrace such small-screen series as *All Creatures Great And Small* for BBC 1 and 1992's *Heartbeat* over on ITV. Among those who succeeded him in the moist basement was the Pop Art virtuoso Sam Walsh.

Unknowingly earmarked for fame or not, student residents did not regard their tenure as the prelude to an entire lifetime of slovenly poverty or even a few weeks of it. As Lennon's departure had demonstrated, there was always the safety net of Mum's home cooking and clean sheets if you needed to get your nerve back for another round of pooling loose change for a trip to the off-licence to see you and your intimates through fireside palaver until dawn.

Number 3 and another student abode in Huskisson Street were the scenes of many gatherings for charades, character assassinations of college lecturers, free-association poetry sessions, séances, and shy-making soliloquys about one's life, one's soul, one's aspirations. Just as undergraduate was Bill Harry's inauguration of a Liverpool chauvinist discussion group when his book idea was still on the boil. He named them 'the Dissenters', 'because I said we're dissenting from having other people's impressions on us. I was fairly convinced that if we really did the thing ourselves, and tried to get publicity, we would make Liverpool famous. Liverpool can be as famous as San Francisco. We've got as much talent as they have over there. Let's get it going.'

To Bill, bohemian Liverpool was then 'a pallid imitation derived of what the Americans were doing'. Its atmosphere was enough like that of New York's vibrant beatnik district, Greenwich Village, that hacks from the muck-raking *Sunday People* were sent up north on a crusade to expose what would be headlined 'THE BEATNIK HORROR!'[2] Local fingers pointed to Allan Williams, thick-set and black-bearded proprietor of the Jacaranda, as publicity-seeking vehicle of the ace reporters' entrée into the *demi-monde* of the dharma bums at 3 Hillary Mansions.

Lavishing drinks on those present, the journalists assured everyone that it was to be a feature on how difficult it is to survive on student grants. It certainly was, agreed John Lennon, who Rod Murray recalled 'saying he had had to go home and scrounge meals off his relatives'. As their nicotine-stained fingers scribbled, the hacks smiled in sympathy, but inwardly they were feeling dubious about the assignment. The situation wasn't up to scratch – or, to be precise, *down* to scratch. Rod Murray's room where they were sipping coffee was mildly untidy but quite clean and agreeably decorated. One so-called beatnik had just come home from an honest day's toil in a suit and a female tenant had said she had had no qualms about inviting her parents round for a candlelit dinner.

Nevertheless, eager to get their pictures in the paper, the young people of Number 3 obeyed a directive to dress down, make the place more higgledy-piggledy, chuck some household waste about, make it more photogenic. You want the readers to think that you're poor, starving students, don't you?

On 24 July 1960, the *Sunday People* published its beatnik article alongside a photograph of Rod Murray's room. It was the first that Britain at large saw of John Lennon. With sideburns past his earlobes and sporting sunglasses, he had pride of place, lolling about on the littered floor among other self-conscious 'beatniks' including Harry, Murray and Williams. 'I think Stuart was around,' said Bill, 'but I think he was embarrassed. He didn't really want to get involved.'

The revelations hurt the followers more than the followed. 'Rod Jones was there,' confirmed Arthur Ballard, 'I remember he was in a terrible state, because his father was a docker and he was so ashamed that he upped and left Liverpool for Toxteth.' You can readily understand why. According to the *Sunday People*, delivered to millions of homes, Mr Jones's son was 'on the road to hell', just like all the other layabouts confronted with their infamy. The hairs rose on parental necks as they read of how one beatnik from Leeds had avoided National Service 'by posing as a psychiatric case'. 'Their object is to seek happiness through meditation.' What's 'meditation' when it's at home? My God! There was more! 'They revel in filth . . . not really orgies – but they get very naughty.'

Backbeat

'An awful lot of the stuff in that article was either blatant untruths or so distorted,' protested Rod Murray. 'All right, we did do silly things. Everyone does when they're young, don't they? I don't think we were quite that odd . . . maybe we were but I don't think we were quite that bad.' From THE BEATNIK HORROR surfaced the enduring legend that either Stuart or John slept at Gambier Terrace in a coffin.[3]

The permissive society was very much in its infancy on Merseyside. What was reported truthfully enough in the *Sunday People*, however, was the student habit of hitch-hiking everywhere, like Kerouac did in *On The Road*. One such journey was to the Welsh holiday resort of Rhyl because Rod Jones 'used to be at Flintshire Tech. My mates from Rhyl were there doing art, and then they crossed over with the Liverpool mob, led by Rod [Murray]. One weekend – it must have been Rod and Stuart – we picked these two birds up in this Flinty dance, and they took us back to their house to stay. It was amazing to us because they were Scandinavian, because I remember we all slept under duvets, and we'd never heard of duvets. I think their parents were there, and we were allowed to stay. That was absolutely strange. I'd never come across anything like that before.'

Another former Flintshire Technical College student, Spike Hawkins, moved to Liverpool 8 where, with Johnny Byrne, he organized poetry readings accompanied by local jazz musicians at Streate's coffee bar. Further jazz-poetry fusions took place at the Crane Theatre. One presentation there was at the behest of Michael Horovitz who launched 1959's *New Departures*, a counter-culture poetry magazine: 'At the party afterwards, Adrian Henri, who was the host, said, "Oh, this poetry stuff is all right. I think I'm going to start doing it." [Roger] McGough had read with us in Edinburgh and [Brian] Patten, who'd sat in the front row of the Crane gig trying to hide his school cap, was this marvellous boy who came up and read rather different, passionate, romantic poems.'[4]

Though they weren't exactly 'jazz', Johnny and the Moondogs framed the declamations of *vers libre* bard Royston Ellis in the Jacaranda's bottle-and-candle cellar. What came across in a *what's-the-matter-with-kids-today?* documentary shown on British television in 1960 was that none of the girls in his native Brighton fancied bespectacled, taper-thin Royston, dancing on his own amid the 'excitement' of a parochial hop. To compensate, perhaps, he turned to a tacky way of getting high and introduced it to John, Stuart and other interested parties in the Gambier Terrace fraternity when he was invited back after the Jacaranda recital. It was flattery of a kind, they supposed, that Royston judged them as 'more of the bohemian ilk than other young northerners, and their pleasant eccentricity made them acceptable'.[5] He also considered them disreputable enough to want to be instructed about buying a Vick inhaler from the chemist's, and isolating the part of it that contained a stimulant called benzedrine. This, you then ate. It is distressing to report that this late 1950s equivalent of glue-sniffing was also taken up by the younger members of Johnny and the Moondogs, guitarists George Harrison and Paul McCartney, who both attended the Institute Grammar School. Of the two, Paul had the most inherent musical talent as well as a moon-faced resemblance to Elvis, though George, said Paul, 'was far ahead of us as a guitarist – though that isn't saying very much as we were raw beginners ourselves'. The pair frequently absconded from school to join in midday rock 'n' roll sessions in the art college's Life Room.

While each tried not to put his foot in it with some inane remark that showed his age, Paul and George tagged along with the big boys from the college. George, especially, 'kept in the background so much,' remembered Bill Harry, 'that he was almost the Invisible Man'. Paul, however, had been John's musical collaborator as far back as the latter's final terms at the 'Police State'. The power structure in the group, in which Harrison was subordinate, had been founded on the handshake that had formalized the Lennon-McCartney songwriting partnership – though the last thing anyone dancing to Johnny and the Moondogs wanted to listen to was a homemade song.

Lennon's newer friendship with Sutcliffe provoked in McCartney an apprehension akin to that of a child viewing another sibling as a barrier to prolonged intimacy with an admired elder brother. Their new 'grown-up' preoccupations with the likes of Jeff Mohammed and, of course, the fanciable girls at art college would have excluded old school chums like McCartney from their day-to-day banter, and provoked a natural feeling of jealousy mixed with awe.

Backbeat

Their wonderment at John spurred McCartney and Harrison to cut classes either for rehearsals or simply to sit at one of the kidney-shaped tables in the Jac, proudly familiar as he held court. Revelling in their wickedness, they would flash packets of Woodbines or a loose handful of a more sophisticated brand filched, perhaps, from parents' walnut cigarette cases. The pair pitched in too when Allan Williams, the latest in a series of Dutch uncles that Stuart would always have, required the painting of murals in the basement.[6]

Sutcliffe, Lennon and the Moondogs plus Rods Jones and Murray were also on hand to assist when Allan hired St George's Hall, one of the city's oldest public auditoriums, for the ninth Lancashire and Cheshire Arts Ball. For fifteen pounds and free admission, the lads, under Stuart's supervision, put together some of the floats intended to lend the event more of a carnival atmosphere. 'We built this giant fifteen-foot thing,' remembered Rod Jones. 'It eventually just collapsed and there was nobody underneath it, but if it had fallen over, it would have killed someone.' By tradition, the floats themselves were torn to pieces at midnight. Unprecedented, however, were diversions not included in the price of a ticket. To the consternation of a head caretaker, anxious to lock up, there followed the letting off of fire extinguishers, the turning on of every tap in the building, the pulling of the main electricity switches, the playing of twelve-bar blues on the pipe organ and the hurling of flour bags. 'They made such a mess with flour and water,' said Jones, 'that it took them weeks to scrape it from around the bottom of the pillars.' The overtime pay demanded by cleaning staff to make good this and the other instances of vandalism put the tin lid on further arts balls at St George's Hall.

The services rendered to Williams were in exchange for his acting in a quasi-managerial capacity for Johnny and the Moondogs. Though his own observations tended to contradict it, Stuart would suck on a cigarette and nod at John's fantasies about the group's engagements. Would anyone like John admit, for instance, that they had taken the stage the previous evening before an audience of the hall caretaker and his barking dog plus two Teds who left after the first number? All Johnny and the Moondogs bookings were triumphs in retrospect – at least, the ones where Stuart hadn't been present.

Stuart had turned over an idea put to him by John of joining the group – but simply appearing casually knowledgeable about rock 'n' roll might not have been an adequate enough qualification for a bandleader expecting instrumental and/or vocal ability to back it up. Lennon, however, wasn't a normal bandleader – or a normal anything. As both a close acquaintance of Stuart and John, and a proficient musician, Mike Evans's well-argued opinion of Sutcliffe as a player and Lennon's motivation for wanting him in the group is worth quoting at length: 'I don't think he [Stuart] was terribly musical. That's the intriguing thing. It was somehow symptomatic of the failure in Lennon that he assumed that because he could do it, other people could do it and the main virtue was "having a go". That was always his attitude – like he had Yoko Ono on his records, and yet Yoko's the world's worst singer. But he had her on his records as a kind of event, an activity justifying the end. This was his notion about art, and I think what fascinated Stuart about John was that whatever was John's art, rock 'n' roll or whatever, he leaped into it with both feet without any training or anything – whereas Stuart's art was academic: he had to work at it. I think this fascinated Stuart. There was this primitive artist and I think, when John offered him the opportunity to do it himself, he just did.

'I think he enjoyed the romantic image of being a rock 'n' roller. What he failed to see immediately, and what John failed to see, was that wanting to be didn't necessarily mean you were good at it. Whereas John was intrinsically good, he failed to see that, in others, enthusiasm wasn't enough for them. It was like Lennon himself was about drawing and painting – he was hopeless. That justified it in his mind. That's what frustrated Ballard – he [John] never wanted to go any further. That's how I see Stuart as a musician.'

Because you didn't have to pretend you liked Stockhausen or Theolonious Monk to be acceptable to rock 'n' roll musicians, Stuart was intrigued not only by Lennon but the entire pop sub-culture as a deliciously 'artless' tangent to more egghead activity. He wasn't alone. Studying fine art under Richard Hamilton in Newcastle, Bryan Ferry was about to cut his teeth with a Sunderland combo, the Banshees, before forming Roxy Music in the 1970s, as Camberwell Art School student Syd Barrett and three architecture students were to form the Pink Floyd in 1964.

A more basic incentive for Sutcliffe to seek an opening as a Moondog was that even the most ill-favoured youth in a pop combo had more licence to fraternize with the gawking young ladies – 'judies' – lining the front of the bandstand than most of the other lads shuffling about with a built-in sense of defeat in the gloom past the burning footlights. You didn't have to look like Charles Atlas to be in a group, and some believed no one would notice a puny physique if your apparel was sufficiently gaudy. There was this myth that, during an intermission or even from the stage, a beatific smile, a flood of libidinous excitement and an 'All right, then, I'll see you later' might secure an appointment after the show in, say, the idyllic seclusion of a backstage broom cupboard.

Another attraction was the camaraderie and bloke-ism of a group, reminiscent of the soon-to-be-repealed National Service minus the barracks discipline. 'I think it's like a guy who is shy and is asked to join the gang,' theorized Bill Harry, confusing shyness with introspection, and 'being in a gang' with the adolescent dynamic of partnering a best friend.

Moreover, though it was early days yet, perhaps Johnny and the Moondogs would get somewhere. Look at Michael Cox, a lanky boy he'd known at Prescot Grammar. He'd sung a bit, and his sisters had written on his behalf to an enthralled Jack Good, producer of television pop showcases like *Oh Boy!*, *Boy Meets Girls* and *Wham!*, on which vocalists and their backing groups followed each other so quickly that the screaming studio audiences scarcely had pause to draw breath. Thanks to Cox's regular plugs on these programmes, his third single, 'Angela Jones', was poised to climb into the Top Thirty.

Michael Cox had shown what was possible. Johnny and the Moondogs might not get that far but, if nothing else, just to appear on stage with them would be something big for Stuart to tell his sisters and their friends.

As the unit was top-heavy with guitarists, the obvious instrument to think about, John had said, was one of these new-fangled electric basses. With only four strings, it was easier to learn than an ordinary guitar. You only have to thrum one note instead of a whole chord. What's more, all groups not wishing to be an anachronism had to have one. Not only did it radiate an infinitely greater volume and depth of sound than a broomstick bass, but, as George pointed out, 'It was much easier to get around, do more gigs and carry it in a case.'[7]

John's proposal that George switch to bass had as much effect as if he had suggested an Indian sitar. He didn't even bother sounding out Paul, who reckoned that bass playing was the lowest of the low, the sort of thing people got lumbered with, rather than chose to do. After all, how many famous bass players are there? No one else John approached was either interested or able to muster up the sixty-odd pounds to buy one – at a time when a ten-bob note (50p) was considered a satisfactory prize in a TV game show.

Stuart belonged to the second category. He wanted a bass but didn't have the money. Like Mr Micawber, he was waiting for something to turn up and, sooner than either he or John had imagined, something did. Between 17 November 1959 and 17 January 1960, the second biennial John Moores Exhibition took place in the Walker Gallery. Over two thousand entries flooded in from all over Britain to be appraised by a panel that included Peter Lanyon, a Cornish painter admired by Stuart, and old Moores himself.

With some misgivings, Sutcliffe submitted what remained of a large canvas entitled *Summer Painting*. Half of it had gone astray during the eviction from Percy Street. 'He started this painting and it was two pieces of six feet by four feet,' explained Rod Murray, 'a great big abstract expressionist painting with sand in, and lots of wax and stuff to build it out.' Perhaps transforming his envy into a friendly gesture, Rod helped Stuart carry half of it down to the Walker, but 'when we got back, we never bothered getting the rest'.

To Stuart's delighted surprise, *Summer Painting* was not only selected for display, but Mr Moores himself bought it for sixty-five pounds. Of less intrinsic value was that John dragged his aunt along to see it – and Charles Sutcliffe, home from the sea for a few weeks, came along too. He glowed with pride as he allowed himself to be led to licensed premises by Arthur Ballard who, past his best, had entered a landscape. The judgement passed on it had prompted a self-consolatory 'Van Gogh never sold a picture in his life' as he advised Sutcliffe junior: 'Don't let it go to your head, it might be ten years before you sell another one.'

Stuart now had the wherewithal to buy his way into John's Moondogs. Before the John Moores windfall, Lennon had offered Rod Murray the job. Rod had been keen enough to start making a bass guitar but 'by the time I'd got round to thinking about strings, Stuart had been out and bought one'. From Frank Hessy's window, he had chosen a magnificent Hofner 'President', for what it looked like rather than its sound.

When told of Stuart's purchase, the Liverpool 8 art community in general felt that he had wasted his money to waste his talent. Bill Harry 'was furious inside. I liked them and believed in them, but I thought he shouldn't be in a band. I couldn't believe it. There was somebody who not only had the talent but the dedication for art. I thought, Why is he dabbling in that? That's not his *métier*. That's not him. Why the hell is he doing it? I asked him why he was wasting his time. I was very disappointed. You channel your energy into something, and if you diversify, it may affect your art – but obviously it didn't because his great art was to come. He had been so deeply intense with his art so that it screwed him up tight.'

Sticking to the contested idea that Stuart was a shrinking violet, Bill went on: 'I think it was a letting go, a release, a relaxation. It was something enjoyable and brought him out of himself. He was one of the boys instead of being the solitary individual only talking to a few people on the quiet. He was one of the gang.'

'Well, all I can say,' sniffed Philip Hartas, 'is that Lennon used to rush about the place and then McCartney and the other fellow, George Harrison, used to come in from the Boys' Institute next door. They would suddenly pick up Lennon and take him out with them, and then Stuart began to be associated with them. I don't know what on earth . . . except, I suppose, that it was a very strange time in this country in that there was a lot stirring ordinary people to buy motor-cars and do extraordinary things, and the sky seemed to be the limit.'

With no axe to grind, guitarist Colin Manley fathomed that, though George Harrison had been obliged by the Youth Employment Centre to become an apprentice electrician on leaving the Institute, 'they [Lennon *et al.*] were born leaders, and it wasn't just their musicianship. They never intended to have ordinary jobs. They just wanted to play music.'[8] Manley was then an executive officer with the National Assistance Board while moonlighting with the Remo Four who, if recognized as Merseyside's top instrumental act, were not prepared then to give up their day jobs for the treachery of full-time showbusiness. Manchester's Peter Noone (later, singer with Herman's Hermits) was similarly cautious: 'Most of us didn't take playing in bands too seriously. We listened to our parents who said, "Put that guitar down and do a job with your hands." [9]

Stuart wasn't immune to twinges of conscience as the enormity of what he had done sank in. His mother, too, wondered what he was playing at: 'I remember the first time I caught him with that guitar. He had this miniature record-player with an Elvis record on it, and this huge, ugly guitar. He was trying to be Presley. I was sorry for him because I knew it was just another attempt at getting rich quick.' [10]

For a long time, he gazed at himself with the new bass in a mirror. At first, he merely posed with it as he had done with the acoustic back in Huyton. With no *Play In A Day* tutor book for bass guitar to help him, what else could he do? The grinning vibrancy that Paul transmitted wasn't for Stuart, neither was John's 'hard man' stance. Stuart wasn't tall enough for that anyhow. Jet Harris, who played bass in Cliff Richard's Shadows, he was, frankly, stunted, but this was overlooked by fans because he had 'image': impassive and detached, he was the James Dean of the group. That was more Stuart's line. He could stand sideways on or even with his back to the audience. As well as being a stylistic affectation, it might also serve to mask what a struggle he was having getting through difficult numbers.

He might have looked good but he couldn't get away with just holding the bass. In virgin territory, he began by gathering what he could from trial-and-error when sweating over sheet music or plucking along to the records he owned or had been lent. At John's decree, George taught Stuart further rudiments. An extra lesson came from Dave May of the Silhouettes who showed the novice how three notes would suffice to play Eddie Cochran's 'C'mon Everybody'. Gradually, it dawned on Stuart that certain cycles recurred *ad nauseam* in rock 'n' roll: the three-chord-trick, the twelve-bar blues and the I-VI minor-VI-V ballad cliché. More often than not, these were complicated by a 'middle-eight' or 'bridge' passage, but the beauty of such loose, simple structures was that variations on them required little instruction. This understanding would be the key to his bass playing for all time.

Positioning his small hands on the thick, taut strings, his fingertips became calloused but not particularly supple with daily practice that dwindled to merely whenever he felt like it, partly because his finger-lacerating effort was having a detrimental effect on his painting.

Nevertheless, he stole nervous glances at the depth into which he might hurtle should he not cut the mustard with a Merseyside adolescent public that had no inhibitions about letting a group know precisely what it thought about them.

Stuart needn't have worried. John wasn't much better on his guitar. However, he was a marvellous Presley-derived vocalist with instinctive if indelicate crowd control that rode roughshod over meandering tempos, flurries of bum notes, clashing slam-chords and long pauses between songs. This was the order of the day when the drummerless outfit entertained in Austin Davis and Beryl Bainbridge's front room at a party that could be heard in all the surrounding streets in an age before phrases like 'noise pollution' and 'environmental health' had been coined.

A more typical engagement was in the dingy fly-by-night jive hive in Upper Parliament Street where Pauline Sutcliffe first saw her brother in action with Johnny and the Moondogs. In a playing area with one white light bulb serving as illumination they did battle with a public address set-up centred on a solitary microphone tied to a broomhandle. Though no amplifiers or speakers were in sight when pop stars mimed their hits on television, amateurs like Johnny and the Moondogs had long been aware that an electric guitar wasn't plugged directly into the mains. Equipment was expensive so you made do by either borrowing or, say, feeding two guitars into a record-player amplifier via a shared jack-plug. This was where someone with electrician's training, like George, was useful, although, after twenty minutes or so, blue smoke might start curling from somewhere or other. You could also try soldering together an amplifier from a kit advertised ('with a ten-watt punch') in *Melody Maker*, and carried to the venue in a school satchel.

By 1960, Johnny and the Moondogs possessed more bona fide means of magnifying their volume, and, if they weren't yet in the upper crust of Liverpool pop, they could keep their ends up not only as an art college support group but as a credible attraction in coffee bars, welfare institutes, far-flung suburban palais, Lancashire village halls, working men's clubs, pub function rooms and at Church youth clubs that had embraced regular 'beat' sessions. Occasionally there was trouble and they weren't rebooked. An amplifier would fall abruptly silent, and a number would shudder to a halt to a desultory spatter of clapping. There would be some fidgeting, and John might mumble something with 'bloody' or even 'bugger' in it, which would occasion squeals of appalled joy from the girls, several of them peeping slyly at the swingin' curate who had ceased clicking his fingers to stiffen with shocked dignity, stare hard at the stage, and look as if he was about to do something. Sometimes he did.

For every door that closed on Johnny and the Moondogs, others opened. The two members most willing to picket for more bookings were Paul and, perhaps to mitigate his musical shortcomings, Stuart. With silver-tongued guile, they would lay it on with a hyperbolic trowel when negotiating with this quizzical pub landlord or that uninterested social secretary. Presenting himself as 'manager', Stuart would weigh every word of his supplicatory letters which stressed the appeal his 'very experienced' clients would have for 'habitués' of a given venue.

He also dreamt up a new name for the group. Buddy Holly had his Crickets and, on a forthcoming month-long tour of Britain, Gene Vincent was going to be backed by the Beat Boys. How about 'The Beetles'? One of the motorbike gangs in *The Wild One* was called that too. A brainstorming session with John warped it eventually to 'The Beatles'[11] – you know, like in 'beat music'.

They tested it on Brian Casser – the 'Cass' in Cass and the Cassanovas, a combo in the first division of Merseyside popularity. An adherent to the 1950s 'Somebody and the Somebodies' dictate, which differentiated between a leader and his accompanists, Casser howled with derision, and, with Robert Newton's role in the movie version of *Treasure Island* lately extended into a television series, suggested Long John and his Pieces of Eight. Warming to this theme, he next proffered Long John and the Silver Beatles.

They compromised with just the Silver Beatles, thus implying no obvious leader and the concept that a unit without a singing non-instrumentalist could be a plausible medium of vocal *and* instrumental expression. While they spurned the synchronized footwork with which the Shadows iced their act, the Silver Beatles were at one with an ancient *New Musical Express* dictum concerning 'visual effect'. 'Some sort of uniform is a great help,' it ran, 'though ordinary casual clothes are perhaps the best as long as you all wear exactly the same.'[12]

One local group, Rory Storm and the Hurricanes, had kitted themselves out in uniform black and white winkle-pickers – gold for Storm – and a starched white handkerchief protruding smartly from the top pockets of bright red suits for the group, light pink for Rory. From another city-centre tailor, Gerry and the Pacemakers had ordered 'G&P'-monogrammed blazers. With such neat professional identities unaffordable, the Silver Beatles settled for saturnine off-the-peg chic: black shirts, dark blue jeans and two-tone plimsolls.

All they needed now was the drummer they had lacked since they were Quarry Men. However, Brian Casser had stopped being facetious for long enough to help secure one in Tommy Moore, a forklift truck driver at Garston Bottle Works. Tommy's frequent night shifts and a very possessive girlfriend bridled him from the outset. At Gambier Terrace rehearsals, 'He used to turn up to do the odd thing in the back room,' said Rod Murray, 'and he'd disappear early, thank God, because his drums shook the floor.' Significantly, the first legal machinations to get the bohemian element out of the flats dated from Moore's recruitment.

It was assumed that, with his heart in jazz, twenty-six-year-old Tommy would do until the arrival of someone more compatible with 'arty' types like the Silver Beatles and their coterie with their long words and insertion of names like Modigliani and Kierkegaard into conversations that would lapse into student vernacular and Goonisms. Not over-friendly, Moore preferred the society of the no-nonsense Cassanovas and other workmanlike semi-professionals who derided the Silver Beatles as 'posers'. With his Pacemakers, Gerry Marsden was not a regular patron of the Jacaranda: 'I went there a few times but it wasn't really my scene. It was a bit too arty for me. The arty types weren't my sort of people.'[13]

George Harrison once suggested that the Silver Beatles, and what they became, were an English grammar-school interpretation of rock 'n' roll and, in 1960, the group certainly contained a representative cross-section of such an institution. When George had first brought his guitar to Quarry Men sessions, his hero-worshippingly friendly overtures were ignored by John, trying to absolve himself from any criticism of hobnobbing with a younger boy. Nonetheless, both he and Harrison were C-Stream reprobates who rejected formal education. Conversely, while not quite front-row smarmers, Paul, then a sixth-former about to take A levels, and Tommy Moore's successor, Pete Best, were less rebellious. Part rebel, part conformist, like his mother, Stuart was somewhere in between.

To a degree, they played up to it. In one incident, they

Top left: Stuart's father, Charles Sutcliffe, taken around 1948. (Pauline Sutcliffe, Private Collection)

Top right: The Sutcliffe family. *From left to right:* Stuart, Pauline, Joyce and their mother, Millie, 1948. (Pauline Sutcliffe, Private Collection)

Above: Stuart leading the choirboys' procession at St Gabriel's, Huyton. His burial service was held in the same church. (Pauline Sutcliffe, Private Collection)

Above: The Liverpool Art School carnival, *c.* 1957. Stuart takes centre position with his friend Rod Murray in glasses and Rod Jones as Dracula. (Pauline Sutcliffe, Private Collection)

Right: 'The Blind Samson' – from one of Stuart's Liverpool Art School sketchbooks, *c.* 1957. (Pauline Sutcliffe, Private Collection)

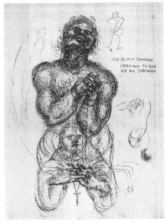

Left: Percy Street studio, Liverpool. Hardly an image of the Beatnik horror later described in the *People* newspaper. (Pauline Sutcliffe, Private Collection)

Above: The Beatles sample one of their first beers in the Grosse Freiheit, Hamburg. *Left to right:* Stuart Sutcliffe, John Lennon, Helmut – a German friend – George Harrison, Paul McCartney, Pete Best. (Pauline Sutcliffe, Private Collection)

Right: Stuart, the inevitable cigarette and bass guitar. (Astrid Kirchherr, Redferns)

Below: Looking cool and casual – Astrid Kirchherr captures the Beatles in a moment of calm. (Astrid Kirchherr, Redferns)

Above: Stu takes a break while the others play on. (Peter Bruchmann, Redferns)

Left: George and Stu play for the crowds. (Peter Bruchmann, Redferns)

Below: Hair swept forward, John and Stu bear witness to Astrid's influence. (Jürgen Volmer, Redferns)

Welding helmet substitutes bass guitar at Hamburg Art School, *c.* 1961. (Pauline Sutcliffe, Private Collection)

Top: Astrid and Stuart. (Jürgen Vollmer, Redferns)

Above left: A self-portrait of Stuart taken in his studio in Astrid's house, *c.* 1961. (Pauline Sutcliffe, Private Collection)

Above right: Self-portrait photograph, in Hamburg studio, *c.* 1961. (Pauline Sutcliffe, Private Collection)

Klaus, Astrid and Stu at a party in Exi garb. (Pauline Sutcliffe, Private Collection)

Above: Millie Sutcliffe gazes at one of Astrid's self-portraits with her son. (Pauline Sutcliffe, Private Collection)

Left: A sultry Stuart responds to Astrid's lens. (Astrid Kirchherr, Redferns)

Left: Stuart and John – a little light relief on the beach. (Astrid Kirchherr, Redferns)

dumbfounded a member of another outfit in the dressing room by pretending to be reading highbrow Russian poetry to each other, each intoning and murmuring appreciatively in mock seriousness. They enjoyed winding people up like that.

McCartney and Lennon's pretensions as composers also caused comment when reputations were made much more easily by churning out rock 'n' roll standards and current hits. Indeed, Gerry and the Pacemakers prided themselves on including everything in the week's Top Twenty when working the dance halls, then virtually the only realistic links outside London between youth-club bashes and seasons in holiday camps, contracts with leisure corporations like Top Rank and Jaycee, and pre-interval slots on round-Britain package tours – with getting a record out a far-fetched afterthought.

Songwriters have to start somewhere but, apart from royalty-earning B-sides of generally unoriginal 'originals', the possibility of a group from the sticks developing songwriting to any great extent was unheard of. Even the exceptions like Cliff Richard's 'Move It' and Johnny Kidd and the Pirates' climactic 'Shakin' All Over' began on the backs of either US cover versions or a piece by a jobbing tunesmith either specially commissioned or procured by grubbing round publishers' offices. In New York's Brill Building, there was even a songwriting 'factory' where such combines as Goffin and King, and Mann and Weill dashed off assembly-line pop for people to hum, whistle and partly sing over a few chart weeks while more ditties were prepared for further instant consumption.

To capture a private gauge of John and Paul's efforts alongside those of the professionals, and to measure their performances against those of rival groups, the Silver Beatles spent a constructive May afternoon in McCartney's living room in Allerton with a Grundig tape recorder. After fiddling about with microphone positioning and tuning up, they plunged into a selection that included cracks at non-originals from such as Eddie Cochran, Gene Vincent and Carl Perkins, but mostly meandering instrumentals and Lennon-McCartney items like 'I'll Always Be In Love With You,' 'I'll Follow The Sun,' 'Hello Little Girl,' 'Somedays' and 'The One After 9.09.' While he helped out vocally here and there, Stuart's principal contribution was still the plonk of a simple bass line, more a presence than a sound.

The story goes that, while finding his way on the instrument, he would take the stage having purposely not connected it to any power point. Ignorant of this strategy, Merseyside promoter Sam Leach imagined he was correcting an oversight by once sidling onstage to plug Stuart in. In the middle of a slow ballad, the resulting electronic grumble in Z minor threw a shift from chorus to middle eight into confusion, and an enraged John chopped an untidy ending in the air while Paul sang on obliviously unaccompanied for a few more bars. Later, Stuart progressed to sheepish audibility though he would still disengage surreptitiously whenever there was a tricky bit coming up. 'He was brought into it as some kind of passenger,' was Rod Jones's not unsubstantiated assessment. His trump card was that he was a friend of John's – the most charismatic and influential member of the group – which added a new dynamic to the complex politics. John could bestow special favours on Stuart because he was a mate, rather than having to choose between the less neutral McCartney or Harrison. Furthermore, he added a touch of class with his artistic leanings and perceptions.

So it was that Stuart and John with Veronica Johnson and Cynthia went separately from the others to the Liverpool Empire that March for Gene Vincent, who was co-headlining his long-awaited tour with the 'C'mon Everybody' hitmaker, Eddie Cochran, a multi-talented Oklahoman Elvis, then in the Top Thirty for the fourth time. For Lennon, the evening was spoilt by girls screaming indiscriminately at all male performers – though within a few years, he would be hearing it no more than a sailor hears the sea.

The indigenous supporting programme included Billy Fury, Joe Brown and Georgie Fame, all on the books of the celebrated pop Svengali Larry Parnes. On the bill too was nineteen-year-old Tony Sheridan, a singing guitarist of unusual flair who had flowered momentarily on *Oh Boy!* before consignment to an obscurity largely of his own making. A spot with Vincent on *Boy Meets Girls* had been cancelled because, in his own publicist's words, Tony 'went haywire (failing to be on time, arriving without his guitar, etc.).' Television was, therefore, closed to him, and only on sufferance did Mr Parnes allow Sheridan just under ten minutes twice nightly on the Vincent-Cochran trek.

Through the enterprising Allan Williams, Vincent and Cochran were scheduled to return to Merseyside on 3 May to spearhead a three-hour spectacular at a 6,000-capacity sports arena near Prince's Dock. The rest of the bill would be filled with an assortment of Parnes's lesser creatures and some top Scouse groups including Rory Storm and the Hurricanes and Cass and the Cassanovas. Williams had to add Gerry and the Pacemakers and four more bands when Eddie was killed after a car carrying him and Gene rammed a lamp-post while tearing through a Wiltshire town in the small hours of 17 April.

Despite fractured ribs and collar bone as well as injuries to his already calipered leg, Vincent insisted, with characteristic obstinacy, that the Liverpool show would go on. Using a microphone stand as a surgical support, Gene paid tribute to Eddie with a mournful 'Over The Rainbow' which only just upstaged Gerry Marsden's equally plaintive 'You'll Never Walk Alone'.

After the show, Larry Parnes had gone with Williams back to the Jacaranda. Though averse to signing groups, he had been sufficiently awed by the local boys' impact on the frenzied audience and Allan Williams's competence as a promoter to discuss a further, albeit less ambitious joint venture. He wanted, he said, an all-purpose backing outfit for use by certain of his singers. A name he kept mentioning was Billy Fury, a Liverpudlian then on the crest of his first Top Ten breakthrough, and predicted to rival Cliff Richard as the nation's titan of teen. Larry would bring him along if Allan could hurriedly assemble some groups for him to see.

Watching Parnes from an outermost table were John, Stuart and George. None of them summoned the courage to approach the Great Man, but in the café two nights later, John asked Williams if the Silver Beatles, now they had a drummer, could audition for the Parnes job at Slater Street's Corinthian Social Club[14] the following week. Doubt, hesitation and final consent chased across the Welshman's hairy face as Lennon spieled in top gear. Allan had witnessed for himself, hadn't he, the group's knack of tuning hostile audiences into their awry absurdity? He hadn't actually been there to see that one, but at the Casbah Coffee Club in Hayman's Green a while ago, they had worked up a wildly enthusiastic response from a full house of three hundred.

On the day, there was a hitch. Tommy Moore rolled up so late that Johnny Hutch from the Cassanovas was requested to drum for the Silver Beatles. A myth has persisted that one aspect of the group that worried Parnes was the fellow with the scrappy beard on bass. Later, Larry insisted that he thought that Stuart could play quite well. It had been the tardy Tommy Moore who had failed to impress.

While they toed no conventional line with fancy Shadows dance steps, at least the Silver Beatles weren't slick to the point of sterility like other bands surveyed that morning. Larry recalled the commotion at Bradford Gaumont recently when as an experiment, Marty Wilde appeared not with, as he put it, 'corny and square' session players imposed on him by his record company, but four youths who had backed him before when he was still just Reg Smith from Blackheath. 'It takes youngsters,' Marty had announced, 'to play and feel the rock beat.'

Apart from their drummer, the Silver Beatles were young enough. Moreover, though the one addressed as John had put down his guitar to sing a Presley opus, they were the only outfit there who weren't encumbered with a flamboyant non-instrumentalist who might agitate to get in on the act. It had been known for such a person to push off the star his band was backing to commandeer the central microphone himself.

'Silver Beatles – very good,' Larry Parnes jotted on a pad. 'Keep note for future work.'

NOTES

1   *Days In the Life*, ed. J. Green (Heinemann, 1988)
2   *Sunday People*, 24 July 1960.
3   And perpetuated (and attributed to John alone) by the media in the mid-1960s because it was commensurate with Lennon's black humour in his books *In His Own Write* and *A Spaniard in the Works*.
4   *The Times*, 24 September 1984.
5   *Generation X*, C. Hamblett and J. Deverson (Tandem, 1964).
6   The murals were still there when the Jacaranda re-opened in 1964.
7   *National Rock Star,* 18 December 1976.
8   *The Beat Goes On*, November 1992.
9   *Let's All Go Down The Cavern*, S. Leigh (Vermilion, 1984).
10 *Disc*, 7 November 1970.
11 Lest we forget, there was at that time a Salisbury group called the Beatniks – who evolved into Dave Dee, Dozy, Beaky, Mick and Tich.

12 *New Musical Express*, 1 November 1957.

13 *You'll Never Walk Alone*, G. Marsden and R. Coleman (Bloomsbury, 1993).

14 Later in 1960, Allan Williams would re-open the premises as the Blue Angel nightclub.

chapter four

POP GOES THE EASEL

'It's a group. We're all in it together. I know he can't play very well – but what he plays is just right. It's rock 'n' roll. The thing about Stu is, he's the greatest rock 'n' roller in the world. He just can't play'

Ian Hart as John Lennon, *Backbeat*

'Future work' came sooner rather than later. Less than a fortnight after the Larry Parnes audition, group and equipment were hurtling from Lime Street railway station for the first leg of an eight-day tour of Scotland, commencing in Alloa. It wouldn't be Billy Fury they'd be backing. It never had been. Instead, the Silver Beatles would be with a lesser Parnes luminary, Johnny Gentle, a square-jawed hunk who, prior to his renaming, had been Merseyside merchant seaman John Askew. While his four singles had all flopped, he had plugged them on *Oh Boy!* and *Drumbeat* and was, therefore, guaranteed a period of well-paid one-nighters before a foreseeable downward spiral.

'Mr Parnes, Shillings And Pence' – as he was called behind his back – had also spoken to Allan Williams about employing the lads as accompanists to other hitless stars who had been rechristened by coupling the commonplace with some facet of the human personality. A name that cropped up often during discussions in connection with the Silver Beatles was Dickie Pride, a diminutive Londoner whose trademark convulsions onstage had earned him the sub-title 'The Sheik of Shake'. Another possibility was Duffy Power, whose second single had been an arrangement of the ragtime stand-by 'Ain't She Sweet'. This had planted unfruitful feet in both the rock 'n' roll and trad jazz camps.

Millie Sutcliffe had been dismayed when Stuart, a-twitter with excitement and childish swagger, had announced that he was about to cut college to go on the road with John Lennon's group and this ridiculous singer. Like the younger Silver Beatles, he was even going to give himself a stage name too – 'Stu de Staël'.

To most middle-class parents, for a boy to become a professional rock 'n' roller was almost the precise equivalent of a girl becoming a prostitute. On television talent contests, this was evinced by soft-hearted celebrity judges like Arthur Askey giving ten-out-of-ten to knife-throwers, comedy impersonators and operatic mezzo-sopranos – everyone, in fact, except pop groups. Millie Sutcliffe shared the general detestation, feeling it more keenly through Stuart's intensifying involvement with the Silver Beatles: 'I was amazed that he was going around with them, and threatened to withdraw my financial support. I thought I was doing my duty. Stuart went around like an orphan of the storm – so I relented and agreed to come and see his group. John knew I was coming. The others didn't. Harrison spotted me and says "Stuart, your mother's here." They thought I'd come to create a scene – but it was a pleasant surprise.'[1]

More able to accept Stuart's membership of the Silver Beatles, Millie would argue that music was harmless as long as it didn't interfere with Stuart's course work, which it was going to do if he went off with them to Scotland – the thin end of the wedge. It wasn't just the neglect of his studies: much more disturbing was the physical danger of dance halls where the entertainment was frequently supplemented with fisticuffs and worse. Aintree Institute was notorious for factions in the audience hurling chairs. Of the same mentality were those who wrecked Knotty Ash Village Hall the night the Big Three – a Cass and the Cassanovas splinter group – were on. Hulking bouncers were usually hired to keep order but if rival gangs showed up – especially just after pub closing-time – there was at least the threat of a Wild West-type showdown.

Stuart, like John, enjoyed being in unusual and potentially dangerous situations – as long as they remained only *potentially* so. However, fists often swung harder than the Silver Beatles, as their music became a soundtrack for beatings-up. At a booking at Neston Hall in the Wirral, a boy was half killed before their eyes. All that could be hoped was that such incidents would flush this Silver Beatles nonsense out of Stuart – but he wouldn't listen as his mother prevailed upon him to be sensible. He truanted from college and disappeared to Scotland just the same.

Only the most fleeting rehearsal was possible before Johnny

Gentle and his group trooped on at Alloa Town Hall. In the teeth of mutterings from Larry Parnes' agent about their slovenly turn-out, they knocked 'em dead with rock 'n' roll set-works plus the simpler sides of Johnny's records, such as the self-penned 'Wendy', a I-VI minor-IV-V ballad. Its lyrical thrust – 'Wendy, Wendy, when? Wendy, Wendy, when?' and so on – may have made John and Paul wonder what they were doing wrong. Whatever they thought of him, Gentle was pleased with the Silver Beatles as musicians, and said so when he rang Parnes with progress reports.

Such a magnanimous gesture was, however, not typical of the predominant atmosphere of the tour which, after Alloa, zigzagged along the north-east coast with its brooding sea mists and dull watchfulness when the van in which the party huddled stopped at lonely petrol stations. In the boarding houses where the Silver Beatles would repair each night, John would decree who slept where, ensuring that he had the least crowded bedroom. As leader, he certainly wasn't going to kip down on the floor if ever they were a bed short.

The further they drove, the more desultory the wit – which turned suddenly nasty as, led by John, Paul and George poked ruthless fun at whichever of the other two seemed likeliest to rise to it. As John's best friend, Stuart was prime butt for abuse from the others when the spurious thrill of 'going professional' gave way to stoic cynicism as each man's eighteen pounds for the week's work dwindled.

Swimming with the tide, Paul no longer had to contain his pent-up resentment of Stuart. Teasing became open harangues that were to increase in frequency throughout the tour and beyond, by turns more subtle and less courteous.

Bickering helped pass the time as they trudged round Scottish ballrooms where Gentle headlined over a diversity of local acts from tartan-clad ceilidh bands to Alex Harvey, 'Scotland's Own Tommy Steele'. The most northerly booking, Fraserburgh Town Hall, was notable for Tommy Moore drumming with his head in bandages, fuzzy with sedatives and missing a few teeth. He had been the sole casualty when the van crumped into a stationary Ford Popular that afternoon. Not of Gene Vincent's show-must-go-on stamp, he had been semi-conscious in hospital when the group and hall manager barged in as showtime approached. They weren't laden with grapes and sympathy either.

Well before they steamed back to Liverpool after the final date, a disgusted Moore, with only two pounds left to show for his pains, had had enough of being a Silver Beatle. This put paid to the group's participation in the second half of Johnny Gentle's Scottish campaign. Instead, it fell upon Cass and his Cassanovas to trek up north for this and another job, backing Duffy Power.

A group without a drummer was no use to anyone. Back on the trivial round of parochial dances, Paul would bash away with bad grace, but once a monstrous Teddy Boy had volunteered only too willingly. Not liking to say no, they had let him inflict untold damage on Tommy Moore's kit, still in their possession even if Tommy himself wasn't. When they had lost Moore's successor, a Norman Chapman, to the army after only three weeks, they were forced to pass the opportunity of another Parnes tour, with Dickie Pride, to another outfit.

Now defiantly trading as just plain Beatles, their local ascendancy was such that they were no longer regarded as a tagalong act. Sometimes, they even topped the bill over older units like those led by Kingsize Taylor, Gerry Marsden and Rory Storm, though this was dictated less by popularity than the others being booked to play elsewhere later that same evening.

Like many Merseyside groups, the Beatles used 'featured vocalists'. John and Paul's respective baritone and tenor were the Beatle voices heard most during the show, but George, Stuart and even Tommy before he went would be brought to the fore too. Apparently, Tommy and Stuart took turns with Carl Perkins's walking-pace blues, 'Matchbox'. However, Sutcliffe's big moment came to be 'Love Me Tender', title song from Elvis Presley's first movie. If a hybrid of plummy ex-choirboy and nasal Scouse, Stuart still managed to exude the required breathy sentence of a man who has been sprinting – and was genuinely surprised when some of the sillier judies made cow-eyed attempts to catch his onstage attention as they clustered, tits bouncing, round the microphone. He wasn't impervious to their coltish charms, far from it, but was, nevertheless, aware of how brittle such adoration was.

Trad Tavern was now occupying the slot once occupied by *Boy*

Meets Girls. From Bristol, where bowler-hatted clarinettist Acker Bilk was king, the pestilence of trad jazz was ravaging the country to the detriment of rock 'n' roll. It had spread beyond the earnest obsession of the intellectual fringe and 'Ban The Bomb' marches to a proletariat where ACKER was studded on the backs of leather motorcycle jackets where ELVIS or GENE once were, and girls fainted to the toot-tooting of trumpeter Humphrey Lyttelton. Next, Bilk and other leading jazzmen breached the Top Twenty. After Acker's 'Stranger On The Shore' came within an ace of topping the chart, a Manchester disciple wrote to ask him if it was about Jesus.[2]

Trad bands were everywhere – and so were places they could play. In central Liverpool, most of the impresarios who counted had applauded the new trend that confirmed the wisdom of their bias towards local trad outfits with plinking banjos, a confusion of front-line horns and 'dads' who thought that a hoarse monotone was all you needed to sing like Louis Armstrong. In the Cavern, the city's main jazz stronghold, proprietor Ray McFall would dock the fee of any band who dared to launch into a rock 'n' roll opus within its hallowed and clammy walls.

With this stylistic stranglehold on many venues, it was small wonder that groups keeping the rock 'n' roll faith were open to offers from abroad – particularly West Germany. In 1959, Mr Acker Bilk's Paramount Jazz Band had been well primed to capitalize on the trad boom after six weeks in a Düsseldorf hostelry where 'you just blew and blew and blew,' exhaled Acker, 'and had twenty minutes off for a drink, and then you were back blowing again.'[2] Within a year, however, bastions of Teutonic trad – from Cologne's Storyville to Kiel's Star Palaast – had converted to rock 'n' roll *bierkellers*, complete with the coin-operated sounds of Elvis, Jerry Lee and all the others.

Among the difficulties encountered by the Fatherland's club owners was that of 'live' entertainment. Patrons were often affronted by indigenous bands who invested duplications of classic rock with complacent exactitude, a quasi-military beat and an unnatural nicety of intonation and vowel purity born of singing in a foreign tongue. German-language chart entries were aimed largely at an easy-listening market. There was no domestic 'answer' to Elvis or even Cliff Richard, but there were plenty of Ronnie Hiltons and Donald Peerses, even in 1960. Among them were Freddy Quinn, a former deckhand, whose first major hit was with a translation of Dean Martin's jogalong

'Memories Are Made of This'; Udo Jürgens, present at every European song festival on the calendar, and Fred Bertelmann, 'The Laughing Vagabond'. Each one was the stock 'pop singer who can really sing', and looked about as sexy as your favourite uncle.

Making tentative enquiries further afield, the more out-of-touch promoters were astounded at the astronomical costs of engaging this Elvis schmuck that everyone's talking about. What was the problem? He was actually in the country just then as a soldier in the US Occupation Forces, wasn't he? 'For the Germans to bring in all these stars from America would have cost a fortune,' reasoned Dave Dee, 'and there they had, just across the Channel, these English blokes that were copying the Americans and doing it very well. So it was easy to bring them in for twenty quid a week and work them to death, so all the English bands were in Germany doing two- or three-month stints.' This policy was most rampant in Hamburg where Dave Dee and the Bostons were to metamorphose from a clumsy Wiltshire group into, perhaps, the city's most adored pop import.

The first was a ragbag of unemployed London musicians who, in 1960, were enticed across the North Sea by an ex-circus clown called Bruno Koschmider who ran the Kaiserkeller, a niterie in the cobbled Reeperbahn – 'Rope Street' – main access through Die Grosse Freiheit, the red-light district just beyond the labyrinthine waterfront of the Elbe. Assembled on the Kaiserkeller's rickety stage as the Jets, their number included Alex Harvey's former keyboard player, Ian Hines; singer-guitarist Ricky Richards, a country-and-western specialist, and Tony Sheridan.

His self-destructive streak had not tarnished Tony's abilities either as a performer or as a bandleader. A wanton dedication to pleasing himself rather than his audience resulted in indefinitely extended work-outs of 'What'd I Say', Jerry Lee's 'Whole Lotta Shakin' and a dash of religion with 'When The Saints Go Marching In'. Like Lonnie Donegan before him, Tony would launch impetuously into items not in the set, unhelpfully leaving other players panicking behind him as he built up a sweaty intensity rarely experienced in European pop before 1960. Seizing songs by the scruff of the neck and wringing the life out them, Tony Sheridan *and* the Jets were an instant and howling success for a clientele for whom the personality of the house band had been secondary to boozing, brawling and flirting.

Rival entrepreneurs cast covetous eyes over Bruno's discovery, and soon Tony and his amorphous backing group were administering their rock elixir at the Top Ten, a newer and more spacious night spot where they were protected by its manager's henchmen from any comeback by Koschmider.

After he had calmed down, Bruno returned to Britain with a cast-iron contract for a comparable draw to Tony Sheridan. Among his contacts was Allan Williams who delivered him Derry Wilkie and the Seniors. Within days of their arrival, the Kaiserkeller was thriving again, and Koschmider's thoughts turned to the Indra, his strip club at the sleazier end of the Reeperbahn. With only a few spectators most evenings, it could only be more profitable to put on pop.

When another Derry Wilkie and the Seniors was requested, Bruno's Man in Liverpool pondered on the groups on his books that weren't either in Scotland or, like Rory Storm and his Hurricanes, resident in holiday-camp ballrooms. Because the Beatles had so gamely gone through with a tasteless job accompanying the cavortings of a stripper in his New Cabaret Artists Club, a well-concealed ledger in his accounts, Allan Williams did not dismiss the idea of sending them – provided they could enlist a drummer. He could take them in his minibus to get there, and the New Cabaret's manager, a West Indian known as 'Lord Woodbine', would share the driving with him. Allan would bring the wife along too – make a holiday of it.

The Beatles' endless search for work had forced them back to the Casbah, the Hayman's Green haunt where they had played as Quarry Men and then Moondogs. Indeed, they had been among those stampeded into getting the place ready for the teenage public by its manager, Mona Best. She lived in the fifteen-room Victorian property above it with her invalid mother, two sons and a moving feast of lodgers. The enamelled Hindu goddess in the hallway reflected Mona's upbringing in India where her eldest, Peter, was born in 1941. He had inherited his sultry good looks from voluptuously handsome Mona. His father, who, like Charles Sutcliffe, was almost permanently away, had passed on to him an athlete's physique, evident when Pete posed for a football XI photograph at Liverpool Collegiate where he also distinguished himself academically. With hardly a murmur, he went along with advice to apply to teacher training college after sitting the cache of O levels his teachers expected him to pass.

Whatever the school thought he should do, Mrs Best would

support any more glamorous life goals that could be coaxed from her reticent son. When he and his pals began to spend hours listening to records in the basement, she suggested turning it into a club. It was Mona, too, who gave it its name.

When John, Paul and George came back to the Casbah in July 1960, bringing Stuart with them, Pete was drumming with the club's regular quartet, the Blackjacks. As he was no longer harbouring any ambitions to teach, his adoring mother had bought him an expensive kit with skins of calf-hide rather than plastic. With the information that he wanted to drum for a living, and that the Blackjacks were about to disband, there was no harm in the Beatles asking if Pete fancied a trip to Hamburg – if they were still going, that is. Following a cursory audition at the Blue Angel, Pete Best became a Beatle, and, to many who heard him play with them, would always remain so – even if he didn't have the same black sense of humour as the others, and wasn't as interested in things artistic as the others, particularly John and Stu.

Pete packed his case with Mona's full approval. With no ties, academic or otherwise, George, too, met hardly any opposition from his mum, who baked him some scones for the journey, and dad, who warned him to boil the water when he got there. As Paul had finished his A levels, his father supposed it was all right for him to go gallivanting off to Germany. At the bottom of the scale, the two oldest Beatles had to jump the highest hurdles of parental opposition. However, after taking heed of his lies about the huge weekly wage he would be earning, and expressing her anxious disapprobation, John's aunt let him go, perhaps admitting inwardly (as he did) that his ignominious art college career was over – though he was never officially thrown out.

Stuart, however, 'was a brilliant potential artist lured away from what he was most serious about and really wanted to do – for twenty pound a week,' moaned Arthur Ballard, who had become almost his second father by now. 'I didn't know about the musical side at all. I knew there were skiffle groups in the school. When I heard that Allan Williams had organized John Lennon and Stuart Sutcliffe to go to Hamburg, I was furious. I swore and cursed and finally got back to Allan Williams. I was really horrified. I was amazed he did that.'

There had been a brief flash of hope when Sutcliffe had got cold feet about Hamburg, but he pressed ahead when the college agreed to let him take a sabbatical. It was like National Service or Voluntary Service Overseas: your old job would be waiting for you when you got back – if you wanted it.

Perhaps the most powerful incentive to flee the country for a while was as a more decisive declaration of leaving home than just shacking up in Liverpool 8. As predictable as Arthur Ballard's grumblings was Millie's distress at what was surely the final abandonment of Stuart's art course, sabbatical or not. She shuddered to think of Charles's reaction – and even Stuart felt a certain trepidation 'as I have made no contact with him for over a year,' he wrote to Pauline, 'and in view of, what must seem to him, my imbecilic choice of coming to Hamburg. Anyway, I will cross those bridges when I come to them.'

His father's ire and Ballard's stuck-record homily about Van Gogh was all very well but Stuart wasn't going to eat very well by selling his paintings at ten pounds a throw, the amount Rod Murray paid for one. This was a minor factor that fuelled Stuart's frustration with Liverpool, now a vacuous and unchallenging environment for an artist such as he. In a letter to Ken Horton – the only friend to keep all his correspondence from Stuart – he griped about being

> . . . washed out with talk, sick of faces, fed up of cathedrals and squares, tired of sitting all day, tired of black and white furniture, tired of seeing so many people jabbering away about nothing. Liverpool! Meaning the Cracke, the Jacaranda, the college, the flat, NDD, tired of 'egg on toast and a tea, please'.
>
> In that Liverpool I know not one thing stands out in my memory. The city sprouts like a huge organism, diseased in every part, the beautiful thoroughfares only a little less repulsive because they have been drained of their pus. Liverpool. When I have something to give, I will give it. When I have something to say, I will say it in paint, in stone or anything my soul touches.

It is possible that these strong words were directed more at himself, but spewing them out in front of Ken was cathartic. As it is with many intelligent adolescents, Sutcliffe metaphysics had a tendency towards the excessive flights of a bad 'kitchen sink' playwright: 'In a piss-pot sits my soul. A rainbow cupola of thought – you're my church!'

Unravelling both these oblique ramblings and his sniping at

Liverpool, it seems that he felt he had never been wholly appreciated as a painter. Boiling with disillusioned anger, he had sworn never to lick a canvas with a brush again. 'Six months ago, I thought I was an artist,' he told Ken Horton. 'I no longer think I am. Everything that was art has fallen from me. No paintings left, thank God. I am a romantic turned sour. I have shrivelled like a sucked grape.'

A more pragmatic if deplorable motivation for the leaving of Liverpool was spicy imagery of fancy-free and affectionate Fräuleins. Stuart had no serious girlfriend then, but was perpetually on the lookout for unserious ones. There was a rumour, later deflected towards another Beatle, that a local girl was expecting his baby. With the oral contraceptive, Conovid, months away from UK chemists' counters, pre-marital sex was as big a step to take then as it would be when Aids and other sexual ailments put on the brake in the 1980s. Condoms still burst, and 'withdrawal' was even less of a guarantee that you wouldn't have either to 'do the decent thing' or procure a back-street abortionist.

A week after the Beatles signed their contract with Bruno Koschmider on 10 August 1960, Stuart and the rest boarded Allan Williams's overloaded minibus outside the Jacaranda. A Beatles biographer would later relate the tale of Millie Sutcliffe, weeping, shrouded in the dark of a shop doorway as Lord Woodbine, resplendent in sharkskin suit and Sinatra snap-brim, nosed the vehicle out of Slater Street.

Homesickness mingled with apprehension as Stuart Sutcliffe breathed foreign air for the first time when the night ferry from Harwich docked at the Hook of Holland. Hot-eyed with sleepnessness, the Liverpudlians passed through the concrete desolation of the customs area, and he slipped into the uneasiest of slumbers with an amplifier on his lap.

He awoke with an eye-crossing headache and the road buzzing in his ears. As they crossed the German border, quips about spy novels and fake passports ignited nonstop badinage as the bus hurtled through the inky firs of Lower Saxony. Villagers peered incuriously as the elated young Merseysiders wound down the side-windows and shouted insults about Krauts or thumped out a beat on the bus roof.

Their exuberance died down a little on the outskirts of Hamburg. Hazy impressions of a desolated Germany of lederhosen and parking lots formed from bomb sites went up in smoke as they penetrated a bustling modern metropolis that had recovered more thoroughly from the war that had destroyed two-thirds of its buildings than Liverpool ever would. Like home, its fully integrated public transport system embraced a railway, a bus and tram network, and a boat service across a winding river flanked by a vast warehouse complex and gaunt 'City Exchange'-type architecture.

After being jolted shoulder-to-shoulder since Holland, the Beatles climbed down from the minibus, giddy and stiff, outside the Kaiser-keller, plusher than any club or palais they had seen on Merseyside. It was, therefore, a disappointment when Herr Koschmider conducted them round the tiny Indra, which had all the tell-tale signs of having known better days: the dust on the carpet and heavy drape curtains; the padded wallpaper peeling off here and there; the depressed forbearance of the staff.

With a face like a bag of screwdrivers, Bruno himself wasn't exactly Uncle Cuddles, but if his manner was cold, he did not seem ill-disposed towards the young Britishers. It wasn't in his interest to be. An antagonized group might take it out on the customers. The Beatles would have more than enough to complain about when he took them to three small, windowless rooms adjoining a toilet in the Bambi Kino cinema over the road. This was where they could sleep. It would have sickened pigs, but the other Englishmen, Derry and his Seniors, seemed to be surviving in two similarly poky holes at the back of the Kaiserkeller.

Stuart and John had had their share of living rough back in Liverpool 8 but even they were too nonplussed to joke about Stalag 13, tunnelling, Red Cross parcels and forming an escape committee. Stuart wondered again what he was doing there with a bunch of lads that, John apart, he wasn't even sure he liked that much, in a strange land in which he could understand only exclamatory phrases like *'Donner und Blitzen'*, *'Schweinhund'*, *'Dummkopf'* and *'Jawohl, Herr Kommandant'*, picked up from *War Picture Library*, a chin-up comic publication which differentiated between *plucky* Britishers and *fanatical* Nazis.

Lennon had recovered enough of his ebullience to bark *'Raus! Raus! Schnell! Schnell!'* when, after a couple of hours of rest, the Beatles had to lug their careworn equipment, including the Students Union amplifier, into Bruno's low-rent palais with its chilly after-hours' essence of disinfectant and flat echo of yesterday's booze and tobacco. The border of light bulbs (not all of them working) round the stage were switched on and, beyond sleep and alert with hunger, the five gave their first ever performance outside the United Kingdom. To the Parnes audition costumes, they had added hound's-tooth check jackets, and replaced the plimsolls with winkle-pickers – all except for Pete who hadn't had time to buy the right gear. His gradual isolation from the others had started before they had even reached Harwich.

During wakeful periods after they had retired, the full horror of the filthy accommodation reared up in the encircling gloom: coats for blankets, George shivering in his sleep, Paul snoring open-mouthed, Pete jerking in and out of his doze, John breaking wind before rising from his pit to shampoo his hair in a washbasin in the movie-goers' lavatories.

With martyred nobility, the Beatles let themselves be pushed in whatever direction fate, Williams and Koschmider ordained – which boiled down to six hours a night, an hour on, an hour off, at the Indra. Derry's Seniors were talking of staying on as a strip-club band when their contract with Bruno was up. The Beatles could hope to step into their shoes at the Kaiserkeller. There was token surly mutiny when the Indra season began but, forgetting the misery of their positions, they perked up, quite tickled when anyone cried encouragement to them. John's runaway tongue unfurled, Pete unzipped his holiday-camp grin, and one or two of the glum old men waiting in vain for the strippers allowed themselves to be jollied along. A more transient clientele of sailors, gangsters, prostitutes, tourists on a night out and teenagers who had stumbled in from the street laughed with them and even took a chance on the dance floor as they got used to the newcomers' endearing glottal stops and their ragged dissimilarity to the contrived splendour of television pop stars.

Up and about by mid-afternoon, the Beatles were recognized occasionally in the immediate vicinity of the Grosse Freiheit. Further afield, they were just anonymous wanderers of the city, one of the oldest municipal republics in Europe and, though sixty miles from the sea, then the world's third largest port. Its recreational facilities included the Alster yachting lake and promenade, a museum containing the largest model railway ever constructed, a zoo, the mammoth Dom funfair – and, of course, the Grosse Freiheit, an erotic funfair since the days of three-mast clippers.

Strip-tease, clip-joints and brothels were to the Freiheit as steel to Sheffield. Germans of all sexes would perform all manner of obscene tableaux, frequently inciting their audiences to join in the fun. It was an eye-opener to anyone who assumed that sexual gratification could be delivered by human tenderness alone.

As Sheridan and his Jets had introduced the Seniors, so they introduced the Beatles as nonchalantly to the Roxy transvestite bar, the shocking 'Street of Windows' and other of the suburb's diversions. *En route*, they had ambled goggle-eyed past hucksters in perfumed doorways extolling the delights of 'beautiful virgins in a bath of pink champagne! Five marks!' In staid old England, Billy Fury had been obliged to moderate his sub-Elvis gyrations, and Penguin Books were about to face legal proceedings over their plans to publish *Lady Chatterley's Lover*.

Time that hung heavy between one night's stint on stage and the next wasn't only spent in sleeping, eating, sight-seeing or practising. Back home, he might have fled if accosted by a prostitute but, with Mum not looking, a young Merseysider might melt eagerly into the robust caress of a lady twice his age who had openly exhibited her seamy goods in a bordello window. 'They usually arrived knowing it all, poor sods,' grimaced Ian Hines, 'taking no advice that I offered them and, sure enough, would return home to the good old UK with crabs, pox, "Hamburg throat" – you name it, they had it.'[3]

The 'cleanest' tarts, he might have informed you, frequented contact cafés along the Herbertstrasse, establishments like the Eros Center and the Palais d'Amour on the Reeperbahn, and hotels such as Luxor, Clubhotel and the Columbus. He didn't need to tell you, did he, not to sniff round 'kerb-swallows' and females in the cheaper bars? Not only will you catch something but, whatever delicate attentions you require, you won't get them for the price originally arranged. Sometimes, however, you could get something extra. 'We spent nearly two months trying in vain to chat up two really gorgeous ladies who used to stroll along the Reeperbahn,' elucidated Ian 'Tich' Amey of the Bostons, 'Just before we returned to England, we found out that they weren't girls at all but two fellows. Thank God none of us were successful with the chat-up lines.'[4]

If you were a musician, you didn't necessarily have to pay for it. When the sixties started swinging, certain famous beat groups were showered with paternity suits. Many of them emanated from the Grosse Freiheit where bartering in sex involved far less pretence than in Britain. Giving in to nature's baser urges, free-spirited Fräuleins would simply lock eyes with the player of a jerking crotch-level guitar up on stage. They would point at him while flexing a phallic forearm, and hope he understood that tonight was to be his night. They weren't too fussy. 'It was funny to witness tearful goodbyes,' laughed Colin Manley after the Remo Four came over, 'only to see someone's sweetheart holding hands with a member of the next group to arrive fresh from England.'[4]

If admirable young men in many ways, the Beatles also had their quota of young men's vices. Not long after their Hamburg début, they were thrilled to discover that the travellers' tales were true. Here, rock 'n' roll myth was hard fact. Aspiring to an orgasm at the thrust of a British pop musician, judies were there for the taking whenever you wished. Without having to display even perfunctory chivalry, the evening's love life could be sorted out by the first beer break. There had been nothing like it even at the art college.

On initiating conversation with the slender Stuart with his slow smile and dark glasses – not entirely for show – these shopsoiled girls were charmed by his bemusement at their interest in him. They were even more delighted that he was not one to deny himself even the most casual erotic exploit. For the more salacious details of the young Beatles' unchallenging appropriation of sexual intimacies you cannot do better than read Pete Best's autobiography[5] with its illustrative encounter between the group and no less than *eight* nubile Fräuleins in the murk of the cinema quarters. The next morning the five didn't even remember what their faces looked like, let alone their names.

Wisely, shadowy thighs and lewd sniggering did not leap out of the pages of Stuart's letters home. 'As far as girls go,' he assured his sisters, 'there are many but none of us can be bothered.' His mother suspected otherwise. He might have inherited her sylph-like physique but, like Charles, Stuart Sutcliffe was the most heterosexual of males. 'Don't imagine that I'm keeping the company of homosexuals,' he wrote. 'There are a few here, but all harmless and very young. They are quite happy to just sit and look. When in Liverpool, I would never have dreamt I could possibly speak to one without shuddering. As it is, I find the one or two I speak to more interesting and entertaining than any others.'

Changing the subject, he chatted to the family about books he had finished lately, and music: 'I heard "Lucille" by the Everly Brothers on the juke-box the other night at the Top Ten. I must say,

I think it's much better than we do it, although we do it completely different to the way we played it in the Jac.' Despite the punishing shifts on stage and any nocturnal shenanigans, he remained a voracious reader. Lying on the frayed sofa-bed in the Beatles' ill-lit lair, he devoured such diverse literature as *The Saint* – Leslie Charteris's stories of a gentleman detective – the sin-and-salvation novels of François Mauriac, and, before the release of the X-certificate film, Vladimir Nabokov's risqué *Lolita* – about a middle-aged academic and a twelve-year-old temptress. In case Joyce and Pauline were tempted by *Lolita*, he promised them that it had 'little literary merit'.

Perusal of Stuart's letters from Hamburg reveals a multi-faceted writer; to friends like Ken Horton, he expressed his fears, dreads, hopes and dreams; to family – particularly his sisters – he kept his darker side out of sight. Instead, he told them about the bread-and-butter of his daily life with frequent requests for domestic news. When necessary, the responsible and responsive 'special son' also imparted 'fatherly' guidance to Joyce and Pauline. He was always careful to elaborate differences in the socio-economics of each community without indicating that he might prefer one to the other.

According to the letters Millie received, he wasn't starving: 'I'm waiting for my main meal of the day – beef-steak and mashed potatoes and a glass of milk.' This was, indeed, the case if he was feeling unexpectedly well heeled as Bruno's musicians could also avail themselves of free beer and salad at night – an advantage as they could be consumed in instalments onstage. Squarer meals could be scrounged from obliging barmaids or by striking up shallow acquaintances with US sailors and similar pleasure-seekers with money to burn.

Outside working hours, the Beatles fed themselves as cheaply as possible. Breakfast was 'cornflakes *mit Milch*' in a Freiheit café. Apfel Kuchen (pancakes with apple purée), Deutsche Bifsteak (hamburger) and Wurst sausage were the recommended dishes at Harold's Schnell-imbiss, the Mambo Shancke, Der Flunde and the twenty-four-hour Nimitz Bar, but more appreciated as a psychological link with home was something with chips from the British Seamen's Mission down in the docks – a source, too, of king-sized American cigarettes.

After figuring out how much a Deutschmark was worth in sterling, Stuart scratched together sufficient emergency funds for the fare home. To Ken Horton he confessed, 'I'm not the happiest man alive. It is now my seventh week here. I came here for a reason I do not know. I have no money, no resources, no hope.'

Both the Beatles and Derry and the Seniors had plenty to grouse about just then. Up at the Kaiserkeller, the group's hours off caused the crowd to thin. Custom was lost, Koschmider presumed, to the hated Top Ten and entrapment by Sheridan for the rest of the night. It was a bit unreasonable to expect Wilkie's boys to work around the clock without a rest but, discontinuing the juke-box, Bruno bridged the gaps by extracting the saxophonist and pianist from the Seniors, and Sutcliffe from the Beatles, and bringing in a German jazz drummer from another club. Stuart borrowed the Seniors' instrument while the Beatles restructured their act with left-handed Paul playing the absent member's bass upside down.

The splinter unit's disparity plus the dissatisfaction of the depleted and inconvenienced Seniors and Beatles combined with complaints about the noise and change of programme at the Indra, but it was the situation's false economy that led the harassed Koschmider to restore the Indra's gartered erotica, and move the Beatles uptown to the Kaiserkeller and extending their contract to December.

To Stuart, the place was 'empty, like a huge pair of dirty underpants waiting for the right tool to pour its rich semen through the ugly distorted slit provided in order that man may piss away the badness from his twenty-four-feet long coil of intestines'. That was certainly one way of describing the Kaiserkeller. A more objective outline would centre on its nautical theme. Among the more obvious features were replica lifeboats as dining alcoves, puffer-fish lamps, and a ceiling decked with fishermen's nets in which were caught fake turtles, dolphins, crabs and lobsters.

At peak hours, harassed waiters dashed from table to table with trays loaded with steins of foaming lager and tumblers of Cola-Rum. Their duties extended to exultant brutality whenever a customer abused the club's hospitality. By comparison, Neston Hall was a vicarage fête. While up to a dozen waiter-bouncers hacked and struck at a single *Schlager* – a fellow actively looking for a fight – amid splintered tankards and upturned furniture, a desultory cheer would ensue when Bruno himself bounded from his office with an ebony truncheon to lend a hand. The blood-splattered and unresisting victim would then be raised aloft, weight-lifter style, and chucked into the

Strasse. 'One night, a drunken sailor staggered on stage, and threw ice-cream,' recounted Tony Jackson of the Searchers, another up-and-coming Merseyside outfit. 'The bouncers dragged the sailor out into the street and kicked him senseless.'

A chap once staggered from the Top Ten with a stevedore's bailing hook embedded in his neck. More conventional aids to keeping the peace could be purchased from a Reeperbahn store called simply 'The Armoury'. Prominent in its front window was a sub-machine gun, a snip at three hundred and fifty marks, but mostly it dealt in coshes, flick-knives and the tear-gas pistols that the Searchers were ordered to buy for self-protection when they first arrived in Hamburg. An off-duty musician was also directed to carry only an essential amount of money – preferably in small notes.

All this was a trifle unsettling for someone of Stuart's temperament, for, guest workers or not, the Beatles' well-being could not depend entirely on the efficiency of *Polizei* at the station on the corner of the Reeperbahn and Davidstrasse. Spreading fear like cigar smoke, local Mister Bigs and the wealthier madames could compel groups to reprise favourite songs over and over again. A fortunate partiality by 'men of respect' for the Beatles was manifested in crates of champagne and even plates of food being sent to sustain them on stage and as pre-payment for requests.

Groups knew better than to show less than the fullest appreciation of these gifts. An advantage of being so frighteningly honoured was extra-legal protection if ever they ran into trouble within such an admirer's sphere of influence. Descending on a clip-joint that had fleeced one approved band, a squad in *Polizei* uniform smashed every bottle, mirror and glass in the building before boarding it up. 'Tony Sheridan was booked to play a gig in Kiel,' recounted Tony Jackson. 'He phoned to say that the owner of the club had refused to pay him – so some hitmen drove to Kiel and destroyed the place with hand-grenades.'

John Lennon liked to point out pockets of violence in the Kaiserkeller to bouncers, even clambering from the stage to defuse it himself. When it came to stopping anyone drawing attention from the Beatles, he would make Kennedy, the USA's new President, vote Communist. The stage act was worth seeing now. It had developed after a week's petrified inertia on the expansive Kaiserkeller podium. This had perturbed Bruno. He had explained why to Allan Williams who had popped back to Hamburg to check how things were going. Herr Koschmider wasn't concerned so much about musical quality as the generation of an action-packed all-night party atmosphere and a subsequent rapid turnover at the bar. Could Allan get that across to the boys?

The Beatles had finally shifted out of neutral when Williams's exasperated yell of 'Make a show, lads!' was taken up as '*Mach Schau!*' by club regulars. This chant – later corrupted to 'Let's go!' – inspired blatant sensationalism. With Stuart and Pete toiling in the background, the group's front line strove to outdo each other in cavortings and caperings; John making the most show with much bucking and shimmying like a composite of every rock 'n' roller he'd ever admired. This, so they and other outfits observed, always elicited a wild response.

Suddenly, the Beatles were home and dry as involved onlookers surged towards the stage or clambered on to crammed tables; worrying when the five flagged, bellowing encouragement as they rallied, glowing when a number or a retaliation to heckling went down particularly well. Rory Storm and the Hurricanes, who were replacing Derry and the Seniors, 'must be very frustrated by the cheers that greet us at most of our numbers,' crowed Stuart to Pauline. What stunned them and another incoming Liverpudlian, a vocalist with the Ivy Benson Band,[6] was that the Beatles didn't care how awful they were – in fact, they prospered on it.

On the creaky stage, you'd never know if they were going to play while perched, smoking lazily, on amplifier rims, or leap into an onslaught of endlessly inventive skylarking and knockabout clowning. Some items might stop abruptly after a couple of muddled verses but others such as 'Whole Lotta Shakin'' and Bobby Comstock and the Counts' 'Let's Stomp' could last a full hour during which Paul or John might abandon his guitar to take it easy and appeal to dancers to clap along to what they identified as Pete's *mach Schau* rhythm – thumping bass drum and smiting hi-hat and snare simultaneous with every beat in the bar. The tension would build to a raving turmoil and then the Beatles would sweep into the wings, leaving 'em wanting more. They had learnt much from watching Sheridan at the Top Ten.

Mention of the Beatles in Hamburg, onstage and off, still brings out strange stories of what alleged 'insiders' claim they heard and saw. Many of the escapades later attributed to them were either improved with age, had taken place under the alibi of a stage act or were the result of elaborations, relocations and retiming of the truth. The one about them urinating over nuns from a Reeperbahn balcony, for instance, is traceable to Rod Murray's and Stuart's hosing of the moped parked in Percy Street.

Perhaps the most documented incident stemmed from their conspiracy with Rory and the Hurricanes to render the unstable Kaiserkeller stage irreparable after an excess of jumping and stamping. Bruno would then be compelled to get a new one. However, although it caved in, he did not. Instead, Koschmider made an example of Storm with a deduction from his pay packet and a temporary dismissal for 'breach of contract'. Stuart's participation in such pranks was sometimes mentioned during prolific letter-writing. To Ken Horton, this also chronicled subtle changes in his mental climate. From a blithe 'I think on the sly I must be a bit mad for packing it in but I must say it is quite an experience living in the mad way we do', while at the Indra, he mutated into a Kaiserkeller fatalist: 'I have ejected myself from the world of sanity like a cartridge.'

Inwardly, he was still gloomily justifying turning his back on painting for 'rocking in Hamburg to thirty-year-old Teddy Boys and fifteen-year-old Teddy Girls. I don't like the repetition but it'll have to do.' At the Indra, the group had stretched out the fifteen or so numbers they had cobbled together after a few hours with the newly enlisted Pete at the Casbah. The monotony of duplicating the same set over and over again had been the main impetus to rehearse strenuously even the most obscure material that could be dug from their common unconscious.

The hoariest old chestnuts were tried, though preference was given to those covered by artists they rated – though 'Ain't She Sweet' bore a closer likeness to Duffy Power's treatment than that of Gene Vincent. Few if any Lennon-McCartney ditties were then unveiled publicly, but a typical bouncer's memory was of the two composing in the bandroom while Stuart was either sketching secretively in a remote corner of the club or joining the others in drinking their pay and being lionized by the clientele. Despite being hand-in-glove with John, he was never certain enough of his position within the group to impose unsolicited ideas.

Musical progress did not correlate with personal relationships within the Beatles. Among them, there was 'no one to whom I can

Johnny B Goode.
Gone, Gone, Gone.
Ain't She Sweet
Hallelujia
Carol
Sweet Little Sixteen
Milk Cow Blues.
Move over.
True Love
Blue Suede Shoes
Honey Don't
Lend me your Comb.
Dana in the streets
Up a lazy River
Somebody Help me
Home.
Winstons Walk
Cats Walk.
Rock-a-chicka
Bebopaluła.
What'd I say
Move on down the line
I don't care (if the sun)
Whole lotta shakin

Page from Stuart's sketchbook noting the evening's set list

communicate even a fraction of my feelings,' he intimated to Ken Horton. It might not have been politic to tell an older best friend that this did not include John. Living in each other's armpits, Stuart, John, Paul, George and Pete had immersed themselves in the bitter intensities that make pop groups what they are. The Beatles' history was and would be punctuated with unresolvable feuds, whispered onstage spite, prima-donna tantrums, backstage post-mortems and interminable sulking.

Once amusing but now annoying him was the ragging of 'baby' George about notices forbidding minors from entering certain Freiheit arcades. Unspoken as yet were vague misgivings about Pete whose part in their on- and off-stage frolics was a duty rather than a pleasure. Neither did he contribute much to the group's studentish restricted code, superstitions and folklore.

John was still prone to antagonizing Stuart just to see his hackles rise, but his inner ear ignored the stark truth that his mate's bass playing hadn't got far past the three essential rock 'n' roll forms after all these months. Had Paul expressed a recent willingness to play bass before the John Moores exhibition, Stuart might have carried on painting, and the group wouldn't have been cluttered with one rhythm guitarist too many, no matter how contrasting McCartney and Lennon's chord shapes could be. If Stuart hadn't been around, Paul wouldn't have felt so redundant, just singing and dancing about with an unplugged guitar, or impersonating Little Richard at the worn-out Kaiserkeller piano, from which aggravating Sutcliffe would snip wires to replace broken bass strings.

There was no let-up in the underminings and sly machinations back in the Bambi Kino rooms which were fouler than ever: receptacles for old newspapers, junk food remains, empty liquor bottles, overflowing makeshift ash-trays, used rubber 'johnnies' and dried vomit. Surrounded by tension-charged ugliness, visible and invisible, Stuart stopped his vocational dithering. When the Beatles' present obligations in Hamburg ceased, he would pick up where he had left off. 'I've just decided that at Christmas I pack in rocking and join the club again,' he reported to Ken Horton. 'You know, the old jeans and sweater gang with a pencil and sketchbook. I've decided that if I get back, I might yet be able to make something of myself. When I come home at Christmas, it'll probably be for good, also without guitar probably. I'll sell it if I can.'

Pop Goes The Easel

NOTES

1   *Disc*, 31 October 1970.
2   *Acker Bilk*, G. Williams (Mayfair, 1970).
3   *Fiesta*, May 1975.
4   *The Beat Goes On*, February 1992.
5   *Beatle!* P. Best and P. Doncaster (Plexus, 1985).
6   From the same dockland suburb as Cilla Black, a vocalist with the Ivy Benson Band 'sings just like Brenda Lee,' wrote Stuart Sutcliffe to his sisters, 'not much to look at but fun, and at least she speaks English'.

chapter five

MäDEL RUCK-RUCK-RUCK

'Tomorrow, I will buy her a white rose, a young boy's thought, a sunny thought and golden one, marred only by the knowledge that I will never have the courage to give it to her'

Stuart Sutcliffe

Stuart Sutcliffe would postpone his return to Liverpool. In October 1960, he clapped eyes on a dashing young German named Astrid Kirchherr for the first time. To begin with she had been just 'some girl' in a letter home but it soon became clear that theirs had been a Momentous Encounter.

Two years older than him, Astrid's childhood had been spent in the genteel Hamburg suburb of Altona, worlds away from the Reeperbahn. During the war, the RAF flattened her grandfather's slot-machine factory, but the reek of burning did not seep as far as 42 Eimsbutteler Strasse, and Astrid's upbringing was undramatic and as free from major trauma as the war and its aftermath would allow.

Almost everyone she knew lived like her own wealthy family in their three-storey house with its tastefully decorated panelled rooms, adorned with old gold and furnished with antiques, Persian carpets and chandeliers. However, with her late father a senior executive in the West German division of the Ford Motor Company she was driving her own immaculate convertible before most of her teenage friends.

Her parents also permitted her a greater degree of liberal nonconformity. Her theatrically arranged bedroom-cum-studio upstairs was excused to visiting relations as an eccentricity that went with her artistic talent. Nevertheless, it caused starchy great-aunts to fight for control of their features when they first gazed upon the black velvet bedspread, the black satin sheets, the walls and ceiling covered with silver foil glittering in the reflected light of concealed spotlights strategically focused on dried flowers in black vases, and the sketches and modern paintings that hung between full-length mirrors.

Mädel Ruck-Ruck-Ruck

As monochrome as her bedroom was her taste in clothes – that she made from her own patterns. Elegantly severe with no distracting jewellery, her attire emphasized her firm-breasted, wasp-waisted profile and honey-blondeness most arrestingly. Unquestionably, she was a stunner. Artfully applied make-up made her dark eyes look enormous in a timorously pretty but deceptively commanding face. The full, almost fleshy mouth was understated with pale pink lipstick, as pale as her flawless complexion. She never lacked male attention.

It raised no eyebrows when she embarked on a course in dress design at Hamburg's fee-paying Meister Schule in preparation for a career in the world of fashion. With her long legs, she was well placed to parade her creations along the catwalk herself. However, Astrid betrayed a more pronounced aptitude for photography during extra-curricular tutorials with the academy's specialist in the subject, Reinhardt Wolf. He persuaded her to switch courses on the understanding that, on completion, he would employ her as his assistant.

Klaus Voorman, a svelte and well-spoken Berliner who was studying illustration at the Meister Schule, began 'going steady' with Astrid in 1958. Not only was this seventeen-year-old doctor's son handsome in an angular Prussian kind of way but he was also socially acceptable to her now-widowed mother, Nielsa, who was happy for him to lodge with them when he became a full-time graphic artist. His passion for rock 'n' roll brought a puffy smile to the lips of both Frau Kirchherr and Astrid, whose record collection contained nothing wilder than Nat 'King' Cole, limp and tasteful Stan Getz, and the politest modern jazz.

Such discs were part of the equipage of Hamburg's 'existentalist' set – the 'Exis' – of which Astrid and Klaus were leading lights. In some respects, their look anticipated the 'Gothic' style prevalent in the late 1970s. Always black, maybe with white collars or ruffs like eighteenth-century dandies, it was predominantly unisex with suede and velvet the most usual fabrics, though you could get by with jeans, polo-neck and windcheater. Exi girls wishing to look more feminine might wear ballet slippers, fishnet stockings and short leather skirts. Exi hair was *Pilzen Kopf* – 'mushroom head' – in style. Though commonplace in Germany, a male so greaselessly coiffured in Britain would be branded a nancy boy, even if Adam Faith, a new pretender to Cliff Richard's throne, was the darling of the ladies with a similar brushed-forward cut.

Backbeat

Astrid and Klaus's crowd was a variant of the Parisian existentialists who, since the 1950s, had been stereotyped by film directors as one of two types of pretentious middle-class beatnik: 'hot' (incessant rapid-fire talking and pseudo-mad stares) and 'cool' (mute, immobile and unapproachable). Both are present at *demi-monde* parties where table lamps are dimmed with headscarves, and Man Ray hangs on the walls. The musical entertainment is scat-singing, bongo-tapping or a saxophone honking inanely. The eyelids of cross-legged listeners are closed in ecstasy. With a nod towards the censor, the drugs and sexual undercurrents are played down. These weirdos are 'good kids' at heart.

'Why kill time when you can kill yourself?' asks a spectral Greco-like girl in 1960's *The Rebel*,[1] a Tony Hancock vehicle set in bohemian Paris, all berets, ten-day beards and holey sweaters. *The Rebel* might have been less resolutely banal and probaby funnier had the great comedian's flight from respectability taken him to either of the *demimondes* of Hamburg or Liverpool.

Klaus Voorman had an unexpected taste of Liverpool after a tiff when he found himself outside 42 Eimsbutteler Strasse's just slammed front door one October evening in 1960. Not being the type to kill himself, he killed time by going to the cinema – at least, his body went: his mind was reaching a conclusion that he and Astrid had now become two old friends who used to be lovers. Sooner or later, one of them would find someone else.

The film ended, and, as his mood hadn't fundamentally improved, Klaus started walking, taking no notice of where he was going. His brooding was interrupted by the realization that he had wandered into the loneliest part of the port district. Dark and misty, the murmur of the Elbe was his only company. Chilled by more than mere cold, he strode rapidly towards a distant glimmer of neon.

He felt no safer in the Gross Freiheit, an area shunned by nice people and crawling with human predators. Klaus dared not let his eyes rest on individuals as he hurried on, but he was brought up short by the metallic beat of a record from within the Kaiserkeller. Obscurely captivated, he listened for a few minutes. It was not a record after all, but a group, a glorious onslaught of pulsating bass, spluttering guitars, crashing drums and ranting vocals. More than mere bravado drew him inside, but once there, he merged into the shadows, torn between a sordid thrill at being out-of-bounds and the desire to run out, never to go there again.

The outfit onstage was Rory Storm and the Hurricanes. They ended their set to a thunderous cheer from an audience made up mostly of a type Klaus recognized as 'Rockers'. The men had an approximate uniform of jeans, motorbike boots, T-shirts and leather jackets. Some of the girls dressed likewise but more frequently it was flared skirts with wide belts, tight jumpers, stilettos, ruby-red lips and beehive hairdos. Had they been British, the boys' brilliantined ducktails would have been descendants of the Teds. Their musical preferences and hostility towards interlopers into the Kaiserkeller – especially students – certainly were.

Young Voorman's trepidation was put on hold when a squeak of feedback heralded the start of a routine Beatles' performance. It veered from a sentimental ballad to a jokey 'Sheik Of Araby' to the blood-curdling dementia of one in the throes of a fit when Chuck Berry's 'Roll Over Beethoven' was attacked by the guitarist with the big mouth, who used coarse language in heated moments. There was no scripted grinning or inoffensive Bobby playfulness with this boy. He'd now taken to breaking into mock-Hitlerian speeches and jibes about the war to a mob uncomprehending, disbelieving or scandalized into laughter.

The initial shock over, Klaus attuned to the situation's epic vulgarity as the Beatles walked what seemed to him an artistic tightrope without a safety net. *Mein Gott*, they were great! He would be drawn back to another Kaiserkeller sweatbath a few days later. When the Beatles stumbled off after exacting their customary submission from the few who hadn't wanted to like them, what could Klaus do but thread through to the bar to congratulate them, having rehearsed mentally what he was going to say and the cool way he'd say it?

'I liked your show. You had fun,' he said nervously to John Lennon, and felt instantly silly. It was all coming out wrong. Smiling fatuously, he tried again by producing a record sleeve he had designed the previous month for the German release of 'Walk Don't Run' by the Ventures. John hardly looked at it before passing it back with, 'Show him. He's the artist in the group.' Stuart at least had the good manners to take an interest. The others, too, were civil enough when

Klaus, his non-specific purpose undeflected, bought a round of drinks, and kept the conversation going in his heavily accented but fluent English.

Astrid had not betrayed the faint revulsion that had swept over her after Klaus had told her where he had been. Not wishing to appear a prude, she accompanied him and a friend, Jürgen Vollmer, on the next visit to the Kaiserkeller. A Stuyvesant smouldering uninhaled between her fingers, Astrid was, if anything, more dumbstruck by the Beatles than Klaus had been: 'We'd not seen boys like this before in our clubs. They played, shouted, made jokes between themselves.'[2] Both she and Jürgen were astounded by their almost wilful scruffiness. 'They looked like their audience, very rough and tough Rockers,' said Jürgen, 'but there was something different about them – for they were basically not rockers. They just had to put up that act in order to please their audience – and, of course, their music was sensational.'

The hound's-tooth coats had now been ditched for lapel-less black leather jackets after George had bought one from a club waiter. They had certainly become more beetle-like in colour and texture, but the collar-length hair combed into glaciers of brilliantine caused more of a stir at a time when veterans of both the Somme and Dunkirk still had their heads planed halfway up the side of the skull.

Though clothed as Rockers, the fact that all five Beatles belonged, technically, to Britain's academic élite might have been a subliminal lure for other Exis who, with good reason, were afraid of Rockers, but dared to trespass into the Kaiserkeller for the Beatles. Among these, the group's first intellectual fans, were Peter Penner, Detlev Birgfeld and Peter Markmann and others from either the Meister Schule or the city's Staatliche Hochschule für bildende Kunste (State High School for Art Instruction).

With quiet pride, Stuart had informed his younger sister that 'we have improved a thousandfold since our arrival and Allan Williams who is here at the moment, tells us that there's no band in Liverpool to touch us'. Nevertheless, it is tempting to imply that the Exis fell for the Beatles like the 'Parisian set' in *The Rebel* did for the verbose but artistically cack-handed Hancock. Yet it was more likely that the Hamburg students were tacitly bored with the 'coolness' of Brubeck, Getz, the Modern Jazz Quartet and other 'hip' music-makers whose LP covers were artlessly strewn about their 'pads'.

Exposure to the uproarious abandon of the British groups in the Freiheit mire inspired in the Exis an appalled urge to reject 'coolness' altogether. Let's dance! Let's get real, real gone for a change – not to Brubeck or even Acker Bilk but to trashy rock 'n' roll. 'We had been Dixieland or [modern] jazz fans,' explained Jürgen Vollmer, 'and ever since then, we really got into rock and roll, and we never went to the jazz clubs any more. Our interest developed after we heard the Beatles, and not only the Beatles but also the other British rock and roll groups – but the Beatles were always our favourite, right from the start.'

Dancing to the Beatles could be perpetuated with the aid of Preludin tablets, appetite suppressants containing amphetamines. Recently outlawed in Britain, they were supposedly only available on prescription in Germany. However, an illicit supply could be obtained with ease. Astrid's, for example, were secured by her mother who 'knew someone at the chemist'.[3] It was no hanging matter even if you were caught. Most policemen couldn't be bothered with the paper-work anyway.

However high on Preludin a mere handful of them were, the Exis did not dance at first, preferring to cower near the sanctuary of the stage, hiding behind the piano when, squinting their way now and then, the Rockers began their nightly brawl. Little by little, the Exis sat more comfortably in the Kaiserkeller and, later, the Top Ten, partly because they had adopted Rocker dress but mainly because of the friendships they had struck up with the musicians who, between sets, were now socializing with them rather than the Rockers. 'They wanted to know what made us tick,' said Tony Sheridan, 'and we found them entertaining. Rather than associating with the real tough characters, we just sort of fell together. They showed us the ropes and a lot of things we otherwise wouldn't have seen.'

A principal advantage that the Exis had in their fraternization was that most of them 'spoke pretty well English that we had learned at school,' explained Vollmer, 'while the general audience – the Rockers – didn't speak English. They were all rather uneducated working class. So we did speak English, and we were something different from the audience. We had a very good understanding because they [the Beatles] were actually artists just like we were.'

It depends on what is meant by 'artists'. In content alone, the Beatles were uncannily like all the other rock 'n' roll groups. However,

Sutcliffe, McCartney and Lennon (when it suited him) were great talkers, using the same reference points as the Exis. After all, they had devoured *On The Road* while up north, and were interested in the same kind of things. He and John might have been able to discuss art, but Stuart, however dormant he was then, was 'the real thing', as Astrid discovered: 'He is a fine artist. Everywhere, he would take out his drawing pad and his pencils and just sketch.'[5]

Relatively passive onstage behind his black-framed sunglasses, Stuart, now clean-shaven, stood awkwardly during the inter-song dialogue. Astrid would sometimes catch him half looking at her, half turning away. 'Stu looked quieter than the others,' she noticed. 'Sometimes he seemed bewildered. I didn't know then that he had not been playing guitar for very long – perhaps that explained the way he was sometimes subdued. I couldn't see Stu's eyes behind those glasses, but I knew, somehow I just knew, he was looking at me. At this first moment, I also knew that one day there would be something real between us.'[5]

Compared to the skirt that solicited him nightly, Astrid was as a fountain pen to a stub of pencil. No question: she had class, a maturity beyond her years reflected in the spellbinding confidence that came from every man she ever met falling in love with her. Like the rest of the British contingent, Stuart was impressively disturbed by her daunting Teutonic directness: the throaty laugh that showed off her dazzling white teeth; the humorous and intelligent eyes that stared appraisingly at whoever spoke to her.

Another element of the fascination was her disarming independence: the car, the separate annex in her parents' house, her refusal to be an adjunct to Klaus – who was still clinging on as her official boyfriend – as Cynthia was to John. It was all far removed from what the Beatles had known of most women on Merseyside.

Her initial interest in the group was as much professional as personal. The day after her first descent into the Kaiserkeller, she had arranged to meet them for a photo session at the Dom, the city funfair. They had to bring their guitars, and Pete his snare drum. Before the viewfinder of her Rollercord, they assumed 'typical Dean poses', so Stuart told his sisters, on the carousel, in front of the freak tent, on the Ferris wheel and, the most usable shot of all, around an ancient truck only a few oil changes away from the breaker's yard, with Stuart in the foreground, sideways on, in a suede jacket he'd bought from John.

After the films had been developed, he was taken aback by Astrid's skill in focusing so tightly on the group's primitive sexuality, and by the grainy texture of her work, 'just like a painting'. The only criticism he had was that 'I wasn't looking so good with pimples and my hair in a mess.' Furthermore, his jacket was dirty, though he assured Joyce and Pauline that 'I'll have this cleaned and it'll be fab.'

The integration of Liverpool slang into Astrid's use of English accelerated through closer association with the Beatles – the Fab Five – and other Merseyside outfits, but it was then intoned with the clipped solemnity often utilized when speaking a language not your own. In turn, Pete and Paul had some schoolboy German, and the others, beginning with phrase books and sign-language, picked up enough to get by.

All five were on their best behaviour – meaning that John stopped a few degrees short of open insolence – when, after finishing at the Dom, Astrid took them to lunch in a Chinese restaurant, and then invited them back to Eimsbutteler Strasse to meet her mother who, wrote Stuart, 'dresses very smartly and soberly and just sits smoking with very sad eyes'. After tea, she drove them back in time for the first set at the Kaiserkeller. They were to dine at the Kirchherrs' on many other occasions, and would gladly submit to further flashbulb *woomphs* from Astrid,[6] Jürgen and anyone else who cared to take pictures of them.

The Beatles got to be quite addictive. Exis would neglect their studies, art, and day jobs to be near them throughout the watches of the night. 'Their natural energy, good humour and wit were seductive,' confirmed Vollmer. 'We felt at times that we had to force ourselves not to go. Astrid and I went to the movies instead – but we had such an urge to return to the Beatles that we let ourselves go into the doorway of the room, way at the back of the dance floor. The Beatles saw us, and, as soon as they finished the number, broke immediately into "Stay".[7] They sang to us.'

Of individual Beatles, Pete, a strong-but-silent type, sent frissons through most nervous systems, though a placard daubed 'I love George', the first of its kind, was hoisted as a fair cross-section of Kaiserkeller males and females shouted for *'Das liebchen Kind'* – the lovely child – to take a lead vocal. None the less, the Kaiserkeller's indomitable head bouncer, Horst Fascher, would insist that Paul, with his chubby winsomeness, was the 'sunny boy'[8] of the group as he scuttled to and from microphones or lilted 'Besame Mucho', a sensual bossa nova and a frequent request from the ladies.

The Exis – and Frau Kirchherr – detected in Stuart and John a strength of personality lacking in other Beatles. 'Lennon, the obvious leader, was like a typical Rocker,' said Vollmer, 'cool, no gestures except for pushing his body slightly in rhythm to the music. Aggressive restraint, a Brando type. The image of James Dean was there, too, in Stuart, mystery behind sunglasses.' It was no coincidence that bass was the instrument that Klaus – already an able pianist, flautist and flamenco guitarist – began teaching himself after being shown the basic principles by Stuart.

From having simply intrigued her, the charismatic Sutcliffe was taking gradual if unknowing possession of Astrid, who discovered herself shivering with pleasure at his rare coy smile from the stage and during his even rarer solo singing spots – a reaction not lost on Klaus. Stuart would boast to his mother that 'everybody says I sing it ['Love Me Tender'] better than Elvis. Moments after I have finished singing, the people all look at me with sad, wistful looks on their faces. Recently, I've become very popular both with girls and homosexuals, who tell me I'm the sweetest, most beautiful boy. It appears that people refer to me as the James Dean of Hamburg.'

A little of Stuart's singing went a long way, but, though no slouch on vocals – even gruffly charming – he wasn't in the same league as John and Paul. As an instrumentalist, he remained limited, even admitting privately to Astrid, Jürgen and Klaus that he wasn't much of a bass player, and had come along mainly for the experience. 'He didn't take it seriously like the other ones,' deduced Vollmer. 'He was such a dreamer that he didn't really pay much attention to the music, and he played a lot of false notes. It's not that he was bad, it's just that he didn't put his mind to it a hundred per cent like the others.' Up on the boards, though, he would intimate to Astrid with an apologetic shrug that he wasn't a genius musician. That, however, didn't matter to her because he had an indefinable something else.

Despite Astrid's frank nature, their shy courtship began with feigned indifference and circuitous enquiry. The main snag was, as Stuart perceived when extolling Astrid's virtues to his sisters, 'but!!!

She has a boyfriend, I'm sure she loves him and certainly he her, although no sign of affection is passed between them.' Mooning over his seemingly off-limits infatuation to Ken Horton, he promised in vain to 'speak little of her for my mind would overflow with tenderness'.

His heart would feel as if it was going to burst through his rib-cage. Song lyrics started to have meaning for him instead of being merely syllables strung together to carry a tune. 'I am aflame,' he wrote to Ken. 'A woman's beauty is not, as the priest says, a temptation of the devil, but may, when in her spirit, work miracles. She's like a rose that has run its dark leaves over the wall to look at the sun. So saintly, she might have walked the waves of a lake and the unshivered lake would have borne her tiny feet.' His worship became less silent during initially frustrating tête-à-têtes in her halting, drawling English and his dog-German. With lessening frequency, the morally generous Klaus was beckoned over to interpret. Soon, the pair seemed to be understanding what each was saying without words.

Though it seemed longer, it took a mere fortnight after their first meeting in October for Astrid to seize an initiative of sorts by giving Stuart a chocolate heart encased in red Cellophane. He wasn't sure how he was supposed to read a signal far more subtle than that of a Freiheit tart punching the air. 'Oh, the heartache!' he wailed to Ken. 'Tomorrow, I will buy her a white rose, a young boy's thought, a sunny thought and golden one, marred only by the knowledge that I will never have the courage to give it to her.' Eventually, he screwed himself up to do so – and, during one Kaiserkeller evening when Klaus was visiting his parents in Berlin, Stuart and Astrid crossed the impalpable boundary between inferred companionship and declared love. Every subsequent day held them tighter in the radiant grip of the same flow of feeling. Above undignified gropings and with the formality of Klaus unresolved, Stuart could assure his mother in mid-November that 'I haven't slept with Astrid yet, in case you think this is just an erotic affair.'

Instead, Astrid would call for Stuart at the Bambi Kino, and they might walk to the Grosse Freiheit's St Pauli underground railway station for outings to central Hamburg's art galleries, theatres and cinemas. Sometimes, they took pot-luck on an unknown part of the city and whatever diversion it might hold. On sunnier days, there were excursions to the Alster with its circling gulls, and to the birch woods beside the Elbe estuary. The Reeperbahn and Klaus could be forgotten as the lovers strolled in the autumn chill, not a leaf stirring, a touch of mist, and a bird twittering somewhere.

When his suspicions proved well founded, Klaus did not erupt with anger. With the same questions coming up again and again, he gently implored Astrid to help him grasp what it all meant. Finally, though his pride was smarting, he was a gentleman about it. It was hardly his new friend's fault that he had fallen under Astrid's spell. Stuart would tell Ken Horton that 'her ex-boyfriend who I love very much is on the verge of suicide'. This may have been an over-dramatization because Voorman is remembered by others as conducting himself with observed good humour as Astrid and Stuart brazened it out until the gossip dried up. The only alternative was not to go to the Kaiserkeller any more.

After ousting Klaus as 42 Eimsbutteler Strasse's lodger too, Stuart began seeing less of the group, even absenting himself from Kaiser-keller bashes now and then to escort Astrid to the kind of cultivated foreign movies he used to attend either with his mother or absorb at the college film society. Their extremes were exemplified by the sub-titled *Ashes and Diamonds* with Zbygniew Cybulski, the Polish James Dean, and *Les Enfants Terribles* with its plot from a Cocteau novel, and its soundtrack from Bach and Vivaldi. 'He'd go to the ballet,' exclaimed Ken Horton. 'He'd do lots of thing he couldn't do in Liverpool because it wasn't available. So obviously, she'd sparked a much more mature desire to dig everything – and he did latch on to jazz, but maybe it was her collection of records.'

Listening to the record-player and other indoor pursuits became more attractive as the seasons changed from gold to marble, and the cold from the Westerweg hit Hamburg like a hammer. Frau Kirchherr liked Stuart, possibly because he took after Klaus in so many respects. Also, after weeks of irregular meals and the Bambi Kino hovel, he looked like he could do with some mothering – someone to see to his laundry and fatten him up with proper meals.

As open-minded as the Scandinavian family in Rhyl had been, there were no old-fashioned looks *chez* Kirchherr after Astrid and Stuart began sharing the same bed. Neither was there any objection in late November when Astrid announced that she was going to marry him.

Mädel Ruck-Ruck-Ruck

NOTES

1   US title: *Call Me Genius*.
2   *Beatlefan* (vol. 1, no. 3, 1978).
3   *John Winston Lennon*, R. Coleman (Sidgwick and Jackson, 1984).
4   A reference to the 1956 novel by Jack Kerouac.
5   *The True Story of the Beatles*, B. Shepherd (Beat, 1964).
6   Including the 'half-light' portrait that was copied for the front cover of 1963's *With The Beatles* album.
7   A 1960 US chart-topper, and UK Top Twenty entry in 1961, for Maurice Williams and the Zodiacs. An exuberant revival by the Hollies made the British Top Ten in 1963.
8   *Good Day Sunshine*, November 1989.

chapter six

HOMESICK FOR ST PAULI

'He only seemed to have known her five minutes. I thought it was a growing-up phase – but he'd fallen so deeply in love apparently that the others couldn't comprehend it'[1]

Millie Sutcliffe

He had asked her during one of the photo sessions that, these days, did not involve any other member of the group. As is the German custom, they had marked their engagement by buying each other a ring.

Stuart sensed that it was the icing on a cake of follies as far as his mother was concerned. While wishing her a 'happy crimbo', he had recalled in a letter written on Christmas Eve ('in a strange city, a strange country – in all a strange atmosphere – I like it') that 'you didn't seem very keen on the idea of me getting engaged. I hope you have become used to the idea by now.' There was also a hint of guilt with 'I suppose you feel that I've found another mother who does all the things for me that you did.' As if to qualify this, he mentioned 'a touch of flu' but 'have no fear though – I am given the best attention, with penicillen [sic] tablets every couple of hours. My back and chest rubbed with the German equivalent of Vick, hot towels around my throat etc.'

The antithesis of these domestic reassurances was the vulnerability of his letter to Ken Horton describing the moment when his proposal was accepted by 'my too wonderful little angel. She flew down a few weeks ago, and big man man Stu said, "I'm better than God – stay with me." Actually, I'm her Church and she's the bells that ring. She pulls the ropes and can she swing?'

John, however, thought there were bats in Stuart's belfry, and, therefore, so did his Beatle underlings. As self-appointed guardian of

Stuart's moral welfare, John dictated the party line: Astrid is a great-looking bird, granted, but fancy tying yourself down when great-looking birds are available in every corner of the Grosse Freiheit. Content to remain the hard nut he never had been, Lennon sneered too as Astrid winkled out Stuart's innate refinement – *ballet*, for Gawd's sake.

The sub-text, of course, was that Astrid had disrupted the intimacy of John's friendship with Stuart: an older love affair. These days, just the subtlest inflexion of Stuart's voice would send John into a foul temper, especially when Astrid was around. When she wasn't, he'd ease up, happy to have Stuart's undivided attention once again. Present or absent, Astrid was often in direct line of fire when Lennon exercised the fantastic boorishness that would explode like shrapnel all around the Kaiserkeller. This could be funnelled to more concentrated effect in less public situations. Still stereotyping Germans, after nearly four months, an aside like 'Rudolf Hess asked me to tell you he was quoted out of context' would issue from the side of his mouth when simply ordering a lager from a barmaid. At first, Astrid couldn't imagine why she had been singled out for worse and more relentless ill-treatment. She would snap back, but John's intermittent retreats were as disconcerting as his tirades.

It cut Stuart like a sharp knife whenever the two people he cared about most reared up at each other. As if watching a tennis match, his eyes darted from lover to best friend as harmless jesting swung in seconds to open trading of insults. He couldn't even fight for the woman he worshipped in this, the severest test ever of the mutual loyalty that was the bedrock of his relationship with John. As Lennon stormed off after another excruciating round with Astrid, Stuart would empty his lungs with a *whoosh*, and begin the case for the defence – as John would have done for him were their positions reversed. Whether beside herself with rage or weak with relief, Astrid would receive the same placatory reassurance that John was a fine fellow when you got to know him.

An assumption that Lennon loathed her, however understandable, was false: she was just the sort of bird he would have liked for himself, closer to a well-mannered Brigitte Bardot than Cynthia, but he felt she was out of his league. Maybe he and Stu weren't so much in a lower league as a different one. If he had been brave enough to chuck Cynthia, and Stuart hadn't been interested, John might have wooed

Astrid himself. As it was, there were long, dangerous moments even at the height of antagonism – but, like many so-called extroverts, he covered a hesitancy with respect to girls by brutalizing himself – in his case, by coming on as the rough, untamed Scouser.

He was childish – and a Right Bastard to boot – but Astrid, and her mother, found it hard to hide a fascination with Lennon, probably the most seethingly angry person they had ever met. On visits to Altona, he would scan the bookshelves and Astrid's record rack, making few exceptions in a string of derisive comments about every author – Cocteau, Sartre, Genet ('all the Left Bank shower'), Poe, Wilde, Nietzsche, de Sade, and composers like Wagner and Stravinsky whose works he might or might not have heard.

Gradually, there came if not a reformed Lennon, then a new mood. The tempest dropped, and he stopped fighting the situation. His manner towards Astrid became not genial exactly but grimly urbane. The exchange of a civil word or two gave way every so often to what might be construed as a compliment. Though his lips never moved upwards, his eyes began smiling almost gently upon her. She was Stuart's, and if she had been John's, he'd feel the same way about her. Suddenly, he was pleased for Stuart. He'd done all right there.

He wouldn't have been the John Lennon of popular acclaim if he had moderated the barbed invective but, with Astrid at least, it was delivered with much the same lurking affection he also reserved for Stuart. Gradually, Astrid grasped the social contradiction that was Lennon. This can be epitomized by a memorable first encounter in Hamburg with Frank Allen, one of Middlesex's Cliff Bennett and the Rebel Rousers. 'Ah yes. It's Frank, isn't it?' acknowledged John after being introduced. 'I've talked to other people in the club and it seems that, next to Cliff, you're the most popular member of the band. I don't know why. Your harmonies are fucking ridiculous.'[2]

The truce between Stuart, John and Astrid did not lessen antipathy towards Stuart by the rest of the outfit, already long-faced about his lackadaisical bass playing. After all, Stuart had been the one to get this stunning blonde creature, when all of them had been hypnotized by her charms. There was always a healthy sense of rivalry when it came to chicks.

As storm clouds continued to gather, Stuart came to prefer the less crowded hours with Astrid and her Exi circle to going through the same shallow rock 'n' roll ritual night after night. He couldn't yet admit even to John that he no longer found it exciting to be a Beatle, even when the Rocker girls were baying for him to sing 'Love Me Tender'. The enjoyment he still derived from being in the group was all for the wrong reasons. For devilment, he would deliberately pluck sickeningly off-key notes. If he was the group's biggest liability, then he'd have fun being it.

He no longer bothered to strain his ears to catch Paul and George's murmured backstage intrigues. They could get John to sack him for all he cared now. He and Pete had been excluded, anyway, from a recording session, financed by Rory Storm and Allan Williams, featuring Paul on bass, John and George with members of the Hurricanes in a minuscule studio behind central Hamburg's Haupt-bahnhof railway station.

In proportion to Stuart's increasing estrangement from the group was the growing friction between them and Bruno Koschmider, who had grown rather wary of his British imports of late. '*Ist gut*,' he would say, with a scowl that said it wasn't, after he had interrogated the Beatles and Rory Storm's Hurricanes about a tale he had been told about them spending their rest periods in the Top Ten. They hadn't even the decency to lie. Impervious to his reprimands, they soon went beyond merely visiting there. When the Beatles joined Sheridan and the Jets onstage, Peter Eckhorn heard not casual jamming but a new backing group for Tony after the Jets' contract expired on 1 December.

On top of higher wages, Peter could offer accommodation two floors above the club. With a balcony facing the church opposite, this dormitory contained a battered old table surrounded by six army camp beds with hard mattresses and lumpy-looking pillows. If plain, it was palatial compared to the unsavoury facilities in the dungeons of Koschmider. Furthermore, both the Jets and the ex-Kaiserkeller staff (notably Horst Fascher) charmed away by Eckhorn found him a fair-minded employer from whom bonuses could be expected when business was brisk. Other fringe benefits included Swiss-embroidered bowling jackets and personalized cigarette lighters, each with 'TOP TEN CLUB HAMBURG' embossed on the side. Rather than racketeers and ruffians, the Top Ten was inclined to cater for tourists and 'Mittel-stand' teenagers whose parents might drop them off in estate cars.

Most of them would be collected just before midnight, owing to the curfew regulation that forbade those under eighteen from frequenting Reeperbahn clubs any later than that.

'When I was first in Germany,' remembered Paul Francis, drummer with the Vibrations, 'I had to alter the date of birth on my passport as I was officially under age. Every time I was asked to produce the passport, I was sure that the authorities would twig.'[2] Seventeen-year-old George Harrison had been unofficially exempted whenever ordered to present his passport for police inspection, thanks, it is presumed, to Koschmider's string-pulling. However, able to read Eckhorn like a book – and a mighty avaricious publication it was – Bruno acted swiftly. Firstly, the Beatles were given a month's notice and reminded of a contractual clause that forbade them from working in any other Hamburg club without his permission, which he withheld. Aware that Eckhorn could grease enough palms to circumvent such legalities, Koschmider was suspected of striking harder by withdrawing whatever immunity he had sorted out concerning the youngest Beatle's nightly violation of the curfew. George Harrison's deportation was arranged by late November.

He spent much of the day before his exile giving John and Paul a crash course in lead guitar the Harrison way as they seemed quite willing to remain abroad indefinitely with or without him. After a month at the Top Ten, there were prospects of a season in Berlin. Another club possibility was a stint at Le Golf Drouot in Paris after the resident British band, Dougie Fowlkes and his Airdales, left. Perhaps Harrison could rejoin after his birthday in February.

Only Stuart and Astrid, both of whom had a soft spot for him, saw George off from the Hauptbahnhof platform. Bewildered and subdued, he flung his arms round the couple before heaving his suitcase, guitar and amplifier into the second-class compartment of the long train. During the depleted Beatles' Kaiserkeller finale, Astrid intended to present them with an emblematic bunch of five long-stemmed roses but, deciding it was a bit silly, let them fall under the table where they were furtively trampled by Jürgen Vollmer.

The reverberations of the sour note on which the Kaiserkeller season finished were heard loud and clear when Peter Eckhorn was obliged to replace the Beatles with a hastily reformed Jets until Gerry and the Pacemakers could be rushed in from Liverpool. The Beatles, after all, were even less of a group after Best and McCartney were handcuffed, bundled into a Peterwagen (Black Maria) and, after questioning, ordered out of the Fatherland on a trumped-up charge of arson.

Tarred with the same brush, Stuart was rounded up too. 'I arrive at the club, and am informed that the whole of Hamburg police are looking for me,' he disclosed to Ken Horton in thrillerish present tense. 'The rest of the band are already locked up, so, smiling and very brave on the arm of Astrid, I proceed to give myself up. At this time, I'm not aware of the charge. All my belongings, including spectacles, are taken away, and I'm led to a cell where, without food or drink, I sit for six hours on a very wooden bench.' He was free to go after signing a statement in German that had satisfied the *Polizei* that he knew nothing about Exhibit A: the charred rag that consti-tuted Herr Koschmider's complaint about the Beatles trying to burn down the Bambi Kino.

So then there were two, and both were forbidden to seek employ-ment as it had also been discovered that the Beatles had had no work permits for their three months at the Kaiserkeller. John had little choice but to follow the other three back to Liverpool. Stuart, who had once imagined he would be the first to go, remained at 42 Eimsbutteler Strasse, 'living in the lap of luxury and contentment' (to Ken Horton). He'd be home for Christmas, he told Millie, who was then maintaining a postal silence. 'Her mother will feed and keep me in cigarettes until then,' he wrote. 'I don't think I've had any letters from you for some time so I assume you are rather annoyed about the whole situation. I don't know what you or my father would have done in the same situation, but I don't feel I've let you down.'

He had the time but not the stomach to dip brush in palette again. However blasé he had been about it in his letters to Ken, he was deeply worried about what would happen if ever he got beyond the endless sketching and crayoning that occupied him as Frau Kirchherr pottered about the house. The outlines between day and night had long dissolved, and, with Astrid on flexi-time, evenings could be spent roaming the clubs around St Pauli. Wisely, the two steered clear of the Kaiserkeller, which, in any case, had been deserted by the Exis since the Beatles and, shortly afterwards, Rory Storm and the Hurricanes had moved on. The Top Ten was the place to be now, even if Gerry and the Pacemakers – straight from the civil service and British Rail rather than art college and grammar schools – weren't on the same wavelength as the Beatles. 'Though we chatted and she was a lovely girl,' said Gerry, 'there wasn't the same relationship that Astrid had with the Beatles. There was a very arty crowd in Hamburg – not for me but it suited the lads.'³

Astrid and Stuart mingled more happily with other guests at the outlandish theme parties, such as the one where all were dressed as famous paintings, that various Exis threw during the festive season. Surreal scenes would ensue in which Whistler's Mothers and Laughing Cavaliers did the depraved Twist – 'the most vulgar dance ever invented'⁴ – soon to be as much the latest rave world-wide as trad had been in Britain alone. Its Acker Bilk was Chubby Checker but, from Sinatra and Elvis downwards, all sorts of unlikely artists would be recording Twist singles. To the delight of the young ladies of Liverpool, an embarrassed Pete Best would be thrust to the front of the stage to demonstrate the dance while Paul struck up its eight-to-the-bar hi-hat rhythm. Little dates a film set in the early 1960s more than the obligatory Twist sequence in which middle-aged socialites rub shoulders with beatniks, pretending to towel their backs while grinding a cigarette butt with the foot.

Exi shindigs were either like this or with Edith Piaf rather than Chubby Checker on the turntable as they small-talked in dim light round a centrepiece of, say, an artful vase of dead black roses. Such gatherings weren't unlike that hosted by the dilettante Parisian artist Jim Smith in *The Rebel*, who when working on a painting would sleep on a canvas. When writing a novel, he would bed down on a bookcase: 'I prefer sleeping on soft wood – oak is so intense, don't you think?' There is a skit in which Hancock explains to a crowd of squatting beatniks, all dressed in exactly the same Astrid-like black garb, that one of the reasons he had to leave London was because he couldn't stand the sartorial uniformity in the accountancy office where he worked. As he leaves them, one beatnik comments to another that 'It must have been very soul-destroying to him; imagine, everybody looking the same.'

Another *Rebel* parallel was drawn in that John could no longer dominate the proceedings from England. The Exis were able, therefore, to put him and Stuart into perspective: John was Hancock, hovering on a current of self-promotion rather than artistic ability; Stuart was his Montmartre flatmate Paul who has real talent.

Just as he had played drums in the absence of Tommy Moore, so

Paul had adapted to bass whenever Stuart had been indisposed at the Kaiserkeller, but George for one wanted their post-Hamburg début in Liverpool to be with a full complement, for reasons he outlined in an appeal by letter to Stuart: 'Can't you or won't you come home sooner, as if we get a new bass player for the time being, it will be crumby, as he will have to learn everything, and it's no good with Paul playing bass, that is if he had some kind of bass and amp to play on.' As Stuart neither could nor would, an ex-Blackjack, Chas Newby, was roped in when the Beatles regrouped for an exploratory bash at the Casbah. Afterwards, wrote George, 'some queer bloke was almost on his knees, asking me if we would play for him.' Because of their lengthy stay in Hamburg – the 'successful German tour' of pre-engagement publicity – they were an unknown quantity locally, but not for long after they were a last-minute addition to a bill at Litherland Town Hall on 27 December. Lennon would recall the Beatles 'being cheered for the first time'[5] in Liverpool after a casually cataclysmic performance which had been wrought as a result of having to *mach schau* for hours on end since August.

You couldn't deny their impact on a crowd who had rippled spontaneously towards the stage when the curtains swept back a few startling bars into John, Paul, George, Chas and Pete's first number, and remained there, spellbound, until the coda of the final encore. Yet musically they were a throwback now that pop was at its most innocuous and ephemeral. Dance craze records on Top Forty radio generally indicate stagnation, and Britain in 1961 would certainly be heaving with that. The Sucu Sucu was everywhere – and so were the Fly, the Mashed Potato, the Hully Gully, the Hitch-Hiker, the back-breaking Limbo, the Madison, even a revival of the Charleston. As well as demonstrations of variations on the Twist and the Cliff-Adam-Billy triumvirate, televised pop was full of Craig Douglas, Mark Wynter and Jess Conrad among a plethora of blow-waved domestic heart-throbs in the US-Bobby mould with slush that your granny liked. They'd be soft-shoe shuffling before you could blink.

In this twee morass, there were few sparkles. Without compromising their rhythm-and-blues determination, Ray Charles and Fats Domino were still chart contenders, while a Texan named Roy Orbison transformed 'Only The Lonely', a trite Bobby ballad into an unprecedented aria with a voice that combined cowboy diction with operatic pitch.

Backbeat

No Beatle would equal Orbison's *bel canto* eloquence but, in the days when vocal balance was achieved by simply moving back and forth on the microphone, the three-part harmonies of John, Paul and George were hard-won but perfected in readiness for what lay ahead. When Paul was on bass, lead and rhythm guitars often merged in the interlocking concord which had also evolved during the group's spell at the Kaiserkeller. The interaction of McCartney's low-fretted throb, Harrison's *Play In A Day* virtuosity and Lennon's good-bad rawness was compulsively exquisite even to more proficient guitarists who could hear what was technically askew. Musically, the three didn't need anyone else – except a compatible drummer.

While the Beatles still fell back on classic rock whenever the set dragged, working the same magic were arrangements of the Marvelettes' 'Please Mr Postman', 'Money' by Barrett Strong and other discs on Tamla-Motown, a promising black label from Detroit that had manoeuvred its first fistful of signings into the US 'Hot Hundred'. Though they paid at least lip-service to the passing joys of the UK hit parade, groups within Liverpool's culturally secluded hinterland did not lean on chart material as obviously as those in many other regions. Tony Sheridan praised the Beatles' 'great talent for finding unusual records'[6] as Bill Harry did the Searchers. The more hip Merseyside bands were also rifling the catalogues of Richie Barrett, Benny Spellman, Chan Romero, Barbara George, James Ray and other Americans unknown to the ordinary Scouser – or ordinary anyone else.

Moreover, while Italy's Little Tony and his Brothers would simply mimic Romero's 'Hippy Hippy Shake', the intention in Liverpool was to make it and 'Money', Barrett's 'Some Other Guy', The Clovers' 'Love Potion Number Nine' and all the rest of them *not* sound like any other outfit's version. It was quite in order, therefore, for both the Beatles and Rory Storm to perform 'Shakin' All Over' and Presley's Latinate 'It's Now Or Never' when appearing at the same venue on the same evening. Later there came the calm precision of the Searchers' go at the Isley Brothers' 'Twist And Shout' and the Beatles' frantic work-out of the same, just one step from chaos.

Key local personalities like the Beatles, the Undertakers, Storm, Gerry, Kingsize Taylor and The Big Three were as much stars on Merseyside as Cliff Richard and the Shadows were nationally – and queuing round the block were any number of substitute Beatles,

Above: John Lennon (played by Ian Hart) and Stuart Sutcliffe (played by Stephen Dorff) in the aftermath of one of their many Liverpool fights. (Mark Tillie)

Above left: Lennon and Sutcliffe present a mean front, in Liverpool. (Mark Tillie)

Above right: A more colourful touch – Astrid Kirchherr (played by Sheryl Lee) photographs the Beatles. (Mark Tillie)

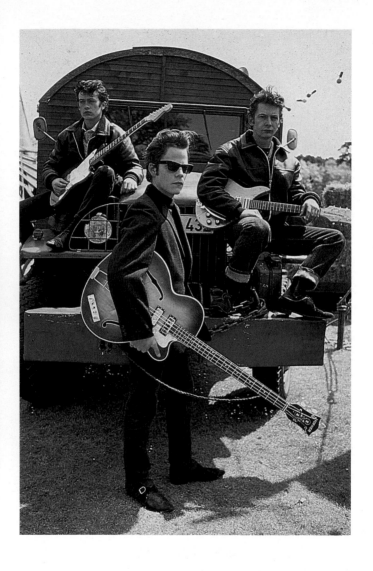

Above: Nightlife sleaze on the Reeperbahn. (Mark Tillie)

Right: John Lennon plays fast and furious to the crowds in the Kaiserkeller. (Mark Tillie)

Facing page: John, Stu and George (played by Chris O'Neill) seen through the lens of Astrid's camera. (Mark Tillie)

Above: Astrid and Stuart escape the mayhem for a few hours. (Mark Tillie)

Below: Leathered up and hair flattened down – the new look Beatles. *Left to right:* Pete Best (played by Scot Williams), Paul McCartney, John Lennon, George Harrison. (Mark Tillie)

Facing page: Totally absorbed, Stuart in his Hamburg studio. (Mark Tillie)

From the oeuvre of Stuart Sutcliffe

Clockwise from top left: 'Elvis Presley' – ink and poster paint, 1957. Elvis was one of Stuart's greatest idols with both his demeanour and his singing voice modelled on the twentieth-century icon. (Pauline Sutcliffe, Private Collection)

'Little Tommy Tucker' – sketched for Millie Sutcliffe to decorate her classroom. (Pauline Sutcliffe, Private Collection)

'Horse' – chalk and charcoal, from a Liverpool Art School sketchbook, *c.* 1958. (Pauline Sutcliffe, Private Collection)

Oil on board painting, *c.* 1958. Obvious influences are Ballard and Bomberg. (Pauline Sutcliffe, Private Collection)

'Summer Painting', 1959. John Moores purchased this painting from the John Moores' Exhibition – Stuart spent the money on a bass guitar. (Private Collection)

Untitled in mixed media from the Hamburg period, 1960–62. (Pauline Sutcliffe, Private Collection)

Left: Untitled, oil on canvas from the late Hamburg period, 1961/62. (Pauline Sutcliffe, Private Collection)

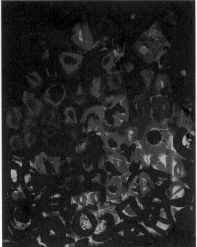

Left: Untitled, *c.* 1961/62. One of the most important works from Stuart's red period. This work was featured in the film *Backbeat* and was one of the paintings that Stu was working on at the time of his crippling headaches. (Pauline Sutcliffe, Private Collection)

Rories and Gerries. For every group that threw in the towel, a dozen sprang up. When Stuart Sutcliffe returned to Liverpool by air in mid-January for some vocational and personal stock-taking, he was astonished to find that the local scene, while not yet erupting, had grown immensely. From Aintree's Faron's Flamingoes to the Path-finders in Birkenhead, each vicinity seemed to have a group enjoying parochial fame. In Huyton, Stuart's Prescot Grammar contemporary Neil Foster was blowing sax with the Delacardoes. Either active or in formation were outfits of every size and description. Most were straws in the wind, in it just for fun as the Quarry Men had been. However, as their hire-purchase debts at Hessy's demonstrated, some meant business.

The Beatles were one such group who required complete commitment from the high command of Lennon and McCartney to a newly acquired van driver, Frank Garner, an erstwhile Casbah bouncer, who was superseded by Neil Aspinall, a ledger clerk who lodged with the Bests. John was pleased to see Stuart, but to the others – for all George's sweet words in December – their errant bass player's reappearance was met with conflicting emotion now that they had become quite used to Paul's more agile bass playing.

McCartney, especially, felt that Stuart was holding them back and that the stakes were now too high to risk mistakes from his bass playing. Neither he, George nor Pete knew how they were supposed to feel when Stuart kept his options open by applying immediately for both a visa to re-enter Germany and for a place on a one-year Art Teacher's Diploma (ATD) course at the art college, starting in September. Each represented an attempt to 'settle down'. Either way, it would not bode well for the Beatles – particularly as John had now issued the naked threat: if he goes, I go.

Consolation for the Beatles' internal anxieties was a full booking schedule within easy reach. From an 'Operation Big Beat' with Gerry, Rory, Kingsize and the Remo Four at the New Brighton Tower to supporting the local heroes in the humblest suburban youth club, 'working in and around Liverpool keeps you busy throughout the whole year', would be George Harrison's earliest quote in the national music press. On the evening of his eighteenth birthday, the group, with Stuart, crammed in two separate engagements, a common undertaking now that dance promoters used to strict tempo had smelt the money to be made from all these young 'Merseybeat' bands, who were glad to have somewhere to make their noise for the hundreds silly enough to pay to hear. Even for the Beatles and other groups that counted, the average turnover was only two or three pounds each per week. Typical too was one night at Orrell Park Ballroom when of the net takings of sixty-seven pounds, only nineteen were split between three acts.

The Undertakers' name would become synomymous with Orrell Park as the Delacardoes would with the Green Dolphin, and the Searchers at the Iron Door. The Beatles would become a fixture at the Cavern where the rot had set in after it had taken a cue from the nearby Iron Door and allowed pop and trad outfits to share the same bill. However, in early 1961, it was still predominantly a jazz venue, but, as a 'rock and dole group' – the words of Bob Wooler, one of its compères – the Beatles were able to make their Cavern début in February 1961 during one of the new lunch-time sessions that were further maximizing the club's profits since it had 'gone pop'.

This was to be Stuart's only performance at the sodden oven that was destined to become as famous a Liverpool landmark as the Pier Head. Its idiosyncratic essence of disinfectant, mould and cheap perfume was still on his clothes twenty-four hours later, as it was on those of Colin Manley who was in the audience on what must have been an off-day for the Beatles who 'still had Stuart Sutcliffe with them, and they really weren't very good.'[7]

Saying much about the Cavern's clientele was the infrequency of the violence that still pervaded pop recitals elsewhere. Musicians weren't immune from it either, as exemplified by hooligans with a grievance against Derry Wilkie who converged, wielding hatchets, on a venue where he was singing. The provocation could be either catching the eye of some bruiser's girl or not playing enough slow ones (or fast ones) to facilitate the undoing of maidens by unattached swains. If pursuit of romance was either unsuccessful or not the principal mass objective of the expedition, it could be mere irritation at a guitarist's narcissistic endeavours while he pretended that he couldn't care less about the more-than-passive interest of the girls near the front.

Beyond sexual jealousy, there were sometimes feelings that perhaps a group's music was not so good. Often it was down to technical difficulties. Sounding puny yet harsh and atrociously distorted, players fought adverse acoustics in the age before the advent of monitors, programmable desks and graphic equalizers. If you couldn't play very well anyway, all you could do was either look cool, as if you were meant to be in a different key from everyone else, or scowl at onlookers, defying them to comment aloud at the flurries of wrong notes hanging flagrantly in the air.

Sentence was pronounced on Stuart Sutcliffe on either 30 January, 4 February or 6 February 1961, though some Beatle annals pinpoint the occurrence as just before the Scottish tour. The group was on at the two-tier Lathom Hall in Seaforth. It was a rough night and no mistake. The baleful nature of the cat-calls and barracking was such that even Stuart lashed out verbally. John was better at outfacing trouble. He was the sort that they laugh at rather than beat up. Yet this new situation was not to yield vintage Lennon.

Maintaining ghastly grins, it was the Beatles' off-mike intention to quit the stage, the building and the district as swiftly as possible. If there was going to be any kind of vendetta against them, they were uncertain of aid from the event's organizers. As long as the teenagers handed over the admission money and behaved themselves while inside, their deeds of destruction in the streets afterwards need be of no concern to palais promoters, who had not let private dislike of pop stop them from turning a hard-nosed penny from it.

Assuming they had to fend for themselves, the group was hurriedly transferring equipment via a fire door from behind the stage down some steps to the van when they came mob-handed: ugly people who wanted to make everything else ugly too. They were going to concentrate on the weedy-looking one. The rest of the group looked as if they might be able to take care of themselves.

On the steps Stuart replied, 'Good evening', to a gruff "Ullo'. For being such a toffee-nosed *get*, he was thumped in the stomach. His glasses toppled from his nose as he collapsed wheezing on to the asphalt. Then they piled in. Beneath the sole back-porch light, other customers were among bestial faces getting an eyeful of unofficial spectator sport as the gang enacted their piston-kick reprisal. Stuart squirmed around to amused jeers, trying to shield head and genitalia.

Someone summoned an elderly man who, hugging a biscuit tin half-full of coins, watched for a few seconds before scurrying away with a look of distaste. Take care of the pennies and the lads can take care of themselves. Anyhow, fighting and vandalism outside the premises was a matter for the Merseyside constabulary.

Backbeat

John Lennon was a past master at verbal fencing if an impresario dithered about handing over the agreed fee, but this was something else entirely. He had dashed out when told by two girls of the fight. Stuart was yelling in panic, and blood was cascading from his face. If he didn't wade in, his hard-man veneer would be cracked for ever. What's more, it was Stuart who was getting a right pasting, Stuart who stuck up for him, right or wrong. Someone caught John's sleeve but he pulled away, charging forward in blind passion to even up hopeless odds. He seized an arm himself, wrenched the owner round and smashed his face so hard that the sleeve tore off. He was in danger of being served the same as Stuart, but with Pete's arrival as reinforcement, he landed a few more indiscriminate punches.

'It's one of the few times when the aggressive Lennon became really violent,' noted Mike Evans, 'as opposed to violent in his manner. It was on this occasion that he, if you like, rescued Stuart from this attack – but, by this time, [Sutcliffe] had been kicked about the head and was bleeding, and they got him home, and that was the end of the affair. Next day, he seemed OK. It was only months after that that he complained about these headaches. If someone complains of a headache, you don't think of a street incident a year before, do you?'

John told his aunt that his injuries, a sprained wrist and broken finger, which would sully his guitar-picking for a while, had resulted from a fall. Stuart's head wound and lost spectacles couldn't be excused quite so easily. He had to come clean with his mother: 'We've been attacked. I got knocked unconscious. My glasses are non-existent. I couldn't even pick up the pieces – but John got one of the thugs, and he broke his wrist giving him what he'd given me.'[1] No, he didn't want any fuss, he shouted as Millie raised the telephone receiver. Instead, she sponged and bandaged him, and he shambled to his bedroom.

The next morning, half his forehead was as black and blue as if he had painted it. He looked so awful that his mother called the doctor whether he liked it or not. There didn't seem to be any serious damage but he ought to spend the next two days in bed. He didn't. 'He had no time to be ill,' sighed Millie. 'He was too fond of life.'[1]

He had gone home to Mother rather than Liverpool 8 partly because home comforts, even in an 'atmosphere', were preferable to wintering in draught and damp; partly because his stay in Liverpool might only be temporary if, perish the thought, he either didn't get on the ATD course or the Beatles went off on their travels again. Another excellent reason was that *l'affaire Beatnik Horror* had drawn intense and unwelcome attention from the freeholders of the Gambier Terrace flat who had set in motion the litigation necessary to flush out all the undesirables mentioned in the article. They began with Rod Murray, vulnerable, anyway, as he had been barely able to cope with the rent after Stuart left for Hamburg. As well as overdue payments, a window broken by a nocturnal visitor was sufficient to obtain a writ for damage to the property. Rod and his sub-tenants vacated the premises in a blaze of glory. 'I was working as a contract gardener in Formby,' reminisced Rod Jones, 'and Rod actually sent me a telegram to get back urgently, and I got back and was given a big stick, and we were supposed to repel boarders. The bailiffs had come to get us out.'

When news of the eviction reached Hamburg, Stuart had been amused: 'At last he is getting paid back for me taking the blame at 9 Percy Street.' Not so funny was his mother having to retrieve his belongings – and some of John's – from Gambier Terrace. Lennon's artwork for his college course had already been consigned to flames while the Beatles were away. 'Outside were all these paintings of Lennon's,' elucidated Johnny Byrne, then still living in the basement. 'The landlord had come and [he] hadn't paid the rent, and the paintings were thrown out into the back yard where they were rotting – and I went out and I got these paintings and I burnt I don't know how many to keep us warm.'[8]

Stuart did not relish going back to that end of the bohemian spectrum. The Bambi Kino experience had cured him of romantic squalor for all time. Though he continued to crash out at various friends' flats near the college, he could be contacted with greater certainty at 53 Ullet Road, a flat on a main road overlooking Sefton Park – very much Liverpool rather than Lancashire – where the Sutcliffes had moved the previous August. This was in accordance with what had become an established pattern of graduating to a home that was an improvement on the one before. Moreover, being a teacher as well as a mother, Millie timed each move to coincide with school summer holidays so that the children's switches from, say, primary to secondary schools, or one form to the next were not too disturbing and their network of friends unaffected.

Backbeat

It was a family joke that house-moving always occurred when Charles was away. He would always say something in the vein of 'If you don't send me the new address, I'll know you've left me.' Both he and Millie enjoyed 'home-making'. Despite her asthma, Millie liked an evening stroll, escorted by one or both daughters, to 'window-shop' other houses, perhaps choosing *the* house to buy 'when we're rich'. She and Charles rarely disagreed about interior decorating, even when he decorated the hall at Sandiway with an unusual salmon-pink gloss paint on a wall covered with armadillo skins, canoe paddles and other artefacts from his travels – stylish, certainly, but he didn't have to see it day in, day out, at a time when Joyce and Pauline, both teenagers now, were not so keen on being thought 'different' by visitors. They wanted modern décor, just like their friends had.

As the girls were old enough to wear stockings rather than socks, and Joyce was 'dating' seriously, Millie considered that being nearer the city centre would enable their late attendance at dances and other social functions to be unblighted by the worry of whether they were going to miss the last bus home. Stuart still had a room at home, bigger than Joyce's or Pauline's, which he rarely used, but he would always notice – and complain – if anything was changed whenever it was used in his absence or tidied up.

Millie's retort might have been that of every other mother of an adolescent – the one about treating the house as a hotel. However, Stuart was keenly aware of the financial burden that he currently represented to the family, particularly as he was still embroiled in hire-purchase payments for equipment from Frank Hessy's. Income from the Beatles was far less now than it had been in Hamburg when he could afford to send Millie five pounds a week. All he could sensibly cling to was the hope – no, the certainty – of getting on the teacher-training course, for which an interview had been set for 23 February. He might qualify for a grant this time.

The only snag was that, apart from holidays, it would mean a year on the opposite side of the North Sea to Astrid. It was a depressing prospect as, less than a month after they had parted at Hamburg airport, he was already tormented with longing, just waiting for her impending visit to Liverpool for a fortnight in February.

I stand void of pleasures [he moped to Ken Horton], for I have forsaken this place. Hamburg and Astrid – I was crushed by the rock of her irresistible weight [*sic*], my heart fluttering like a frightened bird, my alcoves were flooded with radiance and I was swept away like a light feather. For many nights, I had prepared for this. I had washed the windows of my soul and in silence oiled the door to my heart.

Oh how can I help being bored! In the sky above the Earth shine a million stars, each one glittering in a different way, and everything is stationary . . . Astrid. Dear Ken, how sad for you that I write so. Forgive me that I use you as the harp on which I play my comic-opera.

With Astrid's coming centuries away, he spoke of writing a play, even giving it a title – *Mister Man and Queen Elsie*.[9]

There wasn't much space for Astrid either, especially as Millie, not sure if she liked her anyway, wasn't going to let Stuart sleep with her there. Instead, the engaged couple rented a room for the duration in Allan Williams' house. This was all the more convenient for a jubilant Stuart, proud beyond words, to show off his fiancée up the Jac and down Ye Cracke. She was just the sort of incredibly sexy blonde out of a foreign film that teenage schoolboys would invent as a dream date when talking dirty over a communal cigarette behind the bike sheds. What's more, she had read books and used long words – in German, mind, but long words all the same.

Even some of the college lecturers were unashamedly impressed, among them, Philip Hartas: 'The students used to say, "Have you seen Stuart about? Have you seen that girlfriend? He's brought the most extraordinary woman back from Hamburg. You're bound to notice her" – and, of course, she was very attractive and young, and she had this extraordinary leather suit on which you had never seen before, and nobody could afford things like that.'

Astrid was introduced to Bill Harry in the Jac when he and Stuart met for the first time since college broke up the previous July. There was no reason for either to think that this was also the last Bill and Stuart would see of each other as, not purposely snubbing Astrid, they chatted about places she had never been to, people she didn't know. Since the Gambier Terrace débâcle, Rod Jones had vanished.

They'd heard tell he was a night porter somewhere in the Channel Islands. Stuart had seen Mike Kenny the other day, and had congratulated him on his pending scholarship at the Slade in London. Yes, Stuart was aware that Rod Murray was soon to tie the knot. In fact, when the Beatles were playing one night recently in this very building, Rod asked Stuart to be best man. What with him and Astrid, and Bill and his fiancée Virginia too, you wouldn't have a minute to yourself with attending all these weddings.

Stuart hardly touched directly on the Beatles or music at all. Bill remembers: 'He talked about philosophy and the deep things. He'd gone over there and come back an existentialist. He was with Astrid, and she was completely in black and so was he, and he was as white as a sheet. I presumed this was the way existentialists looked. I noticed that he seemed more withdrawn than he'd ever been, less forthcoming.'

When Stuart stuck his head round the door at college, Nicholas Horsfield, who he had glibly put down as a referee on the ATD application form, was left as before with a contradictory impression: 'I can vividly remember him coming in. Maybe I was a bit biased against . . . I mean to say, he came waltzing in with his winkle-picker shoes on and that sort of thing, and maybe he caught me at a bad time. I was taken off-guard by a complete change in his attitude, you know, this very aggressive way of demanding, which I didn't remember before.' Mike Evans put it down to 'the independence he established for himself in Germany, which obviously he never had at home, even though he was living in Liverpool 8. He still had the apron strings effect. Whereas, once he was in Germany, completely independent, there was obviously an assertiveness that perhaps came out naturally.'

A little humility might have lurched the weathervane of approval in Sutcliffe's direction during that pivotal audience with the ATD panel on 23 February. Canteen opinion had it that he hadn't been accepted because it was through him that the Beatles had purloined the Students Union amplifier. Horsfield, however, insists that Stuart's teaching aspirations had been nipped in the bud because, as Nicholas himself had pointed out to the board, 'Stuart was an artist and nothing else – but also I lost patience with him. Perhaps "aggressive" is the wrong word – but he didn't go about it in the way one usually goes about getting someone to give them a recommendation. Also, it would have been frustrating for him as a person. Although it was only a year's course, it would have been so alien to Stuart that he would have rebelled and walked out.'

Stuart gaped at the dumbfounding 'I regret to inform you . . .' sentence on the communication as the full bitterness of the rejection hit him. His mind boggled. Loath to accept the finality of the decision, Stuart persisted for weeks in finding potential champions for his cause among his old tutors, notably Arthur Ballard and John Hart, another ex-serviceman who painted in the post-de Staël manner.

His resentment was almost palpable as he fumed about the college's shortsightedness, its mental sluggishness, its blind ignorance. That finished him with Liverpool anyway. 'This Liverpool that is a brass coffin,' he growled to Ken Horton, 'but they skimped a bit on the handles and they came off, so now we can't lower it into the pit, and the worms and bugs crawl slowly upwards.'

He didn't even stick around long enough either to be Rod Murray's best man or to honour existing local dates with the Beatles. With a character unblemished by a criminal record, Stuart's passage back to Hamburg on 15 March was unimpeded by officialdom as he crossed the Channel from Newhaven. He stared moodily at the flat landscape, and tore the Cellophane from several packets of duty-free cigarettes while enduring the maddeningly slow embarkations at stops *en route* from the Hook of Holland. Nevertheless, all's well that ends well, and he and Astrid fell into each other's arms amid the gusting engine steam and belching smoke at Hauptbahnhof station.

A legitimate colour had been given to his absenteeism from the Beatles whom Peter Eckhorn had pencilled in for a four-month Top Ten season commencing on 1 April. Stuart was to be on hand as Peter's consultant and character witness during negotiations with the West German Immigration Office and Herr Knoop, Hamburg's chief of police. Crucially, Stuart had to support Mona Best's telephoned badgering and Allan Williams' written assurance of good behaviour, especially about fire-bugs Pete and Paul.

'One thing they made clear,' warned Stuart in a letter to Pete, 'if you have any trouble with the police, no matter how small, you've had it forever (drunkenness, fighting, women etc).' However, nominally convinced that it had all been a terrible mistake and that there would be no further harassment from Bruno Koschmider, the German embassy in Amsterdam sent the group's work permits to Allan Williams – who, for his pains, would receive a missive from Stuart a few weeks later that denied the Beatles' professional association with him. Dejected by what he saw as the group's disloyalty – though they had never really been his to manage – Allan found it in him to offer to take them back after making token legal threats.

Grounds for the schism were that, since the Beatles' ignominious return to Liverpool in December, Williams had been responsible for only two of their bookings; the rest had snowballed from those found either by themselves or by Mrs Best for, if there was a storm centre of the Beatles' operation, it was surely the house in Hayman's Green where promoters would telephone the lady to book her son's group.

John, George and Paul had assembled at the Casbah for a final briefing from Mrs Best before the journey. They would be working split shifts with a Nottingham band, the Jaybirds,[10] and, later on, with Rory Storm and the Hurricanes. They would be replacing Dave Dee and the Bostons who, in the Reeperbahn's *Bierkeller* jollity, had become leading exponents of the pounding *mach schau* beat that, years later, would underpin 'Hold Tight', their first big hit as Dave Dee, Dozy, Beaky, Mick and Tich. 'When you played the Top Ten, it was usually a case of an hour on, an hour off,' said Tich, 'starting at around six o'clock in the evening, and sometimes going on to seven the following morning. The money was OK by English standards but didn't go a long way in Germany.'

Now that links with Britain had been established, the Freiheit was providing training for other future hit-parade contenders among the many acts streaming in to serve its clubs. As well as Merseyside and London, other shires and cities had been scoured for talent, and, by 1961, half the dialects of Britain resounded round St Pauli from the Cornish burr of Dave Lee and his Staggerlees to the flat vowels of Birmingham's Rockin' Berries whose vocalist, Clive Lea, had defied all comers in an 'Elvis of the Midlands' talent contest in 1959.

The undisputed Presley of the Reeperbahn, however, would always be Tony Sheridan who shared with the Beatles – except Stuart – the Top Ten's skylit sleeping quarters. Since the Jets' farewell, Tony had had no fixed backing band, performing instead with whoever else happened to be playing the club. The Beatles felt privileged to be on the same stage, learning the tricks of the trade from one nicknamed 'the Teacher' – though Screaming Lord Sutch likened him more to 'a sergeant major. He was really snappy towards them.'

Homesick for St. Pauli

The reason that the dawn set was often as energetic as the first one of the evening was not always down to Tony's gingering them up. The Grosse Freiheit was a narcotic ghetto as well as a sexual one. In Liverpool and during the Koschmider era, the Beatles' only experience of artificial euphoria had been Royston Ellis's Vick inhalers and, producing a similar effect in Germany, Nostrilene hay fever spray. Thanks to his closer association with the Exis, Preludin was not as new to Stuart as the others. However, during the interim between the group's first and second trips to Hamburg, supplies came to be stocked – for purposes other than fighting the flab – in every all-night establishment along the Reeperbahn.

Dave Dee recalled his group's first appearance at the Top Ten: 'We walked in, and they said, "You are onstage in an hour." We said, "Oh no, we've been travelling for two days." This guy said, "Don't worry about it." We went on, came off, the other band went on, came off, we went on again. It got to about 2.30 in the morning, and we were absolutely knackered. The guy says, "Don't worry. I'll take care of things," and he came up with five rum-and-cokes and these little tablets. I said, "What are these?" He said, "Don't ask questions. Just take the tablets. You'll feel great." We didn't know what they were, and, of course, it was speed – actually Preludin slimming pills – but they did the trick. The only problem was that when we finished work, we couldn't sleep and went through the next day waiting for the pills to wear off. Of course, we were knackered again by four o'clock – so we asked for more pills.'

The after-effects of amphetamines vary from person to person. Headaches, rashes, acute insomnia, hyperactivity, loss of appetite, depression and extreme drowsiness are the most common, as is a craving for more amphetamines to remove these symptoms. More sinister are 'the horrors', hallucination and other mental disturbances. Dickie Pride is an instance of one whose dabblings led to death before the age of thirty.

With eyes like catherine-wheels after finishing at the Top Ten, the Beatles would be ripe for mischief, which might begin with five-in-the-morning bar-hopping and end twenty minutes before showtime the next evening with everyone sleeping like the dead, until an envoy from Eckhorn burst in, jabbing at his watch.

At Sefton Park, the only indication that anything was amiss was that, from mid-1961 onwards, Stuart's handwriting became noticeably larger and more spidery in several of his letters home. These expressed preoccupations with an undimmed desire to return to art and with Astrid. 'I'm still a bit sad that you think I've made a mess of my future,' he told his mother, 'but out of it all I have something to really compensate – my love for Astrid, which knows no bounds, and her love for me.' As it had been with Bill Harry, he rarely mentioned the Beatles of which he was now both a founder – and, to all intents and purposes, part-time member. The group were now Sheridan's star pupils. Although the Hurricanes and the Jaybirds had also accorded him competent accompaniment, it would be the Beatles who Tony chose to be onstage with him when Alfred Schlacht, a publisher associated with Deutsche Grammophon, dropped by.

At Schlacht's urgings, Bert Kaempfert, a power on Polydor, the company's pop subsidiary, invited the thrilled Beatles to be one of two outfits, both to be called 'The Beat Brothers', who would cut tracks with Sheridan from which a single and probably an LP could be selected. Thirty-six-year-old Kaempfert's million-selling 'Wonderland By Night', an orchestral sound-portrait of Manhattan, might not have been to the Beatles' taste, but he *had* co-written 'Wooden Heart', the hit single from Elvis Presley's first post-army movie, 1960's *GI Blues*. Kaempfert hadn't said anything about the bass playing, but it was Stuart himself who decided that he would be unequal to this ultimate litmus-test of his musical competence. Very professionally, he suggested that, with a Deutschmark sign over every fretful crotchet in the recording studio, the Beatles would be better off with Paul on the bass for such an important landmark in their career. Though attractive in his matter-of-fact candour, he was slightly disappointed when no one, not even John, made more than a cursory attempt to disagree with his non-participation. Yes, he was quite right, they said, he was wise to stay out of it, but he could come along and spectate if he wasn't busy or going anywhere with Astrid.

One May morning after snatching a little rest from the night's Top Ten stint, the group and Tony were transported to their first Kaempfert session. A minimal budget dictated that the taping would take place not in a proper commercial studio, but on the stage of an infant school while the children were on Whitsun holiday – with equipment that Sheridan reckoned 'was a leftover relic of the British army occupation from some sort of radio station they had'.[11]

Now more confident whenever they heard a ticklish bass run

coming up, the Beatles punched out each Sheridan song in three takes at most. Musicians and producer unwound sufficiently for Bert to lend critical ears to some of John and Paul's songs and 'Cry For A Shadow', an ersatz Shadows instrumental that George had constructed with John's executive clearance. As the latter was more in keeping with current trends than anything Lennon and McCartney proffered, Kaempfert allowed the Beatles to record it as one side of a possible single in their own right. It would be coupled with their arrangement of 'Ain't She Sweet' with John on lead vocal. Neither number could be issued outside the Fatherland until both had acquired historical interest. After fate had taken the Beatles' hand, Bert would recount that 'It was obvious to me that they were enormously talented but nobody – including the boys themselves – knew how to use that talent or where it would lead them.'[12]

Tony Sheridan was the man of the moment in 1961. Nevertheless, the tracks with the Beatles filled half of Tony's *My Bonnie* album, released in June 1962 after the title song[13] had taken him to number five in the German charts a year earlier. Unhappily for the Beatles, they had been paid with a standard session rate rather than a share in Tony's royalties.

Having thrown the race, Stuart, of course, received nothing whatsoever from Polydor. By the time the 45 appeared behind German counters, he had become almost literally the Beatles' sleeping partner. Onstage, he was as nonchalant as ever but usually miles away as George and Paul flinched at hearing another of his fluffed riffs. Even the most diehard members of his unofficial fan club knew the writing was on the wall. 'I'm sure he never had any kind of ambition to become a rock 'n' roll musician,' Jürgen Vollmer concluded. 'The others would be giving their all, but Stuart just did it because it was the thing to do at the time.'

More than ever before, he was physically elsewhere too, so much so that it was necessary to line up a second understudy in Colin Millander, a former Jet who had stayed on as part of a duo in a nearby restaurant. It was getting beyond a joke. Though three years his junior – when such a difference mattered – George's exasperation that 'he was in the band because John conned him into buying a bass' had shown itself in desultory sabre-rattling with Stuart in safe assurance that Paul would support him when John intervened.

Paul, however, was the truer enemy. Their animosity boiled over one evening on stage with Tony Sheridan. Stuart saw red when Paul, seated at the piano, made some remark about Astrid. Flinging down his bass, he bounded across the boards, mad fury in his eyes, to knock the detested Paul off his perch. Manfully, Tony and the others kept the song going as the pair tumbled wrestling to the floor. Used to the Beatles' *mach schau* excesses, the audience emitted whoops of drunken encouragement and bellowed instruction as the number finished and the irresolute fight ebbed away to a slanging match and the combatants glowering at each other from opposite ends of a huffy dressing room.

Characteristically, Paul would pass off the incident as a bit of a lark but he might not have been so jocular had he managed to strike a blow to Stuart's head. Indeed, he might have ended up on a charge of murder before a German judge and jury tacitly prejudiced by his nationality and hirsute appearance. The next day, however, Paul was his smooth, accommodating self again, but neither he nor Stuart would forgive or forget, and, for weeks afterwards, Paul found himself casting an odd thoughtful glance at Stuart sweating over the bass as Sheridan or Lennon hogged the main microphone. Who'd have thought it? Stuart with an unforeseen glint in his eye? Stuart making a stand? Stuart without John protecting him?

Not yet out in the open was another bone of contention: John, Paul and George's desire to be rid of Pete[14] as soon as he had outgrown his usefulness. Only on the periphery of their graveyard-hour japes, private jokes and folklore, Pete was a non-partaker of Preludin and as reliable as he was mature. Like Stuart, his intentions towards his girlfriend were honourable. There was no denying that, to the three guitarists, Best was a bit, well . . . you know.

This might have been tolerated had it not been for the complicity, back in Liverpool, of Pete's volcanic mother who saw herself as the group's *grande dame*. 'Mrs Best wanted to manage the group,' reflected Bill Harry. 'She was one of those people born to manage, have control, do the business. They didn't want her interference.' She, more than Pete, was the victim of intensifying character assassinations by Harrison, Lennon and McCartney over venomous lagers in the Top Ten's murkiest corner.

Why couldn't all Beatle women be more like quiet, faithful Cynthia, and Paul's uncomplaining girlfriend, Dot Rhone, who supplied occasional passive glamour when he made her sit on a bar-stool in the midst of the Beatles' performances at home? For all these ladies' apparent acquiescence, it was still necessary for John and Paul to suspend their philanderings when Cyn and Dot visited them in Hamburg that Easter. Billeted on the Kirchherrs, Cyn felt instantly frumpish and clodhopping on first encounter with Astrid, so elegant and simply beautiful. However, possibly because she might have been expecting someone more devil-may-care to be the alarming John's partner, Astrid was all consideration, lavishing sisterly attention on Cyn, lending her clothes, taking her on a Cook's tour of the sights and shops of Hamburg, and encouraging the exchange of small confidences. 'I used to experience her as a terribly closed person,' said Pauline, 'very difficult to relate to, so much so that I decided she was a very inhibited woman, and yet it is clear that Astrid was very fond of her.'

With their men, there were picnic excursions on hot afternoons in Astrid's car to seaside resorts like Ostsee where, on the beach, John and Stuart would recharge their batteries for the labours of the night. If there was no work that evening, they would drive further to Timmendorf, where it was sometimes mild enough to sleep the night round a camp-fire of driftwood.

By now, Stuart and Astrid were cross-dressing as much as possessors of different sets of hormones generally could in 1961 without risking arrest. It might have led to comments on the streets of Merseyside – even in Liverpool 8 where, said Mike Evans, 'he had long hair in a time when no one had long hair. People used to look at him in the street.' Over in the Grosse Freiheit, however, long-haired males and couples experimenting with swapping clothes were but minor aberrations. In certain flourishing clubs there, you'd get stared at if you *weren't* either transvestite or androgenous. Even relaxing in the orthodox Top Ten, Astrid might be sporting Stuart's leather jacket while he wore her collarless blouse with the front tails knotted, exposing his midriff. On their feet would be crocodile winkle-pickers from England. The tips were stuffed with cardboard to stop them curling up like oriental slippers. Enraptured, Klaus had begged Stuart to import a pair for him, ensuring that there would be no error about the size by tracing on cardboard the outline of each foot.

He was also taken with the form-fitting leather trousers round Stuart's and Astrid's legs – as were Stuart's fellow Beatles. These were, after all, just like the ones Gene and Eddie had worn on that fatal tour. Though John, Paul, George and Pete acquired a pair each too, they were not yet prepared to go as far as Stuart did in emulating the Exi haircut. Astrid had backcombed her hair into a Rocker pompadour now and then, but it drove her crazy when it kept falling forward, and the brilliantine made spots erupt around her scalp-line. Gamely, Stuart submitted to a *Pilzen Kopf*, taking a photo of himself immediately after Astrid had finished snipping and combing. He thought it made him look like Klaus. Was that what she wanted? No, he couldn't visualize himself keeping it like that. Just wait till the lads saw.

Predictably, they fell about with laughter. He'd soon need a guide dog to stop him bumping into things. It was already down to his eyebrows. They kept on about it so much that, with a flash of a comb, Stuart betrayed Astrid by restoring his hair to its original grease-stiffened protrusion. However, before the night was out, it was back the way she liked it. After years of quiffing, it wouldn't cascade naturally into a *Pilzen Kopf* for months, but he had burnt his boats and pledged himself to Astrid more symbolically than a mere engagement ring ever could.

NOTES

1   *Disc*, 7 November 1970.
2   *The Beat Goes On*, February 1992.
3   *You'll Never Walk Alone*, G. Marsden and R. Coleman (Bloomsbury, 1993).
4   *Melody Maker*, 6 December 1962.
5   *Playboy*, 19 October 1964.
6   *Beatlefan*, vol. 1, no. 3, 1978.
7   *The Beat Goes On*, February 1991.
8   *Days In The Life*, ed. Jonathan Green (Heinemann, 1988).
9   'Mister Man' also surfaced as a character in John Lennon's 'Short Diversion on the Dubious Origins of Beatles' essay in *Merseybeat* in July 1961.
10 Featuring high-velocity guitarist Alvin Dean, later Alvin Lee of Ten Years After.
11 *Beatlefan*, vol. 3, no. 2, 1981.
12 Sleeve notes to *The Beatles Featuring Tony Sheridan* LP (Polydor 24-4504, 1971).
13 As shown in its use by Dr Fuchs' skiffle combo (see Chapter One) and in a 1958 recording by Ray Charles, 'My Bonnie' – like its B-side, 'The Saints' – is one of these semi-traditional ditties that never go away. In 1961, it was more in the air than popular. One of the authors remembers being forced to pipe it out in an

uncertain treble at a primary school concert in the same month that Tony
Sheridan and the Beatles taped it.

14 Who had a memorable punch-up with Tony Sheridan shortly after the dispute
between Stuart and Paul.

chapter seven

PEACE OF MIND

**'I believe to this day that he would eventually
have been thrown out as soon as the heavies
moved in and there was some sort of future'**

Rod Jones.

**'True lowliness of heart
Which takes the humbler part
And o'er its own shortcomings weeps with
loathing'**

Bianco da Siena (trans. R. F. Littledale)

After 'My Bonnie'/'The Saints' by Tony Sheridan and the Beat Brothers came out in Germany in June 1961, the final weeks at the Top Ten became very long, itching as the Beatles – or, at least, the four heard on it – were to get back to Liverpool to crow about their marvellous achievement. After all, the first time might be the only time. They had taken their impact in Hamburg and on Merseyside to its limit, but no one, Mrs Best included, knew how to advance to the step between consolidation of a provincial following and the threshold of the Big Time. Nobody even knew what that step entailed.

All five Beatles must have been aware that they were either the same age or older than those who had already Made It, like Billy Fury, all the Bobby goo-merchants, and Cliff Richard, who had been just seventeen when he first donned his pop star crown. Was it time to thrust aside adolescent follies and settle down to a steady job, a mortgage, maybe wedding bells?

On the surface, Stuart seemed furthest along the road to conventional adulthood with his fiancée and attempts to get on the ATD course. In his heart of hearts, all signposts pointed to Astrid and art, teaching it if he had to, but still he stuck it out with the Beatles, perpetually on the brink of fame and wealth. If he left, he might be kicking himself sooner or later. 'Which way are we going, boys?'

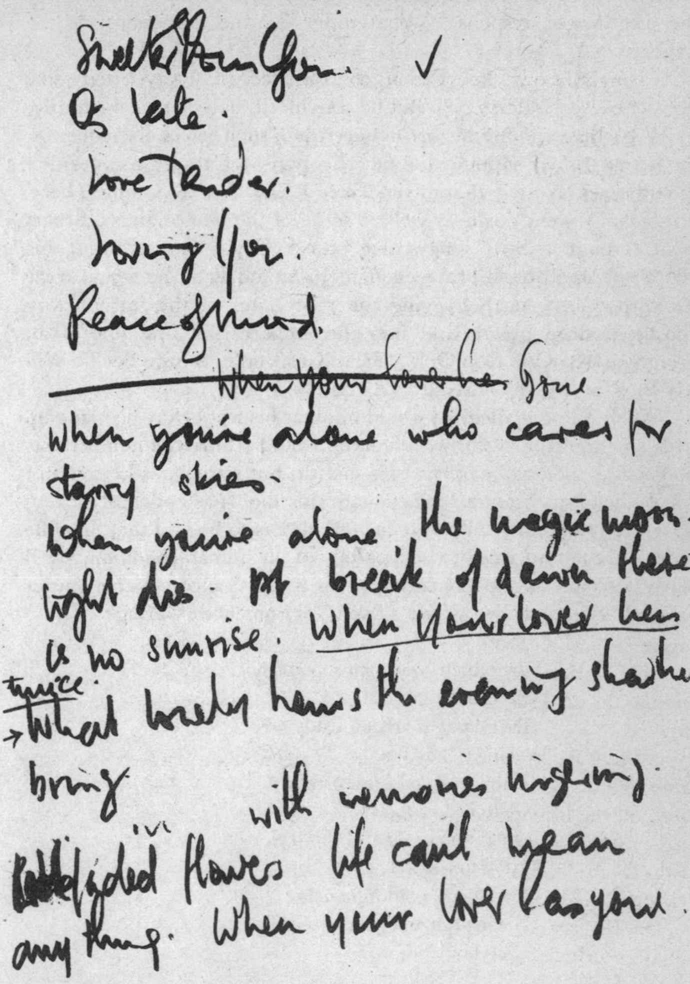

Shelter from You ✓
Of late.
Love Tender.
Loving You.
Peace of Mind.
~~When your love has~~ Gone.
When you're alone who cares for
starry skies.
When you're alone the magic moon-
light dies. At break of dawn there
is no sunrise. When your lover has
twice
What lonely hours the evening shadows
bring
with memories lingering
faded flowers life can't mean
any thing. When your lover has gone.

A page from Stuart's sketchbook with the first draft of one of his songs from around 1961

Lennon would chant when spirits were low. 'To the top, Johnny!' was the conditioned response. 'What top?' 'To the toppermost of the poppermost!'

Though his own observations contradicted this litany, Stuart, like everyone else, couldn't help but be convinced, however momentarily, by John's buoyant optimism. On the crest of such waves of confidence, the group risked slipping the odd Lennon-McCartney composition into the set. Noting that ravers like 'I Saw Her Standing There' occasionally went down as well as some of the non-originals, Stuart went through a brief songwriting phase. Coyly demonstrating his efforts to Astrid or, if brave enough, John and Paul, he would clear his throat and start chugging the root notes of the introductory chords; a deep breath and into the embarrassed first line of an evergreen like 'Ooh Ooh Ooh', 'Yeah 'Cos You're A Sure Bet To Win My Lips' or 'Peace Of Mind'.

When the song died, he would blink at his feet before glancing up with an enquiring eyebrow. Often, he would realize the number was no good as soon as he opened his mouth, but sometimes he couldn't comprehend his listeners' affectionate ridicule. If as guilelessly lovey-dovey as John and Paul's were in 1961, it has to be said that Sutcliffe lyrics were not intended to be a parody of the human condition. We'll leave this dark and lonely corner of his multi-faceted creative output with a few lines of 'Everybody's Ever Got Somebody Caring':

> Everybody's ever got somebody caring
> Everybody but me
> Everybody is getting ready
> Going steady but me
> I stay home on Friday night
> Go to bed at eight
> On Saturday night, I'm all alone
> I don't have a date
> Everybody's out romancing
> Having fun and going dancing
> Everybody but me.[1]

He defended his efforts as just a bit of fun. What had they to do with art, anyway? The first business of any pop group is merely to be liked, not 'appreciated' by highbrows, unless it could be seen as a form of Pop Art. After all, just as you'd lift a pigeonhole flap in a self-service canteen to get cheap, predictable food, you'd go to the Top Ten for cheap, predictable music.

On the boards there nowadays, Stuart was experiencing fatigue without stimulation as, hour after hour, he reacted instinctively to, say, the prelusive 'weeeeeell' that pitched him into another twelve-bar rocker and that changeless four-four off-beat on old Pete's snare drum: a backbeat not even a half-wit could lose. Some stretches up there went by as complete blurs like some run-of-the-mill job you'd done for years. Everything sounded the same, mere vibrations dang-ling in the air. Emitting an almost palpable aura of self-loathing, he would slouch on stage to unacknowledged applause, and glazed listlessness would set in by the end of the first chorus. His mind would drift off further than ever before from the task in hand. Astrid's presence in the audience would split his concentration, and he frequently abandoned the bass mid-set to go over and speak to her. Otherwise, he might be virtually stock-still for minutes on end, with a miserable expression on his face.

Bound to the Beatles by common ordeal one minute and jubilation the next, he could not yet make the speech to John that he agonized over in bed. Shunning rehearsals and venturing only rarely beyond the boundaries of his existing style, he was as good on bass as he was ever likely to get – which wasn't good enough. Paul had long ago run out of patience. 'We can't go on like this! The joke's over,' Gary-Bakewell-as-Paul protests in the *Backbeat* movie. 'Half the time, he doesn't show up. When he does, he's in the Fifth Dimension! I'm not having it!'

Almost all the cards were now on the table. While understanding that the group couldn't carry Stuart any more, Paul allowed his fits of pique to be treated as registered protests rather than ultimatums, intimidated as he was by John's ominous 'If he goes, I go'. Neverthe-less, as Stuart raised hardly a murmur when his solo vocal was axed, John put it to him that he didn't seem interested any more. Stuart conceded that he couldn't envisage being a Beatle for the rest of his life, but then he wouldn't imagine John at thirty still screaming 'Waaaaaah!' into a microphone to signal George's lead break in 'Dizzy Miss Lizzy'. What Stuart wasn't yet able to admit was that he was bracing himself to face the possible loss of his most loved friend to leap into the unknown. 'I haven't had the strength before,' he confided to Millie. 'Always, nervous energy was too completely scattered. I feel more prepared now.'

Lately, he had been head-to-head with Peter Markmann and the sculptor Detlev Birgfeld, pumping them for information and opinion as he groped for reasons why he should or shouldn't recommence his studies at Hamburg's State School of Art or 'Hamburg University' as he would represent it to his mother. He already knew what he had to do.

It was easier to achieve than he had first thought, accustomed as he was to Liverpool Art College's paperwork and tense weeks of waiting. Hamburg, apparently, didn't let talent slip through its fingers quite so unconcernedly. After a discussion amid the academic hush of the assistant director's office, the college kept its options open by allowing the prospective student to begin unofficially by attending sculpture classes three times a week.

In the meantime, Stuart had to find suitable testimonials and documentary evidence of his qualifications to show his interviewers. Millie mailed the second, and both Arthur Ballard and John Hart were pleased to supply the first. Ideally, Stuart would be exempted from a foundation course similar to the Intermediate year of Liverpool Art College, and be able to go directly into a Master Class in painting and sculpture supervised by visiting professor Eduardo Paolozzi, who was to have the final say about who he would and would not teach. He gave Stuart no indication either way when they first spoke on 26 May, shortly after the Beatles' Polydor session.

'It all depends on this Paolozzi man, but I might go to this college for a year, with a grant. Although it's vague yet, this can be a tremendous fillip to my reputation when I return to England. You can't imagine how important it will be for me to have a good reference from this man', so Millie was told by her son.

Eduardo who? Stuart echoed the widely held view that 'Paolozzi must be the most important artist in England or Europe'. Without knowing what he looked like, the renown of this founding father of British Pop Art might conjure up a vision of a slim-hipped demi-god in smock, beret and twirly moustachios. In truth, Paolozzi was not the most prepossessing of men. With frizzy black hair, a caterpillar moustache over thick lips and middle-aged spread, the shirtsleeved thirty-seven-year-old was no Adonis.

Despite the name, Eduardo Paolozzi, like Stuart, had been born in Edinburgh, and was as British as Al Capone was American. Though he became better known as a sculptor, in 1961 Paolozzi was nearly as famous for his proto-Pop screen prints and surreal collages. These dated from his first major exhibition in London fourteen years earlier. Incorporating cut-outs of bulbous automobiles, 'cocktail cherry' coat hooks, monolithic refrigerators and myriad other objects from the beginnings of mass-production, these had period charm – and that is the problem with topical art: what becomes of it when it's no longer topical or the topic gets tedious? Paolozzi's answer was mentally to erase his two-dimensional past and rise anew as a sculptor, albeit one still fixated with the symbolism of popular culture, and the amalgamation of scientific and artistic imagery. In 1956, he stole the show at the 'This Is Tomorrow' exhibition at the White-chapel Art Gallery, London. Of all the elements that fused to produce Pop Art, this showing was among the most inspirational – and it certainly accelerated Paolozzi's brooding climb to international acclaim.

By the turn of the decade, he was regarded as an heir to Arp, Tzara, Braque, Bacon and other gurus of contemporary art. As such, he was a sought-after guest lecturer and tutor at art colleges all over Europe and North America, and, from 1960 to 1962, he illuminated Hamburg's Staatliche Hochschule whenever he was not called away to, say, receive an award at the American Exhibition in Chicago or host a retrospective in Oslo.

Both these events took place during Stuart Sutcliffe's time under Paolozzi because, fortunately for Stuart, his long-cherished scheme to 'join the club again – the old jeans and sweater gang' was realized at last, and he entered a Master Class of hand-picked and mostly mature students 'from all over the school and all over the world . . . all quite mad'. Sponsored by Paolozzi, who had been intrigued by him, Stuart discovered that 'It's quite easy for a foreigner to get a grant at this college', though not a particularly generous one, despite what he had implied to his mother. More accurate was the declaration that he was starting 'not from the beginning, but perhaps I've slipped back a bit (psychologically)'.

Even before the official beginning of the course, he was experimenting with sculpture, and would continue to do so under Paolozzi, who delegated day-to-day instruction to head of department Gustav Seitz while he concentrated on specific projects and educational visits.

Paolozzi had selected for 'intelligence as well as talent – twelve students. There was one girl who dropped out. We worked together the twelve of us, and we did all sorts of things, like go to the shipyards, and that was quite popular. We all worked in a room, and it used to be from eight in the morning to eight at night and then we'd go to the cinema.'

Millie Sutcliffe would 'remember Stuart writing how impressed he was with Paolozzi. The man was so brimful with ideas, so vibrant, that Stuart was at a loss to describe his appreciation of how this man could inspire anybody'.[2] Among Stuart's Hamburg paintings was one that Ken Horton saw 'that looks almost like a Paolozzi sculpture – like machine shapes. If you can imagine a Paolozzi sculpture that has been pressed on to some wet paint or on to some Plasticine, then taken off, the painting looked like that: a flat version of a Paolozzi sculpture. He was influenced while still being highly original.'

This was less sycophancy on Stuart's part than perhaps a demonstration to himself that he hadn't lost his Prescot Grammar knack for imitating any artistic style. Nevertheless, there was inherent pride in his familiarity with the Great Paolozzi – even if Eduardo the person was not always particularly agreeable. Although he, too, was an ex-serviceman, he was no easy-going Arthur Ballard who didn't mind being upstaged by his pupils or even direct artistic rivalry. Some found him charming but to others, Paolozzi came across as a self-obsessed, vinegary man beneath the frightening intellect. The pressure dropped when he swept out of the room.

It could be said that Paolozzi was a living example of Nicholas Horsfield's argument against 'everybody who is any good' becoming a teacher. For such people, an obligation to impart knowledge to others divorces them part of the time from truer vocational purpose. Therefore, some are inclined to show an involuntary disinterest in their charges unless, perhaps, ideas that crop up during tutorials can be incorporated into their own body of work. Possibly out of place in a student-centred environment, Paolozzi proved nowhere near as approachable or helpful as Ballard had been. 'There is no kind of criticism, only a general acknowledgement of one's presence,' wrote Stuart, trying to see the positive aspects. 'This is very confusing at first, even frustrating, but eventually this becomes necessary to one's peace of mind.' In a telling sentence from a later letter home, he mentioned that 'Paolozzi is back in England again, and the rest of the class retired to lick their wounds.'

Of the sculpture department, he would boast that 'some of the things being done here would shock Ballard and the Liverpool College'. However much he wanted it to be, the Staatliche Hochschule was not as lively or as open-minded as Liverpool Art College. 'Even now, I haven't been able to assess the standard,' he wrote. 'It is high but not very original – not so high as the Slade or the Royal College.' In the Master Class, 'there is only two or three of us who really work'.

As Stuart was one of them, Paolozzi's termly reports were golden: 'One of my best students. He is working very hard and with high intelligence.' Later, when both he and Stuart were gone from Hamburg, Paolozzi would praise his former student as 'a very perceptive and sensitive person, and very restless. I think that one could almost use that appalling phrase "child of our time". He was always slightly ahead of the rest of the class. Whatever he did, he'd take things a little bit further than anyone else. We used to get a lot of big cans sent down from the canteen, for instance, and the students would mess about with them any way they liked. Stuart would always be the most imaginative, the most daring. He had brains, and he wasn't inhibited.'

Praise indeed – but Paolozzi might have been in a particular mellow mood just then. Later, he would be far less charitable as he lambasted Stuart's domestic circumstance: 'Unlike his contemporaries, he seemed to be well off because of his girlfriend, much more affluent. Whereas they were living in rooms, he was living in a kind of ritzy apartment – which he seemed to think was his divine right.' In Paolozzi's opinion, 'In my period, he wasn't interested in learning anything. He just wanted to do his own thing.'

Maybe Sutcliffe considered that the encouragement and analytical feedback he received when Paolozzi could spare the time were too meagre to leave him with much choice. At first, he may have resented it, but the appeal of being left to his own devices yielded a renaissance in Stuart Sutcliffe whose most enduring work lay ahead of him. He still preferred not to have anyone looking over his shoulder when he was at the easel. Sighted less and less at the Hochschule, he flowered like an exotic hothouse bloom in an attic studio at the Kirchherrs. Painting once more, he found that the lay-off had wrought in him a sharper technical assurance and a more subtle sense of colour: 'All of it is far superior to what I would have done one year ago.' As to substance, his Hamburg output was so removed overall from his Liverpool work that, to the superficial eye, it could be mistaken for that of an entirely different artist.

Like the latter-day de Staël in reverse, Sutcliffe edged his art far, far away from straightforward depiction, though he would always be wary about being classified as either rigidly figurative *or* abstract. He assured Millie that 'my pictures are still quite conventional in so far as they are two-dimensional. I have only explored colour and shape a little further. There is so much further to push them.' Nevertheless, almost from the onset, there was little that was immediately recognizable or even derived from natural appearance. Within the fragmented, palette-knifed grids, Stuart flew beyond materiality to an open-ended personal universe of squiggles, scratches and circles requiring intense scrutiny to decipher the veiled allusions and messages. The prosaic, Ballard-like titles gave no clues whatsoever: *Hamburg Painting, Hamburg Painting No. 2, Green and Yellow Hamburg Painting*, and so forth. 'You can always invent titles,' commented Paolozzi. 'That often happens when an artist dies. Degas never had titles.'

Adrian Henri would describe Sutcliffe's astounding Hamburg period as 'a synthesis of Parisian abstraction, the dynamic colour field freedom of the New York School'.[3] You could cite further influences – Wols, de Kooning, Michaux, de Staël, Appel. You could also compare his paintings to psychologists' ink blots, or bitch – as Paolozzi did – that 'I can do thousands in a week because there's no upside-down.' Nevertheless, tempering imagination with economy, Sutcliffe knew when to let well alone and the results were still as attractive aesthetically as intellectually.

'I've been painting and drawing on very large paper, and I've made many collages, no sculpture for a long time,' he said in a letter to Sefton Park. 'What I'm really interested in is painted sculpture, but this means complete absorption and concentration, something which needs a great deal of concentrated work for long periods, complete sacrifice of a lot of ideals.' He was to set aside a few hours for painted sculpture, but there was also an abundance of other two-dimensional offerings. As well as collages, generally characterized by German newsprint, there were chalk colourings, lithographs, and monotypes. Especially pleasing were his investigative blendings of two or more such disciplines as exemplified by a blue-black monotype with collage, *Silver Collage*, that struck John Willett as 'austere as the hoar frost of a winter dawn'.[4]

Painting, however, remained the principal concern. His mother would learn that 'I wish to buy stretchers as I'm painting on canvas again. I've just completed four big ones, 4 ft. x 3 ft. I think they're quite good. I bought quite a lot of canvas and paints last week, and I'm bashing away.' He wasn't kidding. As if making up for lost time, he was filling canvases as if there was no tomorrow, losing himself in the action of painting just as a musician on stage can be transported by what he is playing. Sometimes, Astrid and Nielsa had to drag him to bed as he worked furiously away while milk-floats hissed down Eimsbutteler Strasse. His health was already suffering even without these long and feverish hours before the canvas.

While conceding that Stuart was 'very gifted and very intelligent', Paolozzi's first report mentioned too, that his studies had been interrupted by absences of up to three weeks. As well as a preference for his own space, as opposed to the college's, Stuart had been feeling off-colour for some time. Those closest to him had noticed with more than a little concern his frequently ghastly pallor and a habit of half closing his eyes as if in pain. He had been seen sitting pathetically in the dressing room or at a secluded table in the Top Ten with fingers pressed against his temples, or lost in melancholy thoughts. Seeming to snap out of it, he would insist that there wasn't anything seriously the matter, though nausea, dizzy spells, insomnia, increasing pains in his head, chronic indigestion and bouts of depression were plaguing him persistently. He couldn't say specifically where it hurt most; it wasn't localized but seemed to hover all over.

Neither a hypochondriac nor a malingerer by nature, Stuart searched for plausible causes of this general malaise, annotating them in his constant stream of letters home. The headaches were because his spectacles were too strong. Either that or 'It's not too cold outside, but in this weather, I always get headaches.' Next, it was 'The glands in my neck are all wrong. This causes me to be moody and neurotic.'

He blamed everything but what seemed to everyone else the most obvious reason. Long periods of wakefulness in bed might have been rooted genuinely in the problem of where his priorities – and loyalties – now lay. The day wasn't long enough for a double life as student and Beatle.

It went beyond just lateness and skimped essays with their sub-flavour of irritability and temper tantrums. After winding down at the Top Ten, he would return to the attic and, unless Astrid and her mother intervened, paint through till daylight with either records in the background or Radio Luxembourg until it signed off for the night. If he was not frothing over with amphetamines, he might then fit in a few hours' rest. If he was expected at college that morning, more often than not he would either oversleep or turn up for class with glassy eyes.

'This form of life would be a terrific strain on the strongest' was Paolozzi's truism – and, inevitably, both ends of the candle burnt to the middle. With both his art and future happiness with Astrid at stake, Stuart went the distance with the Beatles for the last time one Top Ten night in mid-June 1961. They let him sing 'Love Me Tender' which shimmered over a sea of bobbing heads. The split-second silence at the end was splintered by a barrage of applause, and George's fluffed guitar intro to Chuck Berry's 'Carol'. Onlookers and group meshed as the jigging crowd assumed the role of rhythm section, stamping and clapping on the second and fourth beats of the bar, right through to the big finish with 'Twist and Shout'. While its final major sixth yet resounded, Stuart Sutcliffe grinned, waved and vanished into the wings.

As cigarettes were lit and bottle tops popped afterwards, the prevalent feeling was of release. An unsettled chapter in the respective careers of Stuart and the group had just ended.

The Beatles did not replace him, opting instead for the simpler solution of transferring McCartney permanently to bass. The two now got on well enough for Stuart to lend him his own bass as parting goodwill gesture.

After Klaus Voorman started borrowing Stuart's Hofner President too, Paul invested in a bass guitar of his own. This did not, however, signify any severing of a last link. Whatever bad feeling there had been between Paul and Stuart seemed to evaporate, and an open invitation was issued to the former member to sit in with the Beatles if ever nostalgia for the old days overwhelmed him.

'I believe to this day that he would eventually have been thrown out,' said Rod Jones expressing a commonly held view, 'as soon as the heavies moved in and there was some sort of future. I'm actually surprised that he didn't go before. He couldn't do it, but it was probably the fact that he was a nice fellow, a very amenable guy and virtually in a sense a little bit of a James Dean, although small.'

Whether he fell before he was pushed or not was of less concern to Stuart than maintaining his old affinity with John, the subject of two recent impressionistic portraits. Their finely balanced scale of conflicting emotions – hurt, anger, mutual need and dependence – during these desperate weeks is encapsulated in a *Backbeat* scene in which the wise-cracking pair are so nearly robbed of speech that they are not even able to revile each other in their customary matey way.

Having said it at last, Stuart had read the omen of assault in John's eyes, but if the latter's pent-up rage ever overflowed into violence against Stuart, it subsided and the old brusque tenderness returned. Somehow, they would be together again one day; Stuart might even rejoin the Beatles. John, at least, did not regard this eventuality as unlikely – even if everybody else did.

Because there wasn't even an implied rejection of Sutcliffe by Lennon, the other Beatles continued in their various ways to be frankly jealous of the vice-like grip Stuart and John still had on each other, even when separated by both the footlights and the North Sea. Indeed, there has been speculation that Lennon came close to carrying out his oft-repeated 'If he goes, I go' warning so that he could join Stuart at the Hochschule – though it seems unlikely that Paolozzi would have accepted, let alone tolerated, John in the Master Class.

In the schools, offices and factories of Britain today, how many are the middle-aged employees who, as teenagers, quit pop groups that, in the wake of the Beatles, next became famous and sometimes rich? Perhaps still bitter and twisted about missing the fun are those such as solicitor Jim Spencer, ex-Dave Clark Five saxophonist; guitarist B. D. Smith who left what became the Yardbirds for a career in the civil service, and bass guitarist Paul Arnold whose onstage pumping of 'Peggy Sue' with one condescending hand in his pocket hastened his exit from the Zombies.

Without Stuart, the Beatles now exemplified the two guitars-bass-drums archetype of what would go down in cultural history as 1963's Merseybeat explosion. This would have been unimaginable two years earlier with customer complaints on the Reeperbahn that if you'd heard one Liverpool band, you'd heard 'em all. It also transpired that Bert Kaempfert had wanted Tony Sheridan to have an orchestral backwash on 'My Bonnie', but budgetary restrictions had obliged him to search out a bargain-bin 'Beat Gruppa' instead.

The Shadows would rule 1962's spring charts in Europe with 'Wonderful Land', and their reliance on massed violins upheld record industry bigwigs' suppositions that outfits with electric guitars were *passé*. Such vocal units as there were in the charts – the King Brothers, the Kaye Sisters, the Springfields, the Viscounts and precious few others – were unlikely to be caught titillating Reeperbahn fancies with their rehearsed patter, comedy routines and polished close-harmonies. Since groups were unfashionable, their records were viewed as small time in comparison with more substantial earnings in variety work.

Stuart, therefore, felt little regret about his decision. Neither did Astrid, according to a letter to her prospective parents-in-law, expressing her happiness that Stuart was not playing with the Beatles any more because 'I think this has something to do with his nerves.' The group had been a minor set-back in his artistic career, though without them, he and Astrid would never have met. A secret relief at returning to the fold from the shabbiest nook of showbusiness imaginable betrayed itself most patently in Stuart's short haircut – 'almost respectable,' he told Pauline ruefully, 'I think I must be growing up – anyway, long hair definitely isn't in in Germany.'

He hadn't quite forsaken the old life, however. His twenty-first birthday, for example, was celebrated in the Top Ten. The evening passed happily enough, bar some unpleasantness that dimly echoed the incident during the Beatles' last night at the Kaiserkeller. It blew up over the presentation of a bunch of roses by his Exi friends. 'It was a gesture we considered chic,' sighed Jürgen Vollmer, 'just a sign of admiration, nothing more, but Astrid was furious, because she didn't want anyone to know it was Stuart's birthday. I had actually put the roses behind the piano, but after she and I had the dispute over my gift, I went behind the piano and destroyed them. Then John got a little nasty as he sometimes could. He said they hadn't been all my roses because he'd bought some too – so I told him, very arrogantly, that I'd only destroyed my bouquet.'

With Astrid gripping his arm, Stuart was still drawn back to the club most nights until the Beatles' contract expired. Occasionally, he mounted the stage for a blow with them again – and, later, with other visiting groups he knew. Affirming the respect held locally for ex-Beatles, a German outfit who had lost their bass player to Tony Sheridan offered Stuart the vacancy. For a long second, the now-dormant rock 'n' roller in Stuart peeped out, and he was tempted, but, as he explained to his younger sister, 'I was, however, completely discouraged by Astrid and her mother who were 100% against my playing. Actually, it was quite unrealistic to have considered it, but for a few moments, I allowed myself the luxury of being a "Rocker". I actually went along to see the band last night. Unfortunately, they play six nights a week which was much too much. That's that!'

He wouldn't have been able to stand the pace with his old group either. 'They improved when Stuart left,' noticed the Remo Four's Don Andrew, 'but it was a long time before I appreciated what they were doing.'[5] There were, however, a multitude of Merseyside music lovers several steps ahead of Don. Almost fully mobilized now, the Beatles were at the top of the first division of Merseyside popularity, having won the first readers' poll in Bill Harry's new fortnightly journal *Merseybeat*.

As a testimony to the depth and cohesion of regional pop, the first edition had sold out within a day, such was the strength of demand for its venue information, news coverage and irregular features such as John Lennon's Goonish 'Beatcomber' column. Rapidly recurring dates throughout the region compensated for *Merseybeat*'s main headline demand, 'London, Take A Look Up North'[6] being yet unheeded.

There were signs, however, that certain groups were breaking loose from the bonds of Merseyside. The Seniors had landed a prestigious residency at an Essex palais, Twist At The Top, which, being near the heart of the UK music business, led to a Fontana recording contract, while the Remo Four had broken into the US air base circuit. A feather in Rory Storm's cap was spending a sunnier spring than most Liverpudlians with his combo's first season in a Spanish club. Then living in England, Gene Vincent was pressing Gerry and the Pacemakers to accompany him on a tour of Israel.

The Beatles had also moved up a rung or two in their acquisition of a manager in Brian Epstein, director and sales manager of a central Liverpool department store that contained what could be justifiably advertised in *Merseybeat* as 'The Finest Record Selection in the North'.

Backbeat

As Larry Parnes would have advised him, Brian's first task was to transform the four into 'entertainers'. They had to become what a respectable London agent or record mogul in those naïve times expected a good pop group to be. The Germans have a word for it: *verharmlosen*, which in a free translation, means to render harmless.

Scuttling about like a mother hen, he compelled his new clients to wear the stylish but not too way-out uniform suits he had bought for them rather than the Hamburg leathers. Playing to a fixed programme, punctuality and back-projection were all-important. Stage patter must not include cursing or attempts to pull front-row girls. They weren't to eat or smoke on the boards any more. John was not to sing 'Oh me, oh mv, I've got infection' to rhyme with 'cast an eye in her direction' in 'Ain't She Sweet'. It wasn't nice. The enforcement of this transformation met with tetchy shows of resistance but these lessened after Mr Epstein's clout as a major retailer impelled Decca to schedule a recording test for the Beatles on New Year's Day 1962.

Three of the four had done some structural tampering on their own account. John and Paul had blown a coming-of-age birthday cheque from John's well-to-do Aunt Elizabeth on a fortnight in Paris. As Stuart had informed them in a recent letter, Jürgen was going to be there too. After getting him to try and cut their hair like Stuart's, the two chief Beatles came back with *Pilzen Kopfs* that they wore boldly round Liverpool. Pete didn't bother, but George nerved himself to do likewise.

This adoption of a hairstyle that had once caused howls of derision when he had pioneered it may have raised a cynical smile at Eimsbutteler Strasse when Stuart learned of it in one of John's letters. Raw information like this, however, was dispensed with quickly in correspondence that dwelt at length upon more esoteric issues in which John assumed the role of 'John the Baptist', and Stuart that of 'Jesus Christ'. A substantial proportion of their exchanges under these pseudonyms were in glum existentialist vein about how pointless everything was. The most oft-quoted and evocative lines from these letters came to be John's poetic

> I can't remember anything without a sadness
> So deep that it hardly becomes known to me
> So deep that its tears leave me a spectator of my own stupidity.

Peace Of Mind

Picking these oblique lyrics for meaning, they are reminiscent of 'True lowliness of heart/Which takes the humbler part/And o'er its own shortcomings weeps with loathing' from 'Come Down O Love Divine', a Whitsuntide hymn with which both former choirboys would have been familiar.

Inspired perhaps by these dialogues, Stuart began a novel entitled *Spotlight on Johnny*. Its two main characters were very much based on himself ('Nhoke') and John. 'With John, it was different,' he wrote. 'As I said, he was unlucky. Given the breaks that other people had, he would have been all right. As it was, he brooded, trying to find the answer. He was born old. He'd dried up before his time. He wilted because he knew that someday, he would wilt anyway.'

The real John's mutterings were motivated by the Beatles' lack of success beyond the Liverpool-Hamburg treadmill against Stuart's apparently brighter outlook. George continued to write to Stuart, too, sometimes sending money for more copies of the Sheridan single and the associated extended-play (EP) disc, 'My Bonnie', released in September.[7] Who could say whether this wasn't to be the ceiling of their career, Decca or no Decca? This pop lark was too much of a lottery.

Such pessimism helped dispel Stuart's lingering doubts that he was better off out of it. Showbiz was a silly profession, anyway. All the same, he missed the weekly pay packet from the Top Ten. Though he had sold a few drawings (including two to Astrid's boss) since leaving the group, he was wondering whether or not he needed to supplement his grant either by working one night a week in a newspaper factory as other students did, or taking full-time employ-ment for the summer vacation. That such a choice was even con-sidered contradicts Paolozzi's 'he seemed to be well off, much more affluent', but Stuart concluded eventually that 'to work more is lunacy, particularly as it's so nerve-wracking and inclined to unbal-ance the thought-process'.

Between pictures, he was often at Astrid's elbow in her dark-room, supposedly assisting, 'or rather Astrid worked and I grew tired looking on'. Facing the real world, she now regarded photography as a means to keep the wolf from the door, just like any other occupation. As the breadwinner, she seemed almost determinedly ordinary, 'particularly as she isn't interested in the creative side of her job,' said Stuart.

Backbeat

She was too busy to accompany him on a visit with Klaus to Berlin: 'a very strange city, enormously big and completely inaccessible. I kept out of danger though. Astrid was very worried and only let me go on the vow that I didn't go into East Berlin – which I didn't.' On his return, he and she celebrated the first anniversary of their engagement, not surrounded by a chuckling throng in the Top Ten, but with a quiet meal in a Chinese restaurant. Frau Kirchherr came too.

He seemed nearly as content as his letters home indicated. If he had been a fictionalized character in a happy-ending novel, perhaps the Stuart Sutcliffe saga would have ended there. He could marry Astrid and ease into a prosperous livelihood as a professional artist with little else to worry about, year in, year out. Alternatively, he might become more fêted than Paolozzi, featuring in quality newspapers and on the fronts of Sunday supplements, his works acclaimed as masterpieces.

'Art is a long word which can be stretched' was a Paolozzi maxim that Stuart had practised since grammar school, and it's possible that he would have made a mark in a totally unexpected creative genre – developing his sporadic literary ideas, perhaps, or dipping his toe into a completely new field like *musique concrète* or kinetics. Intimations of one feasible direction were evident in a letter to Pauline:

Yes! Tomorrow comes Paolozzi, and Tuesday, we go once more to this ship-breakers yard we visited last semester.[8] I will have with me a film camera I borrowed off Theo, Astrid's cousin. I'm very quickly trying to learn the technique as I'm enthralled by the possibilities but it's so expensive. He has many films including some of Astrid from a few years ago, very sweet as you can imagine. I'll have to take advantage of the few days I'll have it. I'll probably tire of it all the more quickly because of the complete inaccessibility of all the equipment required.

He did not weary of moving pictures as quickly as he first expected. While there would be no Sutcliffe equivalent of *Un Chien Andalou*, 'I made a film last week when I was at the ship-breaking yard, and I have really caught a feeling for filming; the desire, that is. I made another today and wish to make a long film accompanied by a tape recording.'

Peace Of Mind

The ambitious *Spotlight On Johnny*, likewise, would never be finished – at least, not until the author's health improved. Describing himself in the third person as 'Nhoke', Stuart disclosed that 'he was obviously suffering from dizziness and headaches. When he stood up, he complained of a blackout and tremendous headaches.' The release from night upon night onstage had brought some alleviation of his ailments as sleep became less of a luxury. For a time, he was calm while sleeping, his breathing regular, but, as the symptoms flared up again, his brow would knit and he would look dark and troubled. He surfaced from disturbing dreams with heartburn that a glass of milk might neutralize until the next time. Weight loss was noticeable even in photographs he sent home, and after blacking out on three occasions, once at college, he could make no more excuses that, physically and organically, there was 'overall absolutely nothing dangerous'. A family friend of the Kirchherrs, Peter Hommelhoff, who also happened to be Director of Medicine at a Hamburg hospital, had examined Stuart in late June, and 'said I am a nervous wreck. In his whole experience, he has never seen anyone like me and can't believe it.' X-rays, barium meals, blood samples and other checks winkled out digestive and respiratory problems. Dr Hommelhoff shook his head at the way of life that, thankfully, his patient had now renounced. Stuart's present poor state was, he said, the legacy of too much alcohol, tobacco – and Preludin.

Advisedly, Stuart did not refer to the latter indulgence when outlining the doctor's diagnosis and remedy to Millie: 'I have a shadow on the entrance to my lungs. It is not TB or cancer, and will be gone in a few months providing I do what the doctor tells me' – and later, 'I have gastrittis [*sic*]. What that means is that the lining of my stomach is inflamed and swollen. Also, there is not enough acid in my stomach to digest my food properly. This is why I always had bad heartburn. Now I'm on a diet of special foods. I have tablets and do exercises every morning. I must not smoke or drink alcohol, etc. My appendix must come out – not immediately but in the next few months.'

As he couldn't afford to have it done in Germany, Stuart assumed that it would be a mere formality for his mother to arrange with the National Health Service an admission to a Liverpool hospital for early September when he planned to come over. However, it was not permissible for him to be cut with a British scalpel on the strength of foreign X-rays after he and Astrid arrived towards the end of August with these and a file of correlated notes.

Since March, the family had moved yet again, this time to 37 Aigburth Drive, a road that circled the review ground of Sefton Park. The upkeep of this more spacious flat worried Stuart who, both without a 'proper job' and about to marry, could not contribute. Also, as he was presumed to have 'left home', he no longer had a room with the family and 'couldn't feel any emotion for that big place, and my mummy looked so little and helpless'.

It was due to a quarrel with his mother that he and Astrid stayed for a shorter time than anticipated. Bitterly disappointed because Millie hadn't been able to fix up the appendix operation, Stuart infuriated her by refusing to attend some out-patient appointments, and provoking pointless arguments during those he did. When a consultant from Sefton General Hospital called at Aigburth Drive, Stuart took an instant dislike to him and, with insulting 'politeness', asked him to leave.

Such medical investigations by Sefton General's finest turned up not a single pathological disorder. One disdainful physician dismissed the belligerent youth's afflictions as nervous in origin, and aggravated by a combination of 'artistic temperament' and an over-attached parent. He ought to pull himself together, do a hard day's graft for a change. 'Needless to say, I am very angry with that quack,' Stuart wrote drily from Hamburg where he returned feeling worse than ever.

'Whether staying in Britain would have helped his medical condition or not,' surmised Nicholas Horsfield, 'I think the Sutcliffe family were saying to me that the British Health Service was monstrous, took nothing seriously at all.'

Back in Altona, Stuart resumed a regime of sedatives, bland food, a nap after lunch and – with astounding ease – abstention from all the old Freiheit vices. The dam, however, was already in the first stages of bursting. When not suffering for his art in the attic, he would lie down, lethargically and fully dressed, on the bed. Strangely old at twenty-one, his depressions weren't always clinical these days. Any young man with afflictions that were likely to extinguish his chosen career might well be depressed.

He often wondered why the hell he was there in the first place. Not surprisingly, there was less lust in him now, though this did not mean any tailing off in his affection for Astrid. She was now chained to office hours in a studio in the city centre, out of the house by 7.30 a.m. to be swallowed up in traffic. Testy with the evening rush-hour, she got home just before six. After she had wound down, she functioned less like a passionate lover than a medical orderly with attentive fondnesses.

Missing England as his mother used to miss Scotland, he took to tuning into the Home Service on Sunday at noon for *Two-Way Family Favourites* followed by *The Billy Cotton Band Show* and *The Navy Lark* with their soothing connotations of Yorkshire pudding, Bird's custard and armchair languor. He began firing off even more letters to Liverpool. These he filled mostly with life's small change: the weather (for example, 'every day has been quite cold this last week, which has meant great discomfort etc. The little rivers had special dirty pigeons on their big broken ice floes. Walking was very difficult'); requests for a John Moores Exhibition catalogue and some old clothes to wear for painting; a trip to the ballet to see this Rudolf Nureyev everyone's talking about ('sensational'), and a series of Chaplin films to be shown at the university's lecture theatre. There were also ruminations on the news he had read in the *Daily Express*, bought a day late from Hauptbahnhof station. Then a broadsheet, the *Express* did not label a buyer politically as much as it would later. Nevertheless, Stuart would comment that, 'It's getting worse, particularly on its foreign policy – to my mind completely unrealistic and very inhibited by conservatism. On their treatment of "The German Question", they're quite indecent.'

Living in the Federal Republic for over a year affected not only his perspective on the world, but also his vocabulary, sentence structure, and grammar. Now and then, for example, he began a common noun with a capital letter. He had picked up a smattering of German, though 'I still can't speak very good but I'm learning a bit more quickly now.'

He was only one of many British rock 'n' rollers to become virtually resident in Hamburg. As well as Tony Sheridan, members of Kingsize Taylor's Dominoes (including Kingsize himself) all married German girls as they took the Fatherland for every Deutschmark they could get. Both the Big Three's Adrian Barber and Terry Crowe, singer with Weybridge's Nashville Teens, had opted for secure jobs in St Pauli clubs instead of wasting a lifetime back in Britain trying to be stars.

Rather than modestly coming into their own in a distant land, the Beatles had become a fixture at the Cavern with music as competent as anything in the charts, but played with guts. All kinds of future worthies, from Liverpool XI striker Tommy Smith to Tory Minister Edwina Currie would proudly recall how they had been among the masses jammed in the suffocating blackness. As a regular attender too, Pauline Sutcliffe was pressed to 'tell us a bit about the Cavern' by her brother who also chastised her and Joyce for the lateness of their replies to his letters ('I have always been in a hurry about things, and never got to know you very well'), although Millie wrote often enough to both him and Astrid. Once, she amazed them by remembering Frau Kirchherr's birthday with a fraternal greetings card, for, like John, Mrs Sutcliffe seemed to have accepted Nielsa's daughter as the one for her Stuart. His habit of interrupting sentences with cooings about Astrid were considered too grown-up for Pauline, who was more appreciative of an advance copy of 'My Bonnie' – even if 'not as good as it could have been' – like the one Bob Wooler was plugging relentlessly down the Cavern.

If Pauline was delighted to impress her friends with Stuart's vinyl presents, and his connection with local heroes, the Beatles, nineteen-year-old Joyce was perplexed by his reaction to the announcement of her engagement to a naval officer well known to (and approved by) her father. Why was Stuart so upset about it?

> You must think so carefully, Joyce [he urged]. Please, please know exactly what is important to you, exactly what marriage will mean to you, the break from your home. Love is very primitive, Joyce, the cloaks and guises under which it shelters are very strange and confusing. Joyce, I felt a pang of deep pain when my mother told me you were engaged. I felt I understood the expression 'blood is thicker than water'. I was very shocked and frightened for you, Don't let Pride lead you on – or boredom!
>
> Think of what it's like leaving home. I feel very frightened for my mother and father in that big flat – so much money, so dangerous and insecure. Perhaps your emotions flooded up with Astrid and me because I suppose we must have represented a very romantic figure.

Was there trouble in his Teutonic paradise? Or was it some oblique insecurity about the family unit disintegrating? After coming back into line after his 'wilderness' period as a Beatle, he was muddled about whether his position as surrogate father still stood, especially as Charles, recovering from a recent heart attack, was approaching retirement and would be more at home than he ever had been in Huyton during the war.

Maybe Stuart was losing his marbles. His insistence that 'I'm very much better now, not nearly so nervous or thin' was contradicted by an inclination to flit too fitfully from topic to vaguely connected topic. And what did he mean by 'you must forgive me for not writing very good letters. It's very difficult now because I'm never alone for long enough'? Moreover, his handwriting was deteriorating to near-illegibility.

Occasionally, his script would revert to its former clarity, as when he spoke of a possible journey to Paris with Astrid in April ('and I want to take many pictures with me to try and get an exhibition'). Perhaps debating inwardly what he would wear for the cover photograph in the accompanying booklet, Stuart wrote also to Allan Williams requesting him to arrange an exhibition at the Jac for September – a bit of a cheek, considering who had been the mouthpiece when the Beatles had thrust Williams aside.

For all these proposed small beginnings, he seemed jaded with the state of present-day art. After perusing the glossy catalogue that had wended its dutiful way over from Aigburth Drive, he wrote, 'My impression of the John Moores is that it is crap. I don't know what's happening to painting. Here in Germany, it's the same. They all paint good but very unoriginal.' Close behind came another letter lamenting that 'There is nothing intellectually stimulating here at the moment. I feel in a bit of a torpor, well and truly dumb.'

It was all dispiritingly familiar. As it had been at Liverpool Art College, Stuart's impending ascent to even Ballard-sized fame was blocked by a force-field of parochialism, paralleling that of the Beatles in the pop world, except that now he had the additional burden of failing health. The 'period of worry and struggle if he wants to go into deep water' that he had once advocated appeared interminable. How do you get up to the next level? How do you stay there? Ballard had got there but had lost his grip and fallen back on teaching – and what was Paolozzi doing in Hamburg? Why not cut out the 'fame' phase and proceed directly to the inevitable? As a college tutor with the safety net of a fixed salary, you'd be better placed to make headway as an artist.

If this was the way ahead, then he couldn't stay in Germany as he hadn't sufficient grasp of the language either to teach or be taught how to teach. Now that the ordeal of the ATD rejection had faded, he sent off for details and an application form from the clearing house at Leicester College of Art administrative centre for graduate art teacher training courses. If there was any justice in the world, Paolozzi's complimentary reports would guide him back to Straightsville in September 1962.

This was almost a cheering thought as another Christmas in Hamburg loomed. Though his father was home, Stuart's funds were too low for the fare to Liverpool, although he might manage a week or two after the next grant cheque landed on the Kirchherrs' doormat in the New Year.

Back in the Master Class in late January, he collapsed in a convulsive seizure of shuddering gasps and cold sweat, and Astrid was summoned from work to drive him home. He was confined to bed to await Dr Hommelhoff who, once again, could not point a finger at any particular medical condition. Fräulein Kirchherr's fiancé ought to slow down, relax a little and let time do the rest. Hommelhoff also recommended courses of massage and 'hydrotherapy' at the local hospital. Both he and his colleagues there considered the young Englishman to be very sick indeed. 'Our doctor was very angry,' wrote Astrid to Mrs Sutcliffe, 'when I told him that the English doctors are so stupid and haven't taken Stuart's appendix out . . .' She also mentioned one doctor's prediction of recovery 'in about seven months'. About to undergo exploratory surgery, Millie herself was none too hale. Maybe it was something hereditary, thought Stuart.

The new treatments slowed but did not arrest the progress of whatever was wrong with him. Returning to Merseyside in February, the change in him shocked those who had last seen him as a Beatle. He had an air about him that would haunt them for years. Emaciated and corpse-grey in the face, his eyes had a burned-out look, emphasized by purple-black blotches beneath them like mascara that had trickled and dried. His lips were pressed together as if holding back pain.

In other ways, he was still the Stuart they remembered. Gravitating to Liverpool 8 and the insalubrious beat clubs that now littered the city, he and Astrid – often with sister Pauline in tow – swanned around in Astrid's hand-made corded suits of beige velvet, unusual for epauletted jackets with no lapels, that buttoned up to the throat. There were no unsightly bulges in the high-waisted trousers owing to the absence of pockets around the tight hips. The basic pattern had been taken from a blue-brushed denim get-up sold in the Hamburg branch of C & A's.

'Wearing your sister's suit then, Stu?' quipped Paul when Stuart and Pauline descended the Cavern's narrow stone stairwell. Stuart laughed too – but not at himself. Boys watching the Beatles down there had their hair combed like John, Paul and George's. He'd bet even money that it wouldn't be long before they'd be copying the Beatles' lapel-less suits too. He said as much to Brian Epstein the only time they ever met.

Prompted by John, Epstein sounded Stuart out about a full-time post as assistant manager, art director, whatever he'd like to call it, in the Beatles organization, NEMS Enterprises. For reasons that included frustrated aspirations to be a performer himself, the fastidious Brian's sincerity and faith in the cleaned-up group was even more fervent than John's, if that was possible.

Stuart had seen for himself, hadn't he, the battalions of iron-bladdered girls arriving ridiculously early to fill the stage-front area at the Cavern to gawk at Pete and the other three? So what if Decca – and, thus far, every other label Brian had tried – hadn't been interested? Even without a record deal, the Beatles were now a cut above all other Merseybeat outfits. They weren't above the odd engagement back at the Casbah, but he had nudged them up to golf club dances in Port Sunlight and lording it over Gerry and Rory at Southport's Floral Hall with its plush curtains and tiered seating. No more were they changing in men's toilets or being paid in loose change.

When supporting a hit parade act, Brian ensured that his Beatles appeared second-to-last: the suggestion being that they were giving the bill-toppers cause for nervous backward glances. The Beatles had also risen to the challenge of the ballroom circuit, becoming a reliable draw as their booking spectrum broadened to Yorkshire, Wales and as far south as Swindon. Hamburg? They'd be there again in April to wow 'em at the new Star Club which had given no quarter during a ruthless campaign to outflank the Top Ten as the Freiheit's premier night spot.

After spending over a year expecting to be in the charts next month, Stuart was too long in the tooth to be anything but bemused by Mr Epstein's overtures. Dear, self-hyping John had talked that way for years. Words are cheap. He'd think about it and let them know in April, Stuart told John. Then, like riders in the Wild West, the two old comrades went their separate ways without ceremonial farewells.

During an earlier encounter in a Liverpool jazz club with Michael McCartney, Paul's younger brother, 'he said he had a feeling that something was going to happen to him when he went back'.[9] A few weeks later, *Merseybeat* published a reader's letter that enquired whether there was anything in hearsay that Stuart Sutcliffe had just died in Hamburg.

NOTES

1 A set of three handwritten sheets of Stuart's lyrics (with indications of chord sequences) was among lots in a 1980s pop memorabilia auction. The sale was, however, blocked by Pauline Sutcliffe, and the goods were returned eventually to the Sutcliffe estate.
2 *Music Echo*, 7 November 1970.
3 *Liverpool Daily Post*, 7 September 1990.
4 *Liverpool Daily Post*, 19 March 1964.
5 To Spencer Leigh.
6 *Merseybeat*, 15 February 1962.
7 By coincidence, Astrid was contracted by Polydor for some Tony Sheridan publicity photographs around this time.
8 A term in a German college.
9 *Liverpool Echo*, 16 April 1962.

chapter eight
CRY FOR A SHADOW

*P*auline would always remember the morning of Christmas Day 1961 because nothing was ever the same afterwards. She would remember it not only for what happened at the end of it, but also for the ordinariness that preceded it.

In the living room, she and Mum weren't up to anything in particular as the television babbled like a idiot relation in the corner; Joyce was out somewhere with her fiancé, and lunch was being prepared by Dad – as much an artist with a saucepan as his son was with a paintbrush. It wasn't unusual either for someone to be absent. The previous year, it had been both Charles and Stuart. This time, it was just Stuart.

Postmen worked all hours then, and, owing to the seasonal bottleneck of mail, the parcel from Hamburg didn't arrive until the bread sauce was nearing its climax in the kitchen. Millie stroked a nut-brown suede bag as if it was her faraway boy's wavy hair. Pauline exclaimed with delight at a pair of Dior stockings while Charles was less demonstratively pleased with a grey cardigan which he hung carefully on the back of a chair before returning to his culinary creations.

Presently, he heard a shriek. It was not a normal Christmas morning shriek, but one of love and heartbreak that shot through his nervous system: 'My son is dying!' Abandoning the cooker, he rushed to the fringe of the turmoil in the next room. His elderly wife seemed to have gone crazy. 'My son is dying!', she screeched again and again as, wildly, she wrenched Stuart's oil paintings from the wall, one by one, leaving small craters as the picture hooks and surrounding plaster burst unresistingly away as she blundered about with hysterical vigour.

Lifted out of her Dior reverie, Pauline had been nonplussed for a split second in slow motion. What are you meant to do when you are only seventeen and your mother goes mad? She tugged ineffectually at Millie, but, a moment after Charles arrived on the scene, their heads banged together and, used up, they slumped in a heap on to the carpet.

Charles prised Pauline away and held her to him. As she sobbed and heaved her breath back, blood streamed from her left eyebrow. Some of it had seeped on *to Millie who was kneeling amid the fallen paintings, wailing inconsolably: 'No one is taking any notice! Can't you see that our son is dying?'*

Thanks to Mr Epstein's dogged prodding of Polydor's UK outlet, 'My Bonnie'/'The Saints' by Tony Sheridan and the Beatles was released in Britain on 5 January 1962. NME reviewer Keith Fordyce was generous – 'Both sides are worth a listen for the above-average ideas'[1] – but, unaired on either the Light Programme or Radio Luxembourg, the disc drifted on the vinyl oceans for a few weeks before sinking without trace.

Though there were signs of resistance to the USA's domination of domestic pop, striking back harder was British television. Quickly shutting down *Laramie* and *77 Sunset Strip* were home-produced serials like ITV's *Emergency Ward Ten*, a *Casualty* prototype, after its producer grasped that kidney machines in action made better drama than stolen corridor kisses. Most popular was gritty *Coronation Street* but close behind was *Z-Cars*, also as ingrained with northern working-class realism as censorship would permit. From the same environment arose playwrights such as Shelagh Delaney and Stan Barstow, novelists Keith Waterhouse, John Braine and others with names as uncompromisingly stark. On celluloid, Delaney's *A Taste of Honey* was shot on location in Merseyside dockland – while the new young Turk of British cinema was Liverpudlian Tom Courtenay as Waterhouse's *Billy Liar*.

Enchanting some and sickening others with his 'swinging/dodgy' thumb-sign mannerisms, another Scouser, Norman Vaughan, was master of ceremonies on ITV's long-running *Sunday Night at the London Palladium*. His '*Swinging* In The Rain' in 1962 would tie with the Vernon Girls'[2] 'You Know What I Mean' as the first Liverpool-accented record to make the Top Forty. He was succeeded at the Palladium by Jimmy Tarbuck, a primary-school contemporary of John Lennon and George Harrison. A long way from the social clubs where he began, shock-headed Ken Dodd, 'Squire of Knotty Ash', had been a television fixture since 1960.

With the coming of David Hockney and, by adoption, Richard Hamilton, dawned the realization in the spheres of Fine Art that, as Royal College student Vivian Stanshall commented, 'Clever people could have Geordie and Mancunian accents', Liverpudlian ones too.

Cry For A Shadow

Following a lucrative London exhibition, abrasive Arthur Dooley – who died in 1994 – had become a professional Scouser, often on BBC television's early evening magazine, *Tonight*. Up and coming, too, were other Regional Art College old boys: Rod Murray, Michael Kenny, Mike Knowles (who married Stuart's old flame, Veronica Johnson) and Sam Walsh were all making the most of academic qualifications gained without sabbaticals or like interruptions. Those who could, did; the rest taught. Either way, they were all a credit to their parents.

The college was emerging nationally as a good shop window for gifted students. A protégé of Hamilton, Adrian Henri had reached beyond slapping oil on canvas to performance art and, as he had promised Michael Horovitz, poetry. Other bards and *nouveau vague* artists of the same vintage included Roger McGough, Brian Patten, Peter MacKarell, Alun Owen,[3] Mike Evans and Mike McCartney, who, if no Ken Dodd, would strike much the same note of unforced urbanity.

With more than just Merseybeat happening in Liverpool, Stuart Sutcliffe in Hamburg felt he might be in the wrong place at the right time. Though he didn't begrudge any of his old college friends their luck, he was eating his heart out because, Heaven knows, he could wipe the floor with most of them as a fine artist, and, with his abiding interest in film, writing and whatever else was going, he could hold his own in any of the Henri crowd's audio-visual and literary events that were springing up as alternatives to doing the Hippy Hippy Shake with all o' your might down the Iron Door. As bored with Hamburg's close-knit art world as he had been during the Gambier Terrace epoch, only Astrid mitigated Stuart's yearning to get back before he missed the boat. 'His greatest wish,' said Joyce Sutcliffe after he had missed it, 'was to have an exhibition of his own in Liverpool'[4] – and, in a horrible way, this wish was to come true.

Perhaps it was John who had been on the right track, after all. To crown *Z-Cars*, Hockney, *Billy Liar*, Norman Vaughan and all the other breakthroughs, crass and sophisticated, why not a northern pop group? Who better than the Beatles? If less of a Reeperbahn clubman now, Stuart made what might be construed as one last gesture to recover scrapings of his lost rock 'n' roll inheritance. In a letter to Pauline, dated 14 February 1962, he spoke of having 'played a couple of times in another band, and managed to earn a bit. The day I fell sick, I was practically on the stage to begin. That was horrible. I thought I was dying.'

He was. Fortunately for him, he was unable to view himself with the same hopeless clarity as others did. Despite the motherly attentions of Astrid and Nielsa, he was haggard and undernourished. The hollowed cheeks, parchment complexion and sweat-laden forehead went with the glowing, feverish eyes that made him look even more like the tortured, highly strung Left Bank artist that he and John had once romanced about. He was behaving like one too – and he wasn't playing image. This, unhappily, was for real.

'My students used to complain that he was acting very odd,' remembered Paolozzi. With Astrid, too, there were these moments, leading in one case to a screaming row. 'I have been liberally endowed with the Sutcliffe or Cronin temper,' was his excuse in a letter to Millie, 'and have at times allowed it too free a hand – consequently, people suffer, and often they are shocked.' On other occasions, his mental blitzkriegs would declare themselves – so he told Pauline – 'by wild screams of laughter and sheer delight'.

Painting provided no diversion or occupational therapy as he swung from elation to despair. He entered darkness, and darkness penetrated him as the ringing headaches intensified to muzzy eyesight and even temporary loss of vision. Sometimes, the storm would abate, and he would paint like a maniac while he had the energy. But the foreboding wouldn't lift, and he would go through these placid interludes with much the same attitude as a First World War trench private resigned to the next barrage of enemy shells.

At Liverpool Art College, he kept copious notes of his creative process and its purpose. One eerily prophetic reference began, 'When I paint this picture, I am not, as some people seem to think, outside of myself, but aware of myself so acutely that, at times, this awareness can reach the point of hallucination. This acute consciousness is an essential element of hallucination.' Other attempts to exorcize the bedlam inside his head could be seen in representational exercises such as a charcoal portrait of an amorphous figure with hands supporting head. Jittery and purposely unresolved lines depict the hands in multiple positions to suggest a nervous vulnerability.

With commendable objectivity – and like a true Tachist – he capitalized on, rather than shrank from, his disorientated condition. De Staël and Pollock would have understood Stuart when, during one of his turns, he would hold his arm over a sketchpad or even a canvas and paint the resulting tremors. 'Perhaps a battered gramophone record suggested the motifs which dominate the grey paintings of the last few months,' conjectured John Willett. 'Yet they cluster naturally, almost like leaves and in some it is as though a gentle wind rustled the forms.'[5]

Incorporating coal dust and crumpled-up cakes of sand, the massive oil paintings of 1962 certainly conveyed a more sombre lyricism than those produced earlier. His years of attacking abstract art from new angles had gelled in a style that rebuffed adequate categorization. The emotional cost of this achievement, however, incited fears for his sanity.

One day in class, he had stood swaying and staring vacantly ahead as another convulsive fit loomed. On the floor, his body twitched violently, and he was still shivering uncontrollably after Astrid took him home to bed. He was attended by Dr Hommelhoff who sought two more medical opinions. During the neurological investigations that ensued, Stuart was asked about a blow to the head. The 'grey matter', the most vital part of the brain, has a jelly-like consistency, expounded Dr Hommelhoff, and is protected not by unbroken casing but only by reefs of bone and membrane, which cover it like rafters and plaster cover the floor of a loft. The brain, therefore, can be easily damaged by a knock, accidental or otherwise.

This was but one of many possibilities that might explain his present state. A course of injections ('and they don't half hurt') was prescribed, but, ideally, he should receive residential care in a sanatorium – if only as a respite for his two unofficial nurses because, as Stuart wrote to his elder sister, 'Frau Kirchherr is ill and Astrid is worn out.' Treatment would include days of continuous sleep to 'take my mind out of circulation'. Sadly for all concerned, no room was available just then.

As his mother was ailing too, Stuart spared her the more distressing details of what he referred to as simply as 'the illness'. He saved those for Joyce, second-in-command at Aigburth Drive as Charles was on a voyage to Argentina. The letters that reached Millie sometimes read as if intended for Lennon, Rod Murray or Ken Horton. On 29 March, he pointed out that 'I actually started a letter twice but all they contained were the phantastic hysterical wondering of a very sick little boy' before an unfathomable but alarming 'actually

I'm an acute migraine worker accompanied by my bloodiness so you can try and catch me from there'.

Where mini-eulogies of Astrid had once been, sentences would be cut in two by written cries of agony like 'my head is compressed and filled with such unbelievable pain' or a forthright 'this pain's killing me'. Armed with the X-rays and other medical records he and Astrid had left behind in October, Millie had engineered an audience with the Dean of Liverpool University Medical School. From Mrs Sutcliffe's account of the symptoms as much as the German documentation, the Dean advocated Stuart's immediate return to England for tests, providing he was capable of travel.

That, however, was out of the question.

> I'm very ill, bed-bound [he groaned in another fragmented epistle], can't walk very far without falling over, the only thing is these headaches, can't sleep till the doc comes and injects me, meanwhile I go mad. Actually I'm costing hundreds, the tablets alone. Everyone looks after me fine and chops my food into little pieces. I can't stand being ill, if it happens again, I'll go berserk. Two weeks ill, two weeks to recover!! God, I'll never get anything done.

After another seizure on 2 April, it was downhill all the way. Once again, nobody could diagnose anything explicit. One of Dr Hommelhoff's hypotheses prompted a letter to Joyce to 'find out from my mother and father if there is any epilepsy in the house (in the family I mean)'. What aggravated him most, he said, was the insomnia: 'I don't know why I can't sleep. I've had the right doses and then again, but nothing doing. I hope the concentration of this writing will tire me . . . It's all so horrible and frustrating . . . four days without sleep, I've had all the drugs in the world.' He was even prepared to disobey doctor's orders: 'I've also had a bottle of very thick beer, that is supposed to bring the sleep on.'

A letter written the day after the last convulsion was virtually unreadable in every sense: 'hour after hour . . . from screaming at the frustration, pain and helplessness. I must try and pull myself together . . . I must try hard. It's only twelve now, what am I to do for the other seven hours?' He'd lost eight pounds in a fortnight. Throwing caution to the wind, he also reported a falling-off of libido, though he was 'definitely improving, becoming more manly. I'm terribly spoilt but I know I'm not homosexual.'

Astrid had no doubts about her fiancé's leanings, even when he was debilitated by the illness. 'She's a little queen,' Joyce was told, 'I've wrecked her sleep and nerves probably these last couple of weeks.' The wretchedness of Astrid's devotion cut more keenly than driving herself into the ground physically as, after a day's work, she ministered to his night-long needs and let him bluster through his rages from muttered trepidation to Hitlerian screech.

> I don't think Astrid is completely happy [he had confided to his mother as long ago as January]. I seem to have given her the impression that she is not suitably equipped to live with me. I'm so frustrated at my lack of equipment to deal with myself. She is so very innocent and naïve and so lovely, it's not at all fair that she must suffer. Why should I have been born with such an evil weapon as my tongue? Astrid has buffeted and stood staunch against any such outbursts, but the threat to her poor little heart is too great, and slowly she is weakening. What can I do? Apparently, nothing except wait and hope that she will continue to forgive me.

You always hurt the one you love, and – despite Stuart assuring himself in a letter to Liverpool that 'we are tied together so deeply that we can overcome it' – the illness had assisted an outpouring of home truths and his and Astrid's true feelings for each other. Between them, there now lay an abyss that neither might ever be willing to bridge if or when he recovered.

They could talk more about it later. Marriage, painting, teacher-training, moving to Britain, the Beatles, *Spotlight On Johnny* – none of these mattered any more. On 7 April, Stuart tried to muster some thoughts on paper for Joyce to pass on to the rest of the family as she saw fit. Skipping abruptly from lucidity to confusion and back again, he sent to Aigburth Drive eleven mostly indecipherable pages – as he knew they were:

> I'm really very sad that I can't write more clearly and precisely. I feel so sick and stupid, and I'm evidently spoiled to death, you know. Astrid will have thousands to pay in doctor's bills. They say

Backbeat

I must come home when I am strong enough and be examined (mentally I mean). I'm not mad as I keep saying, but I know many illnesses are caused through psychological suggestion, but we can't keep this up, apart from the expense. My problem seems to stem from an overwhelming self-conceit and lack of respect for others, but if it's not that, why should I feel ill?

A story would circulate later that, expecting the worst but ever the artist, he requested interment in a *white* coffin. However, the letter of 7 April seemed guardedly hopeful, foreseeing at least a short-term future – and one that he expected to spend back in England:

Dear Joyce, I want you to ask what kind of treatment is best. You see, I'll probably be better in the next few days. I don't care if they put me in a lunatic asylum or such a place for a couple of months – or perhaps I have electric treatment. I don't want to make out I'm insane or anything, I think it's more to do with the blood. The moment I have the illness, I'm worried. I'm always sick and the pain for a moment retreats (after an hour or so) but comes back with increased vigour.

Could you please make a synopsis and take it to Doctor E [Endbinder, the Sutcliffes' general practitioner] and find out if it's worth me coming? I have many X-rays from my neck. You see, I'm frightened that I get it again. Perhaps Doctor E is angry with me, but if there is the slightest chance he can do anything for me . . .

Dear Joyce, I feel a little better than before. My illness is almost all psychological, you understand, mental. I'm not mad or anything, just not well-adjusted. Today is Sunday and because she has had so much time off, she is work today . . .

As if fanning the sparks of optimism, Stuart perked up sufficiently for Dr Hommelhoff to allow him to rise and continue with his latest canvas as long as he rested after lunch as prescribed – or, indeed, whenever his powers of concentration failed him. His energy seemed to be gathering and his mind creaked into motion again, but any comfort he might have felt was a reckless sentiment. In the dusty noon light of the attic on Tuesday, 10 April, he felt the tell-tale throbbing and trembling that heralded a collapse.

Downstairs, Nielsa was startled by a choking scream and an accompanying clatter. She half ran, half stumbled up to the attic and found him. He was on his back with his entire body vibrating, every pore on the ashen face bestowed with a pinprick of sweat. His eyes were screwed shut. His teeth were clenched as tightly, and she couldn't force his emergency tablets past them. Panic-stricken, Frau Kirchherr summoned the doctor who arrived at 12.45 p.m. Between them, they carried him to a downstairs bedroom. It was so much more severe than any previous attack that Dr Hommelhoff suspected a cerebral haemorrhage, and advised a transfer that very afternoon to the neurological clinic at Heidbert Hospital. He would telephone to arrange it now.

When he had finished, Frau Kirchherr rang Astrid. The news was not completely unexpected. While she hurtled home through the lunch-time traffic, Stuart was spectacularly sick, and had started to drift into a coma as she strode into the hall. While waiting, she mailed a telegram informing Mrs Sutcliffe that her son was seriously ill.

The flame was flickering lower as the agitated clang of an ambulance bell impinged upon Altona's suburban calm. Inside the vehicle, Stuart sighed feebly and his sticky eyelids parted as if slit with a knife. There was a whisper of a smile as his hand tightened in Astrid's and then went loose. Whichever way their relationship might have gone had he pulled through, Stuart's last certainty before oblivion was that he would be truly mourned by Astrid.

The paramedics tried all manner of procedures, but there was nothing they could do. His breathing slackened, and death took Stuart Sutcliffe without effort on the stroke of 4.45 p.m. Astrid's heart-shaped angel face had been his last vision before he passed over the most absolute abyss – one that he'd be unable to bridge for her.

Millie Sutcliffe had to tear open two telegrams from Eimsbutteler Strasse. Owing to a Post Office foul-up, the one that said he was seriously ill arrived after the second that told her he was dead. Even today, members of the family can hardly bear to mention the disbelieving helplessness of the next few days. Charles was in the middle of the Atlantic and, in view of his heart condition, it was wisest not to contact him via a raw message on the ship's radio receiver. All Millie could do was break it to the girls as gently as she could, and board the next available plane from Manchester Airport to Hamburg.

By coincidence, Brian Epstein and George Harrison, just over a bout of German measles, were also to be on the same midday flight on 12 April. The Beatles' Star-Club residency was to begin that very evening. The news about Stuart had reached NEMS Enterprises, and the least Brian could do was to offer Mrs Sutcliffe a lift to the airport and seat himself next to her on the plane.

'It was to have been such a great reunion,'[6] said Astrid. She and Stuart had been expected to meet the Beatles at Hamburg-Fuhlsbuttel airport the day before the Star-Club opening to drive them in her convertible to the crowded but cosy accommodation laid on at the nearby Pacific Hotel. In the skies, John, Paul and Pete had been raring to go, in then unknowing empathy with 'Homesick For St Pauli', the Freddy Quinn hit that German milkmen were whistling that spring.

They hadn't heard either about Stuart when they had taken off from England, and were consequently still shrill with their first BBC radio broadcast – *Teenagers' Turn* from Manchester's Playhouse – the previous weekend. After performing before the studio audience, the four had been shocked when mobbed outside the theatre by wildly excited females not much younger than themselves. Most had sought Pete who, pinned in a doorway, had lost tufts of hair to clawing fingers while Lennon, Harrison and McCartney had bought their freedom with mere autographs. Despite himself, taciturn Pete had become the region's favourite Beatle. After watching the fan mania sourly, Paul's father had unjustly berated the drummer for stealing the limelight. Nevertheless, regardless of subjective jealousies, it was standing-room-only for the Beatles most nights, and, old troupers now, they had ascertained from a buzz in the air that they were almost there.

John, Paul and Pete were to come down with a bump. After his passport had been checked, John, a mop-topped pop star of a man now, walked towards Astrid with his arms out. Wait a minute. Something was wrong. She was drained of all her usual sparkle. What's up? Where's Stu? 'Stuart died, John. He's gone.'

Her utterance struck home, and John struggled not to lose his cool. He strained his wits for some hilariously appalling remark to show how unaffected he was. He ought to combust with incredulous laughter or at least shrug his shoulders indifferently, not turn an eyelash. At the end of that briefest of pauses, he could manage neither of these pretences. For once at a loss for words, he buried himself in Astrid's embrace.

That night, Paul and Pete moped into their beer for a boy they hadn't understood but had liked because, for all the in-fighting when he was in the group, he had liked them. If neither had been over-complimentary about his musicianship, they had to admit that the Beatles were a better outfit for Stuart's creative instincts, even if his talents and appetites had proved too much at odds with theirs.

Their eyes were still sore the next day when they went with John and Astrid to greet Brian, George and a distraught Mrs Sutcliffe at the airport. Standing apart from the bear-hugging outbursts, John appeared too calm to Millie – like a detached spectator with no interest or stake in the tragedy. Since yesterday, he had made up his mind to be the hard man again: too tough to cry.

The other Beatles barely had time to wipe away the tears before pitching into their first number at the Star-Club with all their customary verve. However, when all the stupid songs about fast cars and girls were over, John could no longer not believe it. The heart and soul of the expected after-hours carousing, he seemed to be quite himself again, but, now and then, he fell silent as shards of memory and disjointed thoughts pierced his already over-stimulated mind. So often they were of trivialities – Stuart flicking away a cigarette end, buying his bass at Hessy's, catching his eye momentarily during the first night at the Indra . . .

As the night wore on, John poured a huge quantity of drink and pills into himself. As a result, his talk got steadily louder, his eyes brighter, and his rampaging round the Freiheit more manic. What amounted to his unspoken wake for Stuart ended with a quarrel with Epstein that you could hear all over some six-in-the-morning bar.

Over the next few weeks, John got worse, giving foundation to many of the embellished tales that would unfold later. Kicking a drunk in the face from the stage; the golden rain that squirted from his bladder onto the wimples of three promenading nuns; the foul-mouthed 'sermons' from the same balcony. All these incidents dated from April 1962.

Beneath it all, however, Lennon was a shaken and downcast man, feeling his anguish all the more sharply for realizing how many functions his best friend could no longer fulfil for him: careers adviser, father confessor, ego massager, straight man in their double-act, the healer of some of the psychic wounds of his childhood, and someone he could bounce his ideas off and be rewarded with honest, constructive answers. There would never be another like Stuart, would there? That's why his death was no misfortune that could be philosophized away but an irredeemable disaster.[8]

Stuart's death had set Astrid along a different route to the same emotional destination. Deeply depressed, she shrouded herself in the solitude of her silvery-black bower. With no glad welcome guaranteed, anxious friends would brave the spiritless gloom to make sympathetic noises and voice possible answers as questions presented themselves. Surprisingly – or not so surprisingly – the most vital source of comfort during those care-worn hours was John who, keeping his bluff guard up, wasn't over-solicitous like everyone else. At first she was in a state of wounded bewilderment as the door to her room flew open and he breezed in boisterously. 'Come on, make up your mind, live or die,' he would boom pseudo-heartily. 'You're coming to the Star-Club with us tonight. Stop sitting at home – it won't bring Stu back.'

Gradually, Astrid's rise from half-death became perceptible. She coped initially by obeying John's hedonistic directives by night, and drugging herself with work during the day. She was seen in the company of many British musicians, ostensibly in a professional capacity with photocalls for, say, the Undertakers on the doorsteps of a Freiheit brothel. 'She was still getting used to life without him,' said Tony Jackson, 'when she photographed us [the Searchers] in the silver-papered bedroom of her parents' house.'

Millie looked at Astrid and wondered. United in grief, the mother and the girlfriend would continue to write to each other until a rift grew over the ownership of Stuart's paintings, correspondence and other effects left in the Kirchherrs' house.

Astrid's letters to Millie were heartfelt and all the more moving for their clumsy English as seen in one letter dealing mainly with the after-life and John's 'terrible mood' because 'he just can't believe it that darling Stuart never comes back'. Apparently, Lennon had assembled a collage centred on Stuart for the wall of his room at the Pacific Hotel – but, affirmed Astrid, all of 'Stuart darling's funny little friends miss him so much'.

As next-of-kin, it had been Millie rather than Astrid who had made the formal identification at the morgue. Her signature was on the necessary forms verifying what he had been wearing when he died, and those authorizing the transportation of the body from Germany. She did not, however, mistake a mere corpse for the person, and consented to the pathologist's request to remove the brain for medical research.

The post-mortem had been conducted in the forensic division of University Hospital, Oppendorf. It confirmed Dr Hommelhoff's suspicions: 'cerebral paralysis due to bleeding into the right ventricle of the brain'. Had Stuart survived, he might have been blind and paralysed. More than one subsequent account of the Beatles' early years would cite a tumour as cause of death. More spurious was a myth that Stuart's end might not have been natural. This gripped hard enough back in Liverpool for another *Sunday People* sleuth who knew Allan Williams to sniff around in vain for a cautionary tale as a belated companion piece to *The Beatnik Horror*.

To local rock 'n' rollers, especially Beatle fans, he was regarded as a phantom from the recent past who had returned to haunt them briefly after being spirited away to Germany. As an artist, however, he was sufficiently well known to warrant a prompt *Liverpool Echo* obituary that told of how he 'went to Germany with a Liverpool skiffle group.'[9]

On Maundy Thursday, 19 April, the day that *Merseybeat* published a more adulatory tribute headlined 'Goodbye Stu!',[10] Stuart, clothed in a suit made by Astrid, was buried in grave no. 552 in the 1939 section of Huyton parish cemetery in Blue Bell Lane. This had followed a service in St Gabriel's Church where he had once carried the processional cross as head choirboy.

His father did not attend. Charles Sutcliffe was not to know of his son's death for another fortnight when a padre met the ship at Buenos Aires. Eduardo Paolozzi wasn't at the funeral either – though from his holiday home in Majorca he had written a note to the deceased's mother assuring her that 'Stuart was a very good boy and worked very hard. He was a sensitive boy with great promise and my deepest condolences.'

Though Mrs Harrison represented George, none of the Beatles was able to make it, owing to their commitments at the Star-Club where they and Tony Sheridan's house band, the Star Combo, were

Backbeat

supporting and proudly socializing with three visiting US idols – Ray Charles, Fats Domino and the ubiquitous Gene Vincent – who had included one-nighters at the place on their European itineraries.

After breaking off her engagément, Joyce Sutcliffe had a new boyfriend, and Rod Murray would help to take nineteen-year-old Pauline's mind off her brother's death by inviting her to join a party from the art college crowd on a month-long holiday, travelling round Europe. Of all Stuart's close friends, Rod was the most sensitive to the family's sorrow, but his dinner invitations and other kindnesses could not lighten the acute melancholia and occasional instability that would bedevil Mrs Sutcliffe for the next two years.

NOTES

1   *New Musical Express*, 8 January 1962.
2   A trio of choreographed singers derived from the choir recruited from among employees of John Moores' football pools conglomerate.
3   Owen was to write the script of 1964's *A Hard Day's Night*, the Beatles' first feature film.
4   *Liverpool Echo*, 23 November 1964.
5   *Liverpool Daily Post*, 19 March 1964.
6   *The True Story of the Beatles*, B. Shepherd (Beat Publications, 1964).
7   Paul's mother had died suddenly when he was fourteen.
8   'In My Life' (from 1965's *Rubber Soul* album) was the closest John came to marshalling his thoughts about 'friends I still can recall' in song.
9   *Liverpool Echo*, 14 April 1962.
10 *Merseybeat*, 19 April 1962.

JuST A BEgINNING

'If he'd lived, he could have been *the* Beatle'[1]

Eduardo Paolozzi

'His posthumous reputation certainly doesn't need the glamour of his former band to enhance it'[2]

Adrian Henri

Everybody knows what happened next. An EMI subsidiary, Parlophone, took on the Beatles in 1962, just before the replacement of Pete Best with Ringo Starr, one of Rory Storm's Hurricanes. The new recruit was hardly less reticent than his predecessor, but he posed no limelight-threatening challenge to the front line, being a Pete Best for girls to adore more as a brother than demon lover.

After Pete turned down an offer to join first Rory Storm (who then poached sixteen-year-old Gibson Kemp from Formby's Memphis Three) and then the Merseybeats, room was found for him in Lee Curtis and the All-Stars, a dependable club draw both in Liverpool and Hamburg. It was the start of something small. During one of their residencies at the Star-Club, Astrid commiserated with Pete but her sympathy wasn't sufficient to mitigate 'continuing with a group not as popular, doing the same old gigs I'd done with the Beatles'.[3]

'Love Me Do', the first single under the Beatles' new regime, was released in October 1962 – and the rest, as they often say, is history. The next year brought the conquest of Britain via hit parade Merseybeat, Beatlemania and the Royal Variety Show. A prosy *Sunday Times* article lauded Lennon and McCartney as 'the outstanding composers of 1963'.[4] Noticing the Beatles months after they had first made the Top Twenty, the general media had seized on them as a sinless, light-hearted antidote to a recent surfeit of 'serious' news of the Profumo scandal, the Great Train Robbery and more east-west black-white tension than usual.

The 'Fab Four' also spearheaded the group boom which finished off the careers of soloists like the Silver Beatles' front man for their aborted 1960 tour of Scotland. Without a recording contract in 1963, Johnny Gentle joined the Viscounts, whose tide was also ebbing, before retiring from showbusiness in the mid-1960s.

Unlike the 'untouchable' image foisted upon Gentle and other would-be idols of old, 'Our appeal is that we're ordinary lads,'[5] pontificated Ringo. As it had in Britain, this did the corrective trick in a USA desolated by its own domestic traumas – notably the Kennedy assassination. Launched with an unprecedented publicity blitz, the group were embraced by North America with a passion that left Beatlemaniacs back home at the starting line.

The rest of the world was a pushover – but, for its conquerors, it was an intrusive and frequently dangerous place, its immensity and richness lying beyond a barrier of flash-bulbs and screeching hysteria. An exceptionally stressful tour in 1966 was followed by a much-mooted decision to down tools as a concert band.

No longer within earshot of each other as they had been on every working day since God knew when, artistic and emotional ties slackened. This was made worse in late 1967 by Brian Epstein's sudden death, and the critical rubbishing received by their television spectacular, the self-produced *Magical Mystery Tour*.

As autumn leaves fell on the Beatles, the average Joe raised sceptical eyebrows as they dabbled with the mental distortions of LSD, then transcendental meditation under the Maharishi, and the 'controlled weirdness' of Apple Corps, a company formed for maverick artistic and scientific ventures. It was jettisoned after their heedlessness over expenditure caused a dam to burst on a river of embezzlement.

Joe Average was puzzled most of all by the behaviour of Lennon who had moved in with Yoko Ono, a Japanese-American who was to art what Lenny Bruce was to comedy – though that might be rating her too highly. As well as taking the place of Cynthia in his bed, Yoko also superseded Paul as John's artistic confrère and filled the void left by Stuart as an adjunct personality. She was a mate in every sense; John describing their bond in a nutshell with 'It's just handy to fuck your best friend.'[6]

Just A Beginning

As it had been with Astrid and Stuart, Yoko and John began styling their hair and dressing the same. Paralleling Astrid again, Yoko was the older and, seemingly, more independent partner. Through her catalytic influence, the world and his wife were confronted with a John Lennon they had never known before, one for whom the Beatles would soon no longer count any more than they had for Stuart after he had made up his mind to return to painting.

Apart from Cynthia, how could anyone begrudge Yoko and John their joy? A writer to *Beatles Monthly* expressed the widespread opinion that Cynthia and John's subsequent divorce eroded the Beatles' magic even more than the absence of the usual Yuletide single had in 1966, but it was the first of a trilogy of non-Beatle albums by Lennon and Ono that annihilated completely any cosy illusions such traditionalists had left. The unmelodious experiments on *Unfinished Music No. 1: Two Virgins* might have been anticipated, even tolerated, but not its cover photographs of the couple doe-eyed and naked, front and back. It was, they explained, an Art Statement. Average Joe was, however, too perplexed to give an Art Reply to this and other of their peculiar pranks like the Bed-Ins, sending acorns to world leaders, 'Bagism' and the film starring John's willy.

When *The Beatles* double-album came out in the same 1968 month as *Two Virgins*, fans listened sceptically to the penultimate track, 'Revolution 9'. Lennon's jarring patchwork of noises not commonly thought of as musical was justifiably praised in the *International Times* as a 'send up'[7] of John Cage's 'Fontana Mix', a classic of its kind. *Rolling Stone* described it as 'an aural litmus of unfocused paranoia'.[8] Could it have also been a Lennon attempt at rendering Sutcliffe's abstract perceptions as sound? It certainly has the same spontaneous character and chance operation used to create the 'unconscious calligraphy' of de Staël and the Tachists.

Even before John turned weird in 1968, John had started doing some pictures of his own, which were not dissimilar to some of Stuart's work – large abstracts, using palette knives rather than brushes. McCartney also took up oil painting, thinking enough of his efforts to have prints of them published in a small paperback book for private distribution.

Had Lennon had time, he may have done the same. Nevertheless, for as long as he lived, so, in spirit, did Stuart – but not, as far as

John was concerned then, the Beatles. Long before Messrs Harrison, Lennon, McCartney and Starkey were disassociated formally as a business enterprise through Paul's legal action in 1971, each, however reluctantly or unknowingly, was well into a career apart through acting roles, solo records or John's antics with the second Mrs Lennon.

In its death throes, the group had shilly-shallied between ineffectual endeavours to get back to its Hamburg-forged genesis and the colour-supplement art of *Abbey Road*. Having soundtracked the 1960s, they failed to dominate the next decade when all but the most snowblinded began to understand how ordinary, even dull and unattractive, the mere mortals behind the myth could be.

If nothing else, the Beatles had put Liverpool on the map. In doing so, the city's art scene garnered more attention than it might have merited in the course of less fantastic events. In return, Liverpool artists remembered the Beatles in paintings like Sam Walsh's *Mike's Brother* (that is, Paul McCartney) and *Lennon*,[9] as well as John Edkins' *We Love The Beatles*, shown in a posthumous exhibition at the Bluecoat in 1966. Less specific homage was paid in the ritual spinning of Beatles' discs during intermissions after the Cavern was reopened that same year to host poetry readings and arty soirées, though a few courageous anachronisms like Rory Storm still cranked out 'Let's Stomp' and 'Twist And Shout' down there for those who still remembered.

Among more recurrent acts now was the mixed-media aggregation known as 'The Liverpool Scene',[10] founded by Adrian Henri and – epitomizing the passing of the old order – ex-members of beat groups, the Roadrunners and the Clayton Squares. Bringing satirical humour as well as pop music to an audience biased against one or the other, the Liverpool Scene drank from the same pool as fellow latter-day Cavern regulars, the Scaffold who, fronted by Paul's brother, were to harry the UK Top Ten via the vexing catchiness of 'Thank U Very Much', 'Lily The Pink' and 1974's 'Liverpool Lou'.

By the 1980s, *a* Cavern had been reconstructed in Mathew Street next to Cavern Walks shopping mall. On the now-busy thoroughfare's opposite side stood the John Lennon pub and, half-way up a wall, an Arthur Dooley statue of a madonna-like figure with a plaque beneath reading 'Four Lads Who Shook The World'. These Beatle-connotated redevelopments were commissioned in the wake of both the city council and the English Tourist Board falling back on Liverpool's cradling of the Beatles just as it had fed off its past as a great port. Pride in the group was stressed further in 1982 by naming four streets on a Wimpey Housing estate after each of the most famous members – George Harrison Way, Ringo Starr Drive and so forth – despite one sniffy burgher's objections that, in the light of Allan Williams' newly published memoirs[11] of 'what went on in Hamburg and their use of filthy language, the Beatles should in no way be linked with the civic name of Liverpool'.[12]

By coincidence, the pre-war Sutcliffe Street was but a stone's throw away. If this wasn't a commemoration of the Fifth Beatle, Stuart's work had, nevertheless, been kept before the Merseyside public since 1964's one-man exhibition at the Walker displayed a selection of his output, mostly the final, and most startling, paintings. The showing had come about through the enthusiasm of John Willett, who had been in Liverpool to research his book, *Art In A City*.[13] A record-breaking ten thousand attended during the Walker's three-week run, testifying not so much to a lessening of national antipathy towards abstract art than an insatiable appetite for anything to do with the Beatles at an optimum moment in their career. They had just been immortalized in wax at Madame Tussaud's; their singles, even the antique Sheridan sides, were swamping North American and Australasian Top Tens five or six at a time; *A Hard Day's Night* came to cinemas beyond the Iron Curtain, and their sacked drummer was about to milk his links with the group via a US-only album, spin-off 45s and a six-month string of sell-out dates with his Pete Best Combo.

The only direction should have been down for the Beatles but, even after disbandment, their records continued to sell by the ton, and Stuart was subject of further major retrospectives patronized by a significant minority who wouldn't normally step inside a gallery. With Nicholas Horsfield heading the steering committee, three more exhibitions took place in Liverpool between 1965 and 1967.

Over the next twenty or so years, Sutcliffes were seen in prestigious galleries in London,[14] Glasgow, Cologne and once more in Liverpool. In the mid-1980s, his contributions were a key selling point in *The Art of the Beatles*, a travelling exposition which, containing items by all manner of artists that had breathed the air round the group, was seen as far away as Japan.

In January 1990, a one-man show in London brought together

representations from every trackway of Stuart's life – and afterlife. The paintings were mostly from Hamburg, but among those viewing them were sister Pauline (the event's co-sponsor), Beryl Bainbridge, Adrian Henri, who regarded them 'like artefacts of a lost civilization',[15] Roger McGough, John Willett and, called upon to say a few words, Peter Blake. It was a celebratory, companionable occasion of coded hilarity and mutual nostalgia about the old days back in Liverpool when the world was young. It seemed so far away: the art college, Arthur Ballard, the Jac, three-in-the-morning word-games at Gambier Terrace, the smell of turpentine, the Silver Beatles, beehive hairdos, Kingsize Taylor, Vick inhalers, Mr Epstein – and poor, dead Stuart, the boy who had had everything it took.

Some of his exhibitions were instigated and even organized by Millie and, later, Pauline Sutcliffe, who founded StuArt, a company dedicated to promoting her brother's work. Though individual Beatles lent practical assistance to lesser artists like Yoko Ono and ex-Liverpool art collegian Jonathan Hague, no such support came Stuart's way. Though he had left them well before 'Love Me Do', Millie was wounded by his wealthy former comrades' apparent reluctance to use their celebrity if not their finance to thank one who was 'an integral part of them at the foundation – and quite likely it's on the memory of the things he instilled in them then that they've gone on to become what they are today'.[16]

After her only son's death and her husband's retirement from the sea, Mrs Sutcliffe quit the teaching profession and withdrew from local politics. Widowed in 1966, she decided to spend her twilight years in the milder climate of Sevenoaks, Kent. Until they were passed on to Pauline, now an eminent psychotherapist, most of Stuart's canvases were lovingly preserved in his mother's new home. Over the years, a few had gone missing. A self-portrait popped up in the Netherlands in 1986 when it was offered to the highest bidder via a boxed advertisement in a Beatles fanzine.

A blue abstract by his late friend had been John Lennon's since he and Bill Harry paid a surprise visit to Aigburth Drive after a Beatles concert at the Liverpool Empire in November 1964. Both selected an item each at the invitation of Millie, who also returned *How To Draw Horses*, a book John had won at primary school, and lent to Stuart. John's hard-as-nails pose was suspended that night as

'He kissed us all and was most tender and affectionate,' said Millie, who would tend to claim him vicariously as a son by proxy. That was, none the less, the last the Sutcliffes saw of John Lennon. His aunt, however, stayed in touch until Millie died on 8 December 1983.[17]

After John left England for ever in 1971 to settle eventually in New York, the blue abstract went with him. Quite a number of Stuart's other paintings had been distributed among the Hamburg crowd; Klaus Voorman, for example, had several. He, Astrid and other old faces from the Kaiserkeller days had stayed in contact with the Beatles and were present at a reunion gathering on 26 June 1966 during the last weeks of the group's most public journey. The old dormitory above the Top Ten had been made available for this purpose as soon as they finished at the Ernst Merck Halle, their first Hamburg appearance since a disinclined Star-Club residency that had disturbed the 'Love Me Do' chart campaign in Britain.

A knees-up over the Top Ten became impractical but a few pals were admitted to an Ernst Merck backstage area almost as security-protected as Fort Knox. Squired by Gibson Kemp, Astrid was there, apparently, to present a gratified John with the letters his younger self had written to Stuart.

Gradually, the party loosened up with selective reminiscences about the struggle back at the Kaiserkeller and Top Ten. Someone also passed round ancient snaps of the Beatles between quiff and *Pilzen Kopf*. It was agreed that, attributable directly to Astrid and her Exi contingent, the Fab Four's mop-tops had helped greatly to make them what they were now. The 'look' had proved as critical for most of their contemporaries. The Rolling Stones' calling-card, for example, was longer hair, aggressive scruffiness and an embellishment of the transfixing androgyny that Astrid had brought out in Stuart. Before them, Johnny Kidd and the Pirates had gone in for nautical stage outfits with galleon backdrop. With 'Wreck Of The *Antoinette*' and similar succeeding singles after 1968's 'Legend of Xanadu', Dave Dee, Dozy, Beaky, Mick and Tich would present a different costume drama on BBC television's *Top of the Pops*.

The Beatles' more overtly 'arty' aura, exemplified by the hiring of Peter Blake to design the *Sgt. Pepper* sleeve, showed others the way. Light shows and other audio-visual aids would simulate psychedelic experience as 'bands' – not groups – like the Pink Floyd and Soft Machine played on and on and on for 'idiot dancers' and hippies in a stoned trance in 'underground' venues such as London's Middle Earth and Amsterdam's Paradiso. During the next decade, the glam-rock of Roxy Music and David Bowie and, later, the more theatrical post-punk acts appealed to 1970s and 1980s intellectuals as the Beatles had to Hamburg's Exis.

Backtracking to the 1960s, ex-art student Pete Townshend of the Who alluded to the German-British artist Gustav Metzger as the doubtful inspiration for 'auto-destruction', that is, the Who's practice of closing their act by smashing up their equipment. In the same 'Mod' bag, the Creation had climaxed their set in a more two-dimensional manner by splashing on to a canvas backdrop a painting that owed less to Jackson Pollock than to Tony Hancock. With Moseley Art College old boy Roy Wood at their creative helm, the Move first impinged upon national consciousness with a stage show that involved singer Carl Wayne charging onstage with a chopper to hack up effigies of world political figures before turning his attention to imploding televisions – and if that's not art, then what is?

In June 1966, the Move landed the recording deal that would set in motion a five-year chart run, but Hamburg performers of the old school hadn't forgotten an outfit called Carl Wayne and the Vikings making their nervous Star-Club début in 1965 any more than they had five callow Liverpudlians with eyes out on stalks who had arrived to play the Indra five years earlier. Now what remained of the original Beatles were about to leave the Ernst Merck Halle in a fleet of Mercedes with *Polizei* outriders. They would leave Hamburg on a train usually reserved for royalty – from the selfsame station where Stuart and Astrid had waved a pale and very young George into exile for staying up past his bedtime.

Down on the Grosse Freiheit, the bands played on. Guided by Star-Club proprietor Manfred Weissleder, a native ensemble, the Rattles, had modelled themselves profitably in the British beat image. Among their first recordings was a version of 'The Hippy Hippy Shake', but such Merseybeat antiquities were far behind them by 1966. In the Star-Club too, the Remo Four were trying jazz-rock these days.

Two years earlier, Tony Sheridan, though well placed to grow fat on Beatlemania, had been plucking jazz guitar as drinkers chattered in a Reeperbahn Bar. Just then, a re-released 'My Bonnie' was registered as a million-seller because the Beatles were on it. Therefore, drawn from Hamburg by pragmatism, Tony combed his grey-flecked hair forward, recorded a new album, was 'special guest' on a tour with the Searchers, and appeared on the ITV children's programme *Five O'Clock Club*. On this jaunt, Tony had also met up with the Beatles in London for 'talk of the old times, laughs about some of the German raves and best wishes for the future'.[18]

Having kept in sporadic touch, Ringo and George were there at a Star-Club anniversary show in 1977 when, flanked by former Elvis Presley sidemen, Tony brushed aside the millennia since 1962 like matchsticks. For sale in the foyer was his new LP, *World's End*, produced by Klaus Voorman who had also made a prodigal's return to Germany.

Stuart's former bass guitar protégé had retained his boyish good looks, but his journey to middle age hadn't been peaceful – and is worth chronicling at length. In 1965, Klaus had forsaken the security of graphic design to thrum bass in his first group with Gibson Kemp and ex-Big Three guitarist Paddy Chambers. As 'Paddy, Klaus and Gibson', they secured a recording deal with Pye and a residency at the Pickwick, a fashionable night spot, frequented by London's 'in-crowd'.

In with the most exlusive in-crowd of all, Klaus gave Ringo guitar lessons, and landed the plum job of crafting the sleeve of the Beatles' *Revolver* album. His liaison with Gibson and Paddy was nowhere as lucrative: three consecutive flop singles contributed to the break-up of the trio in May 1966. Chambers joined the Escorts, Gibson, the executive body of a record company, while Voorman served the Hollies briefly before filling a vacancy created by Jack Bruce (later, of Cream) in Manfred Mann, in which he doubled on flute.

Well before Manfred Mann's break-up in 1969, Klaus had found it convenient to live permanently in London and turned out to assist on records by the Lennons, George Harrison and, especially, Ringo Starr. Whenever each ex-Beatle warmed up for a take, Klaus would react instinctively with some rock 'n' roll classic half remembered from the Kaiserkeller.

Inevitably, rumours of the impending formation of *a* Beatles had him like the stock Hollywood chorus girl, thrust into a sudden headlining role. See, as writ-happy Paul was *persona non grata*, the other three were going to try again as John, *Klaus*, George and Ringo. 'New Beatle Goes Into Hiding!'[19] *Melody Maker* had bawled the spring when Klaus and his wife spent a few days at George's country estate in Oxfordshire. *Disc* saw him less as McCartney's successor than 'a natural replacement for Stuart Sutcliffe, the Beatle-Who-Died'.[20]

This was backed up with a convincing quote from Bill Harry: 'Stuart was an artist from Liverpool who went to Hamburg. Klaus was an artist from Hamburg who came over here. It's always been obvious that he was particularly ideal to be a Beatle. Like Stuart, he's more of an artist than musician, and the Beatles have always admired his work. He would add another dimension to them. There is a charisma about him. He has a fantastically interesting face. He's a thinker.'[19]

The plot diluted after Harrison, Lennon and Starr issued a statement refuting any re-formation involving Klaus or anyone else. The nearest their Hamburg friend was to come to Beatlehood was as one of the all-star band assembled by Harrison for the *Concerts For Bangla Desh* in New York in 1971, and on a 1973 Starr track that also happened to feature John and George.

By then, Klaus had become a stalwart of the Los Angeles studio scene where, at its most mundane, his work schedule ranged from pot-boiling hours with showbiz diehards such as Andy Williams, and unknowns, like Patti Dahlstrom and Geoff Muldaur, to thrumming the snappy rhythmic jitter deemed essential to boring solo albums by Bobby Whitlock, Bobby Keyes, Leon Russell and other inter-changeable 'super-sidemen'. Looking infinitely more impressive on Voorman's musical curriculum vitae were such diverse legends as Donovan, Lou Reed, Lonnie Donegan, Bob Dylan, Howlin' Wolf, B. B. King, Jerry Lee Lewis and even Screaming Lord Sutch.

Living in California, too, were Ringo and John, both in the grip of marital turmoil and premature male menopauses, but keeping them at arm's length with booze and classified drugs. Sometimes, their tipsy musings slopped over on to albums like Lennon's *Mind Games*. On its cover photograph he didn't look much different from the way he did in *The Beatnik Horror*. Several degrees more regressive was 1975's non-original *Rock 'N' Roll*, its content telegraphed on the sleeve by Jürgen Vollmer's 1961 photograph, and the artist's own sentiment: 'You should have been there.'

Though welcome to drop by at John and his cronies' rented Santa

Monica villa, Klaus was more inclined to enter into an after-dinner discussion of a metaphysical nature than the woozy, kerb-crawling escapades that more often occupied idle hours there. He'd have his eventual fill of Tinsel Town, its aggressively friendly passing strangers, and the squeaky-clean precision expected of him every time he plugged in his instrument.

Come the early 1980s, and Klaus was back in Hamburg where it had all started. Nevertheless, the decades in close proximity to every grade of pop star from the Beatles downwards stimulated demand for his services as a record producer – and a very competent and adventurous one he proved to be. This was demonstrated in 1982 when his 'Da Da Da' by Germany's own Trio came within an ace of topping the British chart.

The *Backbeat* film was lent authenticity by the involvement of Voorman and Astrid Kirchherr. The two have always remained friends, and, as director Iain Softley observed, it would be true to say that one of the bonds between them is the shared memory of their friendship for Stuart.

Astrid's life since 1962 has been a conundrum. Was the pragmatism she later displayed admirable or was she another disillusioned artist reconciled to the fulfilment of what might have been only a fraction of her potential? In 1964 she abandoned photography, having, so she said, lost confidence in her ability. She had also become weary of the shadier aspects of the profession she had once chosen with such hope.

The morning after the Ernst Merck Halle party in 1966, she returned to work as a barmaid. However, her acquaintance with the Beatles did not become as distant as others' did after they stopped touring two months later. As a favour, she took time out from the real world in 1968 to photograph George Harrison for the jacket of his *Wonderwall* soundtrack. In the credits for this, the first album release by Apple Records, she was listed as 'Astrid Kemp'. Eight years her junior, Gibson Kemp was the first of two husbands.

Almost perversely unremarkable now, she pursues a career in music publishing in Hamburg. Among few public indications of the other life Astrid had led *circa* 1961 is the infusing of her English (when she needs to use it) with Scouse slang, and the intermittent wearing of earrings fashioned from plectrums given to her by Stuart and John.

She has remained in touch with the thrice-married Cynthia

Lennon, a 'liberated' divorcée whose business interests include a London restaurant named Lennon's which serves dishes like Penny Lane Pâté and Rubber Sole and Chips.

Cynthia's former husband's status as the most famous and notorious product of Liverpool's College of Art had little to do with his skill as an artist if the sub-Thurber doodlings adorning the text in his two best-selling books, and 1970's scrawly lithographs of himself and Yoko having sex are anything to go by. To the untrained eye, he was no Arthur Ballard or Stuart Sutcliffe. Yet Ballard reckoned his former student 'had talent. If I'd had my way, he'd have never have become a Beatle.'

Let's transfer to a parallel dimension for a few minutes. In it, John quit the Beatles, an obscure 1960s beat group, in 1965 for a hand-to-mouth existence as a jobbing commercial artist in Liverpool. For a while, he was on the periphery of the Liverpool Scene before a chat with Arthur Ballard got him a post as technician in Ballard's department at the college. As his marriage to Cynthia deteriorated, he became a virtual fixture at Ye Cracke. In his cups, he often rambled on with rueful and misplaced pride about the Beatles' meagre achievements.

For beer money and a laugh, Lennon re-formed the group for bookings in local watering-holes. They became as peculiar to Liverpool alone as Mickey Finn, a comedian unknown nationally but guaranteed work for as long as he can stand on Merseyside. A typical engagement was providing music after Finn's entertainment at a dinner-and-dance at Lathom Hall on 12 April 1980 when the Beatles left a dancing audience wanting more. They encored with smoochy 'Love Me Tender', 'dedicated for sentimental reasons to Stu Sutcliffe, our old bass player'. The group's personnel on that night-of-nights consisted of Pete Best, deputy manager at Garston Job Centre on drums; George Harrison, a Southport curate, on guitar; Paul McCartney, a Radio Merseyside presenter and amateur songwriter, on bass – and Lennon, his singing voice darker and attractively shorn of 1960s ingenuity, now a slightly batty art lecturer who'd wed a Japanese performance artist he'd met at a 1967 'happening' at the Bluecoat.

Unreal life isn't like that – at least, it wasn't for John. Reunited with Yoko after his Californian roisterings, five years of cheery artistic lassitude ended with 1980's *Double Fantasy*, a husband-and-wife effort that could almost be filed under 'Easy Listening'. In 1964, Lennon had answered a question about retirement with a rhetorical 'Who'd want to be an eighty-year-old Beatle?'[21] On 8 December 1980,[22] two months after his fortieth birthday, he was shot on a New York sidewalk by a 'fan' who was Beatle-crazy in the most clinical sense. 'Are you John Lennon?' asked one of the cops in whose squad car the victim was hastened to hospital. 'Yeah,' gasped John. Then he died.

Like it was with Kennedy and, in 1977, Elvis Presley, everyone remembers the moment they heard. The very next day, estate agents discussed who would be doing the probate assessment; publishers liaised with biographers; hack composers got going on tribute songs, and record moguls pondered what tracks by Lennon or associated with him they were entitled to rush-release. Under the editorial lash, pressured hordes of the media cobbled together hasty obituaries. One of the more memorable comments reported in the press was by the recently retired Arthur Ballard:[23] 'I think his death is more significant than that of a leading politician. Like Michelangelo has never been forgotten, neither will John Lennon be'[24] – and Allan Williams was the first to point out the unsettling particular that 'Three people connected with the Beatles have died so young. First Stuart then Brian Epstein and now John.'[24]

The latest tragedy increased the already vast amounts of money being poured, mostly by American and Japanese visitors, into the English Tourist Board's coffers for twice-daily guided Beatle tours round London and Liverpool to such venues as the Abbey Road zebra crossing and 3 Gambier Terrace. A similar service was not, however, implemented in Hamburg although a statue of John Lennon was unveiled in 1981 by Horst Fascher, now running both an advertising agency and a Star-Club relocated to the Grossneumarkt, away from the disreputable heart of the Reeperbahn which, now under government licence, is not as liberal about human frailty as it once was.

Some old haunts are recognizable only by their names. The Kaiserkeller, for example, thrives today as a transvestite hang-out. The Top Ten, however, has long gone – as has Peter Eckhorn – though Bruno Koschmider is still in the club business, his main concern being a place called the Alodria.

The original Exis are seldom seen in St Pauli any more. Living in

New York, Jürgen Vollmer mourns for his lost youth: 'That was a unique period that could not be brought back. That period I definitely would say was the greatest time of my life. I mean, every day sitting there and having the Beatles right in front of you. I was totally in ecstasy. I didn't think whether they'd be big stars. I just enjoyed that moment.'[25]

At the huge 'Beatle Conventions' that have become annual events in cities throughout the world, groups whose *raison d'être* rests solely on impersonating the Fab Four tend to go down better than the trivia quizzes, showings of film footage and lifesize displays of LP covers enabling you to be 'photographed with the boys'. However, even the youngest ticket-holders, who were not even born when Lennon was slain, could not pretend that the Beetle Brothers, Russia's Beatles Club and, most accurate of all, the Bootleg Beatles were what the genuine article must have been like in 1960 in the bowels of the Indra.

For some attending these celebrations, the Beatles have become a craving, almost a religion. Beyond just fitting a few extra shelves to accommodate more accumulated records and memorabilia, and combing thinning hair in a mop-top, certain fans have been known to make a start on the canons of unconnected acts simply because they recorded on the same labels as the Beatles, and holiday in a different foreign country every year just to seek out and buy up Beatle discs issued with an alien label, matrix number and, possibly, an additional second of reverberation on the closing major sixth of 'She Loves You'.

They file, catalogue and gloat over their treasures, finding much to notice, study and compare. They are able to talk with great authority about their interest, and are at a loss to understand why others don't find it just as absorbing. You could argue soundly that being a Beatle fanatic is a more acceptable form of obsession, even autism, than collating information about swimming-pool lockers, learning by heart the door colours of every police station in your county, or being mad about the Dave Clark Five.

A reason given for the Five's relegation to also-rans after their 'Glad All Over' knocked the long-standing 'I Wanna Hold Your Hand' from the top of the UK chart in 1964 was 'If you go off Dave, you're off the group.'[26] Conversely, as each separate Beatle was as much the outfit's public face as the others, fans could maintain overall loyalty yet still be fickle in affections towards individual members, past and present.

Just A Beginning

Because of his consistent commitment to performing and public relations, Paul is generally recognized as the most popular living Beatle. However, the *Backbeat* movie might result in Stuart closing the gap on John as the most favoured one from beyond the grave. Even before silver screen exposure, Sutcliffe had been the subject of a stage play, *Stu – Scenes from the Life of Stuart Sutcliffe* by Hugh O'Neill and Jeremy Stockwell, and had cornered a considerable cult following among Beatle people. When in Liverpool, certain of these would make a point of staying at 37 Aigburth Drive, converted to the Gamblesby Hotel after Mrs Sutcliffe moved. Thrilling at the thought that they might have just spent the night in Stuart's bedroom, devotees would then complete the final stage of their pilgrimage to the burial ground, enduring a knotted stomach gladly while hoping for tombside tears.

With or without the Beatles, Stuart Sutcliffe satisfies every requirement of a doomed pop hero. Gilding the overall aura of fated youth are dark glasses hiding restless eyes, prominent cheekbones in an ember-white complexion, the slouch, the kismet supercool, the Brooding Intensity, and, to round it off, the 'beautiful sadness' of an early grave.

For good measure, a question mark hangs over his fatal brain haemorrhage. Is it really traceable to a violent incident? If it is, which one? Was it delayed reaction to the 'Kiss Me Honey Honey Kiss Me' fight that kicks off *Backbeat*? On the other hand, supposition in Liverpool traces it to the gang ambush as the Beatles were loading up after the Seaforth dance in 1961. His mother blamed a tumble down a flight of stairs, and his younger sister recalls him falling off a bicycle at the age of six. One of the more infamous biographical portrayals of another ex-Beatle has it that Sutcliffe shuffled off this mortal coil as the result of an altercation with John on a Hamburg street. A more sinister cause might have been his not inconsiderable intake of amphetamines.

Nourished by half-truths, apocrypha and tidy-minded media fiction, the myth took hold, and he is spoken of in the same awed breath as James Dean, vulnerable and enigmatic. Dean's and Sutcliffe's respective images are not dissimilar to those of Syd Barrett,[27] Jim Morrison, David Bowie, Liverpool's own Billy Fury and, if his publicist is to be believed, the film actor River Phoenix who died in 1993 at the age of twenty-two.

Yet comparison of Sutcliffe to modern pop luminaries is superficial. He belongs to an older romantic tradition that encompasses the short and unquiet lives of such as Raphael, Chatterton, Keats, Kierkegaard, Brooke and, inspired by their own deliberated self-destruction, Rimbaud and Verlaine – not to mention stock 'tortured' *vie bohème* painters like Van Gogh, Seurat, Modigliani and old idol Nicholas de Staël.

'Artists whose lives are cut short are interesting,' agreed Nicholas Horsfield. 'In most cases, the artist had fulfilled himself. Part of Van Gogh's suicide was because he realized this, and he feared success. Raphael, of course, had fulfilled himself. Seurat who died at thirty-two, had not, and it's fascinating to wonder how Seurat might have changed. Stuart's work ended abruptly at a much earlier stage, ten years earlier than Seurat. All Seurat's development took place in that ten years which were denied to Stuart. Stuart only had virtually two years, didn't he?'

According to Detlev Birgfeld, 'He didn't believe his pictures to be masterpieces. It was just a beginning.' So it was – but while it may have pointed the way to more important achievements and a legitimacy as an artist lost through his affinity to the Beatles, Sutcliffe left behind more than enough to be getting on with, including canvases that plenty of discerning artists alive today would be proud to call their finest work.

John Willett has been a long-time admirer, and the late art historian Lord Clark[28] and Sir Harold Wilson[14] have been among the many illustrious names, lay and expert, who have also supported the tireless efforts of the Sutcliffe family to get Stuart's work recognized as being worth more than just a tiny and disputable footnote in the history of English art. Decades after the oils had dried, Adrian Henri, speaking at a 1990 Sutcliffe retrospective at the Bluecoat, acknowledged that some of the self-directed Hamburg abstracts 'look as good today as when they were painted, and as relevant. His posthumous reputation certainly doesn't need the glamour of his former band to enhance it.'[29]

Just A Beginning

NOTES

1   *Disc*, 6 November 1970.
2   *Liverpool Daily Post*, 7 September 1990.
3   *Merseybeat*, 29 November 1962.
4   *Sunday Times*, 27 December 1963.
5   Milwaukee press conference, 4 September 1964.
6   *Loose Talk*, compiled by Linda Botts (Rolling Stone Press, 1980)
7   *International Times*, 4 December 1968.
8   *Rolling Stone*, 22 January 1981.
9   However, Walsh's most famous work was a portrait of the late Cuban *guerrillero* Che Guevara. As a poster print, this became a fixture in student hostel rooms in the late 1960s.
10 Later heard a lot on John Peel's BBC radio shows. They would also record several albums for RCA, tour with Led Zeppelin, and be on Bob Dylan's supporting bill at 1969's Isle of Wight festival.
11 *The Man Who Gave The Beatles Away*, A. Williams and W. Marshall (Elm Tree, 1975).
12 Local Merseyside journal (name and precise date obscured), December 1981.
13 Any student of post-war art on Merseyside should go first and last to *Art In A City* (Methuen, 1967), and *Liverpool Seen*, Peter Davies (Redcliffe, 1992).
14 In a letter to Millie Sutcliffe, Prime Minister Harold Wilson expressed his pleasure that her son's work had been exhibited in London.
15 Henri's programme notes for a 1976 exhibition.
16 *Disc*, 31 October 1970. A possible explanation of the Beatles' lack of support is a crisis of loyalty following the estrangement of the Sutcliffes and Astrid over the proprietory right to Stuart's belongings.
17 Mrs Sutcliffe spent her final weeks in a hospital in Tunbridge Wells, visited daily by the nuns of St Francis, the order she had entered as a teenager between the wars.
18 *New Musical Express*, 20 March 1964.
19 *Melody Maker*, 27 March 1971.
20 *Disc*, 27 March 1971.
21 *New York Times*, 20 December 1964.
22 Did you notice, Beatle freaks? Millie Sutcliffe died three years to the day after John.
23 Ballard still possesses some Sutcliffe paintings but evidence suggests that Eduardo Paolozzi (now knighted) does not. Neither, incidentally, does Paul McCartney who, nevertheless, does own a Paolozzi.
24 *Reading Evening Post*, 9 December 1980.
25 *Beatlefan*, March 1981.
26 *Sunday Times*, 13 November 1964.
27 To certain of his fans, it was Syd's misfortune to live on after shedding his creative load (and some might say the same about David Bowie).
28 In a letter thanking Mrs Sutcliffe for a catalogue of a 1976 exhibition, Lord

Clark judged Stuart to be 'a most talented artist. What a tragedy that someone so beautiful and so gifted should have died at the age of 22. I am glad that you sent me the catalogue as it has introduced me to an artist I would never have known, and a remarkable human being.'

29 *Liverpool Daily Post*, 7 September 1990.

APPENDICES

CHRONOLOGY

Born 23 June 1940 Edinburgh, Scotland

1943 Family moves to Merseyside

1946–50 Park View Primary School, Huyton

1950–6 Prescot Grammar School

1956 Enters Liverpool's Regional College of Art

1959 Meets fellow student John Lennon

Painting selected for the John Moores exhibition at Liverpool's Walker Art Gallery, subsequently bought by John Moores

Joins John Lennon's rock 'n' roll group, then known as Johnny and the Moondogs, on bass guitar

1960 Tours Scotland with the group, renamed the Silver Beatles, as accompanists to Johnny Gentle

Leaves the Regional College of Art

Travels with the Beatles to Hamburg where they work from August until late November, during which time he becomes engaged to photographer Astrid Kirchherr

1961 During the Beatles' second visit to Hamburg, he enrols at the city's Staatliche Hochschule für bildende Kunste (State School of Art), and leaves the group

1961–2 Studies in Eduardo Paolozzi's Master Class

Dies in Hamburg 10 April 1962

EXHIBITIONS

1959 John Moores Liverpool Exhibition, Walker Art Gallery

1964 Major retrospective, Walker Art Gallery

1965–7 One-man shows in Liverpool at the University, the Neptune Gallery and the Bluecoat Gallery

1967   *Art In A City* exhibition, ICA, London
1972   One-man show, The Room, Greenwich
1976   One-man show, South London Art Gallery
1984   *The Art of the Beatles*, Walker Art Gallery, Liverpool (Merseyside County Council)
1984–7   *The Art of the Beatles* tour of Japan (Seibu Stores/Toshiba)
1988   *The Art of the Beatles*, Cologne (British Council)
January 1990   One-man show, Sotheby's, London
May 1990   One-man show, Barbizon Gallery, Glasgow (Mayfest)
August 1990   One-man show, Bluecoat Gallery, Liverpool
December 1990–January 1991   One-man show, BBK Gallery, Cologne
December 1992   Mixed exhibition, Bluecoat Gallery, Liverpool
March 1994   One-man show, Japan (Della Corporation)
May 1994   One-man show, Govinda Gallery, Washington, USA (in association with Genesis Publications)

TELEVISION DOCUMENTARIES

1990   *Midnight Angel*, Granada TV (networked)
1991   *BBK Exhibition*, Cologne TV

'DISCOGRAPHY'

Stuart Sutcliffe cannot be heard on any official Beatles discs. However, defying every known copyright law, various bootleg albums featuring him with the Silver Beatles prior to the enlistment of Tommy Moore, have been circulating since the 1970s. Titles include *The Bass Drum Used To Roll Away Across The Stage*, *Quarry Men* (sic) *Rehearse With Stu Sutcliff* (sic), *Spring 1960* and *Liverpool, May 1960 – John, Paul, George And Stu*. The latter is a double album, promising 'over eighty minutes of vintage home recordings'. Indeed, all these under-the-counter commodities have been culled from tape recordings of rehearsals at Paul McCartney's house (20, Forthlin Road, Allerton, Merseyside) during the spring of 1960.

Documentary rather than recreational, the quality of sound and performances are what might be expected of music by amateurs filtered through hand-held domestic equipment from the medieval period of recording technology. Selections include 'Hallelujah I Love Her So', two versions of 'The One After 9.09', 'I'll Always Be In Love With You', 'You'll Be Mine', 'Matchbox', 'You Just Don't Understand', 'Somedays', 'I'll Follow The Sun', 'Hey Darling', 'You Must Lie Everyday', 'When The Heartaches Begin', 'Hello Little Girl' and some meandering instrumentals.

1967   *Art In A City* exhibition, ICA, London
1972   One-man show, The Room, Greenwich
1976   One-man show, South London Art Gallery
1984   *The Art of the Beatles*, Walker Art Gallery, Liverpool (Merseyside County Council)
1984–7   *The Art of the Beatles* tour of Japan (Seibu Stores/Toshiba)
1988   *The Art of the Beatles*, Cologne (British Council)
January 1990   One-man show, Sotheby's, London
May 1990   One-man show, Barbizon Gallery, Glasgow (Mayfest)
August 1990   One-man show, Bluecoat Gallery, Liverpool
December 1990–January 1991   One-man show, BBK Gallery, Cologne
December 1992   Mixed exhibition, Bluecoat Gallery, Liverpool
March 1994   One-man show, Japan (Della Corporation)
May 1994   One-man show, Govinda Gallery, Washington, USA (in association with Genesis Publications)

TELEVISION DOCUMENTARIES

1990   *Midnight Angel*, Granada TV (networked)
1991   *BBK Exhibition*, Cologne TV

'DISCOGRAPHY'

Stuart Sutcliffe cannot be heard on any official Beatles discs. However, defying every known copyright law, various bootleg albums featuring him with the Silver Beatles prior to the enlistment of Tommy Moore, have been circulating since the 1970s. Titles include *The Bass Drum Used To Roll Away Across The Stage*, *Quarry Men (sic) Rehearse With Stu Sutcliff (sic)*, *Spring 1960* and *Liverpool, May 1960 – John, Paul, George And Stu*. The latter is a double album, promising 'over eighty minutes of vintage home recordings'. Indeed, all these under-the-counter commodities have been culled from tape recordings of rehearsals at Paul McCartney's house (20, Forthlin Road, Allerton, Merseyside) during the spring of 1960.

Documentary rather than recreational, the quality of sound and performances are what might be expected of music by amateurs filtered through hand-held domestic equipment from the medieval period of recording technology. Selections include 'Hallelujah I Love Her So', two versions of 'The One After 9.09', 'I'll Always Be In Love With You', 'You'll Be Mine', 'Matchbox', 'You Just Don't Understand', 'Somedays', 'I'll Follow The Sun', 'Hey Darling', 'You Must Lie Everyday', 'When The Heartaches Begin', 'Hello Little Girl' and some meandering instrumentals.